THE
JUDGES

THE
JUDGES

A PENETRATING EXPLORATION OF AMERICAN COURTS
AND OF THE NEW DECISIONS—HARD DECISIONS—
THEY MUST MAKE FOR A NEW MILLENNIUM

MARTIN
MAYER

TRUMAN TALLEY BOOKS

ST. MARTIN'S PRESS 🎗 NEW YORK

AUTHOR'S NOTE: Many of the people mentioned in this book, including those quoted, will not on publication day hold the positions by which they are identified. This book was more than five years in the making, and the author, trained initially as a writer for periodicals, retains the habit of enhancing immediacy by using the present tense wherever possible, identifying the subjects of interviews by their job when interviewed. Those who wish to find someone mentioned here should use a search engine on the name itself rather than seek by title. Even then, there is no safety: The William Vickrey who runs the California courts, for example, is entirely different and distinct from the Nobel Prize–winning economist of the same name.

www.stmartins.com

Library of Congress Cataloging-in-Publication Data
Mayer, Martin, 1928–
   The judges : a penetrating exploration of American courts and of the new decisions—hard decisions—they must make for a new millennium / Martin Mayer.—1st ed.
      p. cm.
   Includes bibliographical references.
   ISBN-13: 978-0-312-28975-1
   ISBN-10: 0-312-28975-8
   1. Courts—United States.   2. Law—United States.   3. Justice, Admisistration of—United States.   I. Title.

KF8700.M354 2006
347.73'1—dc22

2006050124

First Edition: January 2007

10 9 8 7 6 5 4 3 2 1

In Memoriam
Gerald T. Dunne of the St. Louis bar,
Sol M. Linowitz of the District of Columbia bar,
and Martin Feinstein of the Washington Opera,
who played poker with the justices

CONTENTS

THE
JUDGES

1 THE MONASTIC BENCH

The law, the working of the law, the daily application of the law to people and situations, is an essential element in a country's life. It runs through everything; it is part of the pattern, like the architecture and the art and the look of the cultivated countryside. It shapes, and expresses, a country's modes of thought, its political concepts and realities, its conduct. One smells it in the corridors of public affairs. . . . It hangs together whether people themselves wish or acknowledge it or not.

—Sybille Bedford[1]

The chief lawmakers in our country may be, and often are, the judges, because they are the final seat of authority. Every time they interpret contract, property, vested rights, due process of law, liberty, they necessarily enact into law parts of a system of social philosophy; and as such interpretation is fundamental, they give direction to all law-making . . . and for the peaceful progress of our people during the twentieth century we shall owe most to those judges who hold to a twentieth century economic and social philosophy and not to a long outgrown philosophy, which was itself the product of primitive economic conditions.

—Theodore Roosevelt, December 8, 1908[2]

PERIODICALLY IN AMERICAN HISTORY, QUES-tions about the judicial branch of government rise to the surface of political discourse. Locally and nation-ally, the executive, the legislature, and the courts all draw their authority independently from the same short written constitutions. And as Alexis de Tocqueville observed in the 1840s, the United States is a country where great disputes get simplified into lawsuits and resolved, at least temporarily, in the courts, which have assumed and grudgingly been granted the franchise of determining the meaning of those written constitutions.

Government works more directly on its publics through the courts than through any other institution. As Supreme Court justice Tom Clark once said, the courtroom is where legislation finds its teeth. People believe that decisions in court cases expressing the wishes and fears of individuals and organizations far away will powerfully affect their own lives. Ours, for good or ill, is a time when decisions by and about judges occupy considerable political space. In Senate hearings, on radio and television in the states where judges face election, in the offices of the state governors whose powers include judicial appointments, temperatures rise as the politically committed seek judges who will rule their way.

The superstructure of policies that may be devised, enforced, or rejected by the publicized and brawled-over "supreme courts" rests on a rabbit warren of daily business done by 30,000 judges and a million lawyers and the "working groups" in the courthouses managing a docket of almost a hundred million cases a year. Here history enormously complicates understanding, for there is no one court system or, indeed, legal system in the United States. There are fifty sovereign states (plus Puerto Rico and the District of Columbia), each operating its own system of many county courts, enforcing its own laws and constitution. Each has its own legislators writing laws for their state only. Each has its own judges interpreting state and county laws, hearing cases, rendering decisions, bound only by the precedents of their own states, if those. Then there are administrative judges, paladins of the bureaucracy, whose realm forever expands. And on top of the local jurisdictions there is a federal system of laws and courts, more prestigious and better financed but much smaller, charged with providing a national framework of law to span a continent, but at the same time constitutionally constrained to accept and follow the local rules of procedure and local law where applicable.

In Randall Jarrell's wonderful novel about the American liberal arts college, *Pictures from an Institution*, a refugee German professor of music hears a colleague say, "There is no book of which it can be said that all your students have read it"—and realizes that he has learned something about America. Other than the insistence on decorum ("All rise!" "May it please the court") there is no statement one can make about the courts or their judges in the United States that can be considered correct everywhere. "The courts are very byzantine," says Juanita Bing Newton, deputy chief administrative judge in New York, in charge of the criminal courts. "When I got this job, I told my mother, 'I've finally found a use for that course I took on the Holy Roman Empire.'" In the words of the Bureau of Justice Statistics of the U.S. Department of Justice, "there is no generic court system in the United States."[3]

One starts then with the question of whether a judicial profession exists at all in the United States. Judges in different courts lead very different lives. The nation has fifteen hundred or so appellate court judges (about 350 of them judges on "supreme" courts—every state has one, and so does the federal government—more than 175 on the geographically divided federal "circuit courts of appeal"). They breathe a refined and perfumed air totally unlike the polluted stuff breathed by the judges in traffic courts, family courts, criminal courts. They see no litigants or witnesses, hear argument rather than evidence, command the services of young and brilliant "elbow clerks," new graduates from the top of the top law schools who work only for them, to find citations and draft memos. Trial judges sit alone and shoot from the hip all day long. Appellate judges confer in groups before deciding, and can indeed change their minds behind walls of secrecy as a result of those discussions.

What gnaws at them is uncertainty about whether the result of the case is "right." Appellate judges inevitably live and work, as Justice Frank Kennison of the New Hampshire Supreme Court brilliantly put it in the 1940s, "in the partial vacuum of the printed record."[4] In theory, the appellate courts exist to correct errors in the trial courts and to assure justice. But as Judge Jerome Frank observed more than half a century ago, if it's justice you seek, you'll find it much more often in the trial court, for justice relates to the persons present in the trial court, not to the abstractions of law. Appellate judges never meet the accused in the criminal case, neither plaintiff nor defendant in the civil case, nor do they lay eyes on the witnesses. "Up there in our ivory tower," Judge Patricia M. Wald wrote while chief judge of the D.C. Circuit Court of Appeals, "we have limited expertise and resources to absorb, synthesize, and accommodate all of the facts and evidence presented by parties throughout the adversarial process. Even if we immerse ourselves ad infinitum and ad nauseam in the technical details of the record, a practice of which I have often been accused, still we are often left groping for the more elusive, intuitive grasp of the essence of a case."[5]

In trial courts, by contrast, the judge sits on her bench alone and makes decisions bing-bing-bing, in the glare of attention not only from counsel and the working group in the court but also from a public beyond the railing. Sometimes these decisions are en route, about the admissibility of evidence or testimony or lines of argument; sometimes they are decisions she keeps to herself, about whom to believe, sometimes final decisions of guilt or innocence, liability for injuries, obligations to perform under contract, acceptance of agreements, imposition of punishments. And of course, at least for the immediate purpose of the trial, the judge is always right; counsel can take an exception, but the caravan moves on. The judge is a queen in her courtroom, which is to a significant degree a separate realm. What happens to litigants in the American judicial system is very much a function of which judge hears the case. But the trial judge is subject to instruction by a legislature that also decides how much she will be paid, how heavy a load of cases her court will carry, how large a staff of clerks and secretaries and bailiffs and police and legal advisers she will have, how long or short a sentence she may impose on a convicted criminal defendant. And the appellate judges can of course reverse her decisions.

Judges come to the bench from all sorts of backgrounds, some with much experience trying cases, some with almost none. We don't train judges; there is no licensing exam, and no criteria that relate to the performance of the job are applied before a judge takes her chair on the podium above the well of the court. Most appellate judges (and all federal judges) are appointed either for long terms or for life. Their daily experience hearing and deciding appeals permits them to believe that they are not part of the nation's political turmoil and serve only what they are pleased (very pleased) to call the rule of law. The great majority of trial judges, on the other hand, not only come in daily contact with the public but must seek public approval in periodic elections: 90 percent of our trial judges are elected from their state or district or serve subject to voters' verdicts in "retention elections." And judges who have to stand for reelection live daily with the great political truth that people never remember what you did *for* them and never forget what you did *to* them. A Connecticut judge, beneficiary of a system in which judges are appointed by the state governor for eight-year terms and then more or less automatically reappointed by the legislature (a system unique to Connecticut), went to the National Judicial College in Reno for a two-week course to hone her skills after fifteen years on the job. "I was appalled," she says, remembering what she heard over cups of coffee from her fellow judges from other states. "Ninety percent of the conversation was about how you had to watch out in the courtroom in case what you did would impact on your election."

But the most important, formative, in-courtroom experiences are shared by all the judges, appointed or elected, trial or appeal, and are exclusive to them. As I started work on this book in 2001, my late feminist wife's feminist sister, the law professor Mary Moers Wenig, sent me off to the annual convention of the National Association of Women Jurists. To them, clearly, there really was a job description, not just a census category, behind the word "judge." The panels included and mixed together a range of judges, from traffic court judges to justices of state supreme courts, but they all clearly felt themselves to be sisters under the skin, sharing the pleasures of deference, the power of rarely challenged decision making, and the pains of overload, time pressure, and the testosterone-soaked atmosphere of trial work. They were pioneers: When they first had thought of the law as a profession, there were virtually no women on the bench. They considered themselves the vanguard of an army, for the predictability of the hours has made the job especially desirable for women. Listening to the participants in their convention, no one could doubt that whatever their rank, they were all in the same line of work. Every court system is a process for forcing decisions on parties compelled to accept the decisions. The people who preside over this process we call "judges."

Writing about judges, however, one must offer the reader observations, attributes, and attitudes: There seems to be no way to communicate how it looks from inside the system. The judges themselves don't—apparently, can't—tell you. Felix Frankfurter noted in a talk before the American Philosophical Society in 1954 that "the most illuminating light on painting has been furnished by painters, and the deepest revelations on the writing of poetry have come from poets. It is not so with the business of judging. The power of searching analysis of what it is that they are doing seems rarely to be possessed by judges, either because they are lacking in the art of critical exposition or because they are inhibited from practicing it.

The fact is that pitifully little of significance has been contributed by judges regarding the nature of their endeavor."[6] That continues to be true more than half a century later.

In *The Ways of a Judge*, Judge Frank M. Coffin of the federal First Circuit Court of Appeals (Boston) summed up more than a decade on an appellate bench by describing what he "did"—what he would have done if these had been the facts— in three cases. Two of them were entirely made up; the third was more or less real, but the discussions he reported with his clerks were admittedly fiction. "Judges in recent times," he notes, "have largely left to others the writing about their craft and calling. There are ample reasons for this. One is that the judge's code of ethics precludes his writing about what he knows best—the steps he took in arriving at his last or his most widely known decision—for that decision must be judged solely by what he or his court wrote to justify and explain it. Barred from backstage reporting, the would-be judicial essayist faces the hard fact that judging is infinitely complex. It does not lend itself to an authoritative how-it-is-done book."[7]

It is of the essence of the work that judges cannot be held accountable anywhere for the decisions they make as judges. They are accountable only to the law itself. This is what we mean when we say "an independent judiciary." Which means on the other side of the coin that judges cannot talk about their work, because discussing a case opens the door to challengers. Someone once asked for an explanation of an opinion from New Jersey Chief Justice Arthur T. Vanderbilt, the inventor of the twentieth-century court reform movement, chairman of the state Republican Party before he became a judge. "I don't explain them, Madam," he said courteously. "I write them." Judicial opinions do not argue that the judges have found the "right" answer, and do not necessarily reveal the arguments that informed the result; instead, they assert the consonance of this decision with others from the past, and insist that this is the answer compelled by the law.

The most common code of judicial ethics actually forbids judges to explain to the public their interlocutory rulings on motions by the lawyers presenting the case, and some of the old canons prohibit judges from discussing any phase of the cases tried before them. Frankfurter, advancing to the Supreme Court after decades as a freewheeling law professor, described himself as "one who is ex officio compelled to deny himself freedom of speech."[8] When a judge rules, he speaks from Olympus; when he discusses his work, he is, nearly always, an ordinary joe. For the judge who made the decision to defend it would be to demean it, to reduce an expression of authority to a mere argument. In 1957, when a committee of the American Bar Association adopted a resolution critical of Supreme Court decisions in matters of "subversion," Chief Justice Earl Warren did not participate in a reply, but quietly resigned from the ABA.

When courts are attacked, they cannot respond, a truth obvious to the judges themselves since the early days of the republic. Chief Justice John Marshall sent a letter to Justice Bushrod Washington (George's nephew), commenting on the likely fallout from a decision to uphold and enforce an act of Congress: "We shall be denounced bitterly in the papers &, as not a word will be said on the other side, we shall undoubtedly be condemned as a pack of consolidating aristocrats. The legislature & executive who have enacted the law, but who have power and places to bestow, will escape with impunity, while the poor court, who have nothing to give & of whom nobody is afraid, bears all the obloquy of the measure."[9]

And of course judges feel themselves physically exposed out in the center of the pedestal in their courtrooms, an inviting target for one of the criminals they have punished or litigants whose cause they have ruled against. Irving R. Kaufman, who sentenced Julius and Ethel Rosenberg to death for helping the Russians penetrate our atom bomb development, had a policeman at the entrance to his apartment house day and night for all the almost fifty years of his life after that decision. Judge Leonard Sand, who presided over the case of the blind sheikh who plotted the first attempt on the World Trade Center, in 1993, has chambers in an otherwise almost deserted floor of the courthouse, because it's easier to keep an eye on a corridor nobody uses. Chicago has installed bulletproof glass between the public and the business sections of its criminal courts. Almost everywhere, the police assigned to courtrooms carry guns. One cannot think offhand of another environment for professional work where guns are visible in holsters on hips.

There is some motion toward giving judges the right to reply to criticism. In North Carolina, the legislature marked the arrival of a new millennium by passing a law that for the first time permits judges to reply to critics. In Connecticut a couple of years ago, the conference of Superior Court judges (most judges in the unified Connecticut system are Superior Court judges) voted to suspend the code of judicial ethics and let a family court judge tell the press that a prosecuting state attorney had lied when he said his office had warned a judge against returning a child to the abusive parent who thereupon killed her. But in general the judge has to stand and bear it in a world where in any event the riposte is always weaker than the thrust.

AT DAGGERS DRAWN: THE COURTS AND THE PRESS

The truth is that judges do not want to talk to the outside world about what it is they do. "The judiciary," the political scientist and court reformer Frances Kahn Zemans told a meeting at the University of Southern California Law School, "had been and remains our least visible branch of government. By and large, judges like it that way."[10] And they especially don't want to talk with the press. Joyce Purnick of *The New York Times* has had an amusing running battle with her state's judiciary to get them to publish a directory of the state's 1,211 judges, something that happened for the first time early in 2005.[11] It wasn't very well done. Purnick reported that the directory completely misses about a tenth of the judges, and that the president of the state Association of Family Court Judges wound up with an entry that lists a non-working telephone number for his chambers.

Judges who can't answer questions about the cases they have heard (let alone the cases currently before them), naturally want to make sure that the grunts on their front line don't talk, either. "Journalists," says the *Chambers Handbook for Judges' Law Clerks and Secretaries*, an official publication of the Federal Judicial Center, "frequently telephone chambers to inquire about a case, or attempt to provoke a conversation at a social affair. There should be as little communication as possible be-tween chambers staff and representatives of the media." The federal code of conduct for judicial employees, adopted by the Judicial Conference in 1995, says that "a judicial employee should never disclose any confidential information received in the course of official duties except as required in the perfor-mance of such duties. . . . A former judicial employee should observe the same restrictions on disclosure of confidential in-formation that apply to a current judicial employee. . . ."[12]

I had been around this barn before, forty some years ago, when I wrote *The Lawyers*, a substantial bestseller that set a record for number of times stolen from the Mid-Manhattan Branch of the New York Public Library. (Tells you, said a li-brarian there, what kind of kid goes to law school these days; it should also be noted that there was a much larger theft by the law schools themselves, many of which duplicated and distrib-uted to students scores of pages from the book without the consent of or payment to the author or publisher.) Many of the lawyers with whom I had wished to speak then did not wish to speak with me. In the 1960s, after all, Canon 27 of the American Bar Association Canons of Professional Ethics pro-claimed that "indirect advertisements for professional employ-ment such as furnishing or inspiring newspaper comments . . . in connection with causes in which the lawyer has been or is engaged . . . offend the traditions and lower the tone of our profession and are reprehensible." Even in the early 1960s, this canon of ethics was mostly an excuse to avoid answering questions. Then as now, whatever the canon of ethics, it was part of the repertoire of every trial lawyer to play upon the consumers of publicity for his own and his clients' benefit, perhaps his opponents' detriment. Soon the U.S. Supreme Court in a rather mischievous decision authorized all kinds of advertising by lawyers as part of their First Amendment rights, licensing even the most vulgar and hyperbolic self-promotion. Then the elite bar began today's practice of hiding behind the bushes of client confidentiality.

On reflection, the hostility breathed by the lawyers' and judges' canons is not surprising. Antagonism between the courts and the press has deep roots. "The courts and the press do not get on very well with each other," I wrote in 1975, "never have and never will. What the lawyers and judges have to sell, after all, is procedure, and the press couldn't care less about that. But they do share two fundamental characteristics. Both are strongly oriented toward individual events and individual participants in those events, drawing their general conclusions from particular incidents rather than from statistical representations. And both look backward toward what is already on, or can be placed on, the record; for better or worse (it cuts both ways), they judge principles by the applications as observed. Justice Holmes once noted in a letter that he had heard law described as 'the government of the living by the dead'; the newspaper story is notoriously good for one day only (the broadcast news report, for less than that). At best, both the court and the press are intensely responsible to the reality of the immediate past, but they are unavoidably (though they pretend otherwise) irresponsible to the reality of the future."[13]

The tendency always is for each side to blame the other. "Public ignorance of the real workings of the courts," Roscoe Pound said in 1906 as part of his call for significant reforms in his great talk to the American Bar Association convention, "is due to ignorant and sensational reports in the press." Movies and television have obviously made the ignorance even worse. Frances Zemans notes cautiously that "local judges feel picked upon; there is actually some evidence that news coverage generally has evolved into what has been characterized as 'attack journalism.' "[14]

"Them" and "us" attitudes are further promoted by the sense that the system is not working very well, and that there seem to be few ideas about how to keep things from getting even worse. At least to keep them from *looking* worse. As long ago as 1967, the sociologist and law professor Abraham Blumberg argued that in the world of criminal law "managing the trauma produced by law enforcement and administration [requires] almost pathological distrust of 'outsiders' bordering on group paranoia."[15] An Alabama judge on a court of criminal appeals wrote in 1993 that "like vultures perched in a barren tree on a desert plain, the media and the public watch for a judge to stumble and fall."[16] Writing in *The Court Manager* magazine, John Martin and Brenda J. Wagenknecht-Ivey mention among their list of requirements for the court systems of the twenty-first century "a need to inform and educate the public directly about the courts without the filtering, interpretation, or intervention of the press."[17] Others know that this simply cannot be: "Rules," writes (very conservative) federal appellate judge Frank H. Easterbrook, "must be publicized to be effective, to be 'rules of law' at all."[18] And there is no publicity without the press.

Judges in public pronouncements pay generous lip service to "freedom of the press" as a necessity of democracy. "An independent judiciary," recently retired Justice Sandra Day O'Connor wrote while still on the bench, "is necessary, but certainly not sufficient, to the maintenance of a free society. The second principle I want to emphasize is the *importance of a free press*. A judiciary that stands apart from the other branches of government is able to perform its function without fear or sanction. Likewise, a responsible press free from government control is able to perform its function of comment and criticism."[19]

Alas, they don't mean it—sometimes very obviously. Most judges dislike "the media," which propagates wrong notions about the law and spreads information untested by cross-examination and inadmissible in a trial process. They resent the press for efforts, not always unsuccessful, to push the courts around. "Justice Felix Frankfurter," we are told, "recorded in his diary that in the fall term after the first Flag Salute case [*Minersville School District v. Gobitis*, 310 US 586] . . . Justice Douglas remarked to him, 'Hugo [Justice Black] would not now go with you in the Flag Salute case.' Frankfurter wrote that he replied, 'Why, has he reread the Constitution during the summer?' to which Justice Douglas replied, 'No, but he has read the papers.' "[20] The greatest threat to the independence of the judiciary is often a press campaign associated with a heinous crime.

Attorneys cheerfully leak to the press in an effort to prejudice the pool of potential jurors, or simply for self-aggrandizement, and the press plays along. The lawyer-novelist Scott Turow served on a committee investigating the use of the death penalty in Illinois and found, rather to his surprise, that juries were *more* likely to convict innocent defendants in capital cases than in other prosecutions. Death penalties are imposed only for truly heinous crimes. Such crimes arouse the community, which puts heavy pressure on police and prosecutors to bring the monster to justice. The announcement that a perpetrator has been caught takes the heat off the institutions, which leads them to invest even more heavily in the guilt of the first person accused. The prosecutor exploits what the great trial lawyer Francis X. Wellman called "that dangerous ground of intimacy that arises between any set of jurymen and a District Attorney whom they soon come to regard as, in a sense, one of their own number in his attempts to suppress crime in the neighborhood where they all live."[21] The judge is also part of the community and may face unpleasant criticism in the press if his rulings impede the course of the prosecution.

Courts are the repositories of secrets, and wish to keep them. They therefore tend to be less than neutral arbiters when people who have exposed secrets seek to conceal their sources. "News," said Lord Northcliffe, who owned *The Times* of London in its great days, "is what somebody somewhere wants to suppress; all the rest is advertising." Reporters are snoops by profession. "It's their job to keep secrets," Walter Mears, executive editor of the Associated Press, told ABC's *Nightline* when Ronald Reagan's defense secretary, Caspar Weinberger, accused the news service of "giving aid and comfort to the enemy" by reporting the payload of a satellite launch, "and it's our job to find out about them."[22] In their hearts, judges sympathize with the corporations and the agencies of the executive branch, which hate the sight of those fellows in raincoats skulking about in hopes of pumping somebody.

It's a serious problem. Perhaps the most pernicious form of government control of the press is the classification of important information to hide it from prying eyes. In China and Russia, they lock up journalists who print things the authorities regard as state secrets. In America, much public exposure of misbehavior in government—and some official investigation of such misbehavior—starts with a tipster on the public payroll telling secrets to a reporter. Invariably, the information is conveyed "on background"—that is, the source of the story is not to be revealed. In theory, "whistle-blower laws" protect the insider who bears bad news about government agencies, but in fact people who are known to have complained about their bosses and/or their colleagues have a less pleasant life than people who keep their mouths shut and play along. Thus reporters promise to protect their sources, and in thirty-one states and the District of Columbia local laws shield statements to reporters with a "privilege" similar to that they give to statements by penitent to priest, client to lawyer, patient to doctor, husband to wife.

In 1972, in the case of *Branzburg v. Hayes*,[23] four justices of the Supreme Court signed on to a typically vigorous opinion by Justice Byron White rejecting the arguments for a newsman's privilege in federal courts. Reporters for the Louisville *Courier-Journal* had found some juveniles preparing and selling hashish, and federal prosecutors (because drug laws are national in scope) had summoned them to a grand jury to identify the youths. Relying on a Kentucky "shield law," the reporters refused. White insisted that newspaper reporters like anyone else had an obligation to tell a grand jury what they knew about the commission of a crime, and regardless of state law a federal judge could jail a reporter who refused to testify: "[T]he evidence fails to demonstrate that there would be a significant constriction of the flow of news to the public if this Court reaffirms the prior common-law and constitutional rule regarding the testimonial obligations of newsmen."

This issue got on the front pages in 2005 at the end of a complicated process gone bad. In 2003, people in the Bush administration leaked to selected reporters the fact that a former ambassador who had spoken out against the invasion of Iraq had a wife who was a CIA operative. The suggestion was that the CIA was conspiring with the State Department against the Bush White House. Because she was undercover, the revelation of the lady's name was a crime. The newspapers, led by *The New York Times*, insisted that the administration could not be trusted to investigate itself, and demanded the appointment of a special prosecutor. Note the role reversal: The newspapers that published the leak were now demanding that the miscreant who leaked must be caught and punished. Logic said that the most likely candidates for knowledge of who spoke with the reporters were the reporters themselves, several of whom claimed a constitutional right to protect their sources. To which the judges—district, appellate, and Supreme Court—said, Your father's mustache, with the upshot that a reporter for *The New York Times* spent eighty-five days in jail in contempt of court for refusal to tell a grand jury about the sources for an article she had never written. And then she did indeed testify.[24]

This farcical episode had serious real-life consequences for the reporter, for the *Times*, and for the status of journalism in America, and it is by no means clear that these consequences were in any way necessary. David Santelle, the senior judge of the three-man panel of the D.C. Circuit Court of Appeals that heard the appeal of the jail sentence, insisted that defense counsel distinguish this case from *Branzburg*, and threw out the newsman's privilege argument with an interesting statement in open court: "You just shut down leak investigations if we give you this privilege."[25] He did not seek to explain why public policy should exalt leak investigations over the rights of the people to a press that tells them what their government is doing. As Justice Hugo Black put it in *Times Co. v. US*,[26] "The press was protected so it could serve the governed, not the governor." Against which, perhaps, one should set the comment by Justice Oliver Wendell Holmes, when chief justice in Massachusetts, that publishing a newspaper is "very like firing a gun into the street."[27]

ALONE ON THE BENCH

Partly because the judiciary has walled itself off from other sources of information, both incoming and outgoing, its reputation has deteriorated in an age of information technology. Many judges worry that the job no longer carries the high rewards of respect and admiration that were once part of the culture. Fifty-some years ago, a friend who was already a rising star at a big Wall Street law firm—who would make more than $50 million over his career as a lawyer, and knew he would, and cared about money—said that if somebody offered to make him a federal judge, he would jump for it: "*Everybody* wants to be a judge." The judge still drives to work in a car with a license plate that guarantees he won't get a ticket, and he wears the robe on the job, and when he enters his courtroom everybody rises. Senior federal judge Richard Owen, prominent in 2004 (at the age of eighty) as the judge who was removed from the trial of Credit Suisse stock salesman Frank Quattrone, is also a composer who writes operas that get staged (and the leather that peeks out from under the robe is cowboy boots). He has on a wall of his chambers in downtown New York a neo-Cartesian sampler that reads, "I Said, Therefore I Am."

To quote former federal judge Herbert Stern (who has since returning to private practice tried cases fun enough to write books about) wearing a robe is still proof that one is important. But it is no longer true that everybody wants to be a judge, and there are many former judges who are pleased to be out of it, practicing law again or serving as arbitrators in the commercial world, doing much the same work, better paid, equally immune from suit for what they do as arbitrator or mediator, not bugged by the need to impose or approve death penalties—and not subject to reversal by higher courts. The National Judicial College in Reno now offers summer programs in mediation for judges looking to quit the bench and get rich in the private sector. Stern himself generously cut his fee to $500 an hour in 2005 while he became monitor of the troubled University of Medicine and Dentistry of New Jersey.

There are also, of course, many judges deeply content with their own experience, people like former chief justice Tom Phillips of the Texas Supreme Court, who according to his wife wanted to be a judge since he was four years old. (But even

Phillips retired young, in 2004, to escape the hassles of Texas politics and make some money.) Or the lordly Norm Davis in Phoenix, "presiding judge" of Maricopa County's family court (which provides work for twenty-seven of the ninety-one superior court judges in the immense county), efficient, openly results-oriented, who may settle seven cases a day in chambers while trying one in open court. Or Milton Pollack on the federal bench in the Southern District of New York, ramrod straight at age ninety-seven, still beating up counsel and forcing agreements in cases which have been assigned to him in violation of his court's rule of random selection because he's the financial market expert and tough guy of that bench. Or the scholarly Robert Katzmann on the Second Circuit Court of Appeals (New York), who after eighteen years as an academic sees the courts as "the means by which the problems of individuals can be addressed, the bedrock of a peaceful society. It's a great privilege to be part of that system."

There continue to be lots of candidates, especially for federal posts (some places with family courts are running out of applicants to be a family court judge, a terrible job), but increasingly they come from within the system, from other government jobs and from academia. Congressmen, senators, and governors (the two great chief justices of the twentieth century—Charles Evans Hughes and Earl Warren—both had been state governors) no longer wanted those jobs. Successful practitioners simply cannot afford to make the move: The monetary penalty is too great. William Rehnquist, when chief justice, testified repeatedly before Congress that insufficient salaries were driving away the judges you'd want to keep. Supreme Court justice Antonin Scalia noted recently that after two years on the job one of his clerks, who had come to him one year from law school, was paid a signing bonus by a Wall Street firm almost as large as the annual salary of a Supreme Court justice. State judges are paid less and worked harder, with much less control over the dockets they must get through.

For someone like myself, trained as an economist, the best explanation of the decline of the legal profession and its judicial branch was what William J. Baumol and William E. Bowen, writing about the performing arts, called "the economic dilemma." In a world where the productivity of the factory worker and the farmer and the clerk has been dramatically boosted by technology, the string section of the big-time symphony still has sixteen first violins, and it takes them more than thirteen minutes to play the first movement of the *Eroica*. The barber still needs twenty minutes to cut your hair. School classrooms still have twenty-five children and one teacher. Only the surgeon's hands can tie the sutures, one at a time. Thus even after the computer contributes efficiencies, the relative costs of the service sector rise very rapidly by comparison with the costs of the goods sector, and society squeezes the service providers, seeking to reduce inputs and increase outputs.

This pressure has been exerted with great success on the judiciary. "Today," says Martin Redlinger, a retired New York judge, "Nobody cares how good you are. Just how fast you are." Chief Justice Kathleen Blatz of the Minnesota Supreme Court says, "Sometimes I feel as though I work for McJustice—we're not good for you, but we sure are fast." There is simply too much work. Professionalism implies collegiality, with loss of reputation and shame as the shillelaghs behind the door. Jack Weinstein, who came to the federal bench in Brooklyn from a law professorship at Columbia University in the early 1970s, remembers that when he started there were only seven federal district judges in the Eastern District of New York. "We had breakfast together every day," Judge Weinstein says, "talked about interesting cases before us, sentencing problems. Now there are thirty-five judges on this bench, and I don't recognize most of them in the halls." For the country as a whole, twice as many federal judges as we had in 1970 are asked to handle six times as many cases. And the federal load is much lighter than the state load. Chief Justice Rehnquist warned in 1993 that "both lawyers and judges will be subjected to additional rules and regulations designed to maximize the efficient use of the federal and state court systems."[28] And so it happened.

Approaching a book on the judiciary, then, I saw the mushroomlike growth of court administrators and case-flow managers as an invasion of professional autonomy caused by the same factors that were deviling and sapping the confidence of the other professions. There are some remarkable sidebars to the story of the relationship between trial judges and clerks, who report up their own hierarchy and spend their own funds, paid to them by litigants. Even the "administrators," a much more professional cadre, usually appointed by the judges rather than elected on their own ballot lines, have acquired unsuspected clout. One notes the astonishing political muscle of the federal court administrators who snuck a pay raise for themselves (but not for judges) into the 480 pages of the bill that established the Department of Homeland Security.[29] I expected judges to want to talk about these vandals as the doctors talk about the clerks at the insurance companies who approve (or do not approve) what they wish to do for patients. Court administrators, after all, have a power over the lives of judges much greater than insurance adjusters and their kind have over the lives of doctors. A North Carolina court administrator can (and does) order a Raleigh-based judge to sit for a week or two in Asheville, and an Oregon administrator can (and does) assign a judge who has never dealt with such matters before to hear a horrifying case of domestic violence. (Oregon has a rule that every judge must spend some time each year on a family-court bench.)

But I was wrong. Many judges *do* resent the change in the hierarchy of judges as courts "consolidate" and supervisory opinion about individuals replaces the older geographical and functional distinctions. In places like California and Illinois, for example, nearly all judges are now "superior court" or "district court" judges, and the administrative apparatus allocates work and evaluates quality behind the scenes. Comparably, in New York State, the administrative apparatus has created a special "commercial court" in Manhattan to handle the interesting stuff, leaving the rest of that county's huge bench stuck with personal-injury and dysfunctional-family litigation. Judges are increasingly annoyed by the need to keep peace with administrators ("[E]very new administrative or non-case-related chore or function," First Circuit Court of Appeals (Boston) judge Frank M. Coffin objects, "carried with it a cost, measured by judges' diminished availability to reflect on cases. Eternal busyness is a virus, draining serenity."[30]) But the judges know their courts are inefficient and need administrative help—and, anyway, they don't want to talk about it, and they don't want anybody else to talk about it, either.

Greatly heightened sensitivity to possible conflicts of interest—much of it unquestionably driven by self-consciously virtuous media—has further isolated the judiciary. Chief Justice William Howard Taft socialized considerably with Calvin Coolidge and Herbert Hoover—Justice Frankfurter with Franklin Roosevelt, Chief Justice Fred Vinson with Harry Truman, and Justice Abe Fortas with Lyndon Johnson—and nobody worried much about it. In the early years of the twentieth century, when the justices of the Supreme Court worked at home, their wives often had a Monday open house at teatime for the community of clerks and lawyers who worked in the Court. Today that would be unthinkable. Donning robes, a judge accepts at least the appearance, and often the reality, of a monastic life. "A federal judge," said Luke Bierman of the American Bar Association, "is a lifetime of loneliness."

When presidential adviser, saxophonist, and lawyer Leonard Garment let it be known to the press that he played in a Wednesday night poker game that included two Supreme Court justices, a judge in the circuit court of appeals and a pair of federal district court judges, he was exiled from the game, for life. In 2004, Justice Antonin Scalia was put in the public stocks and threatened with tar and feathers when he insisted that he could go duck hunting with Vice President Richard Cheney and still treat him like any other defendant. (Cheney had refused demands from public interest groups to name the oil industry executives with whom he had met when putting together the Bush administration's energy proposals.)

Most judges get itchy about lunching with lawyers who were good friends in the old days. For those on the bench who would be more gregarious if they could, it's a drag. As a group of new judges taking a course at the National Judicial College in Reno explained to a visiting political scientist, "We're all old pols put into a new world; we miss our support groups."

For judges are, of course, human. One of the few nice stories from the 1970s tells of the direct telephone to the White House that sat on the desk of Harold "Ace" Tyler, deputy attorney general (formerly a district judge) in the administration of President Gerald Ford. Not long after the new president pardoned Richard Nixon, and had been blasted with negative comment in the press, the phone rang on Tyler's desk. It was a call from the president himself to make a strange request. Judge Tyler remembers President Ford saying, "It seems to me that this impeachment business has been hard on the federal judges, too." Tyler did not deny it. "I'd like to give them a dinner at the White House," the president said. "Could you pick fifty good judges for me and send me their names, and we'll invite them to dinner." Which he did, and it is reported that a highly respectful good time was had by all.

2 CONFRONTING THE MYTHS

Lawyers have framed our political theory, which accordingly abounds in fictions.

—Morris Raphael Cohen[1]

Our Anglo-American legal system postulates an active popular interest in justice. In communities which are too busy to take an active interest in the maintenance of right through law or too heterogeneous to have reasonably fixed and generally accepted notions of justice, such a system does not operate efficiently.

—Charles W. Eliot, Louis D. Brandeis, Moorfield Storey, Adolph J. Rodenbeck, and Roscoe Pound, for the National Economic League of Boston, 1913[2]

Everything secret degenerates, even the administration of justice; nothing is safe that does not show how it can bear discussion and publicity.

—Lord Acton[3]

EVERY TEN YEARS OR SO, A NEW POLITICAL pollster finds that the American people would resoundingly reject the substance of the Bill of Rights if it were put before them in a referendum, and indeed James Madison's purpose in pushing the amendments was to restrain the actions of majorities. Especially in wartime—most urgently in a war as vague in its boundaries as the war against terrorism—anyone disaffected from the government has a stake in the vitality of the courts as the protector of civil society. Only a national supreme court can take on the concentrated power of the president or the Congress. Those who think most about the Court—including not only law professors and political activists but the president who nominates justices and the Senate that must consent to their appointment and the press that reports on confirmation hearings—naturally confuse the work of the justices with the work of the judicial system. University of Chicago law professor Cass R. Sunstein has gone so far as to posit a collection of horribles—from the return of prohibitions against contraceptives to the elimination of all federal steps to protect the environment and all affirmative action programs—if the Scalia-Thomas minority of the Court should become the majority.[4]

It makes a difference who is on the Court and what the Court does. Sunstein shrewdly observes that the kinds of cases that will be considered by the trial courts is a function of the attitudes on the highest appellate levels. But the protection of our liberties is not what courts do best. The anarchists of 1920 and the communists of 1950 went to jail; the Japanese-Americans were interned. Judge Learned Hand, speaking at the 250th anniversary of the Supreme Judicial Court in Massachusetts, in 1942, observed "that a society so riven that the spirit of moderation is gone, no court *can* save; that a society where the spirit flourishes, no court *need* save; that in a society which evades its responsibility by thrusting upon the courts the nurture of that spirit, that spirit in the end will perish."[5]

There are pieces of the ideology that stand simple and strong enough to persuade even the most routine judiciary that they must intervene. As an appeals judge setting a standard for the trial judges of his circuit, Hand wrote: "Few weapons in the arsenal of freedom are more useful than the power to compel a government to disclose the evidence on which it seeks to forfeit the liberty of its citizens. All governments, democracies as well as autocracies, believe that those they seek to punish are guilty; the impediment of constitutional barriers are galling to all governments. . . ."[6]

Judges have few opportunities, and few of those who do have opportunities have the desire, to seek glory. What judges do all day has long departed far from the ideology. But the ideology survives, taught in junior high schools as well as in law schools, informing newspaper editorials and appellate court opinions alike. This book deals with the daily work of the courts, overwhelmed as they are by the volume of business and trapped in inherited institutional structures unsuited to the modern world. We do not see the prospects for crisis because our vision is blocked by certain myths presented as truths.

The destruction of these myths, which is where one must start any serious exploration of the American judicial system, is a dangerous thing to do. God knows we need judges and our judges need courage. But it is by no means clear that we need the court system we have now, with its generalist judges dominated by advocacy and avoiding the statistical modes of information that have conquered both the academy and the learned professions. Instead of discussing the legal profession and the court system we have, we wander in a haze of rhetoric about the rule of law and the role of law, equal justice under law, the adversary system as a search for truth, fair trials, due process, et cetera. This rhetoric is false, and in no small part dishonest. This book attempts to deal with the realities of an occupation that has not in fact achieved the status of a profession, and a political institution still in the process of finding its function in governance.

2

We must start, then, by discarding the slogans. The slogans stress, for example, the equality of citizens before the law, which means the law is supposed to be the same everywhere. Equal justice under law is engraved in stone atop the lofty columns of the facade of the Supreme Court building. "It will not do," said then New York State Court of Appeals judge Benjamin Cardozo in 1921, "to decide the same question one way between one set of litigants and the opposite way between another." Twenty years later, Supreme Court justice Robert H. Jackson said, "It is obviously repugnant to one's sense of justice that the judgment meted out to a defendant should depend in large part on a partly fortuitous circumstance: namely, the personality of the particular judge before whom the case happens to come for disposition."

But that is precisely what happens every day, even within a single state. The lawyers who take their suits against automobile manufacturers or pharmaceutical companies to obscure counties in Alabama know exactly what they are about. It happens, indeed, within a single courthouse. In Chicago's criminal courts building on Twenty-sixth Street, Judge Daniel Locallo tells reporter Steve Bogira that its thirty courtrooms "are like thirty different countries." Bogira notes that the computer that randomly assigns cases to judges "blesses a defendant with a benevolent judge or consigns him to a banger; it sends him to a courtroom with reasonable prosecutors or cut-throats, with energetic PDs [public defenders] or mopes."[7]

Three miles from Locallo's courthouse, Judge Richard A. Posner of the Seventh Circuit Court of Appeals writes opinions and many books promoting conservative views. He does not disagree with Locallo: "[W]e must acknowledge if we are clear-eyed, . . . that the goal of uniform justice is unattainable in the United States. At every level of the judiciary, judges exercise discretionary power, which means that two different judges faced with the same issue may reach different results without either judge being reversed. Trial judges exercise expansive discretionary powers with respect to factfinding, the admission and exclusion of evidence, the application of law to facts, and case management that often determines the outcome of a case without realistic prospects for correction on appeal."[8] In the end, Judge Jerome Frank said sixty-odd years ago, the judge "as a fact-finder . . . is a witness—a witness of witnesses."[9] Thus the training of judges is of paramount importance. And we don't train our judges.

Another hearty myth speaks to the role of the trial in American jurisprudence. "Property can be taken by the state," Justice Antonin Scalia told a Princeton symposium in 1997, "liberty can be taken, even life can be taken; but not without the process that our traditions require—notably, a validly enacted law and a fair trial."[10] That's the view from the top of the skyscraper, where the people below are so many ants swarming around ant heaps. At street level, the truth is quite different. "To most lay people," said Timothy J. Murray, then director of Program Development in the Bureau of Justice Assistance at the U.S. Department of Justice, "the criminal justice system doesn't make sense. When they go to a courthouse, they go to a place that is architecturally designed, staffed, equipped, and populated with people trained for something that hardly ever happens in that place, and that is a trial. All of us in this room know that trials hardly ever happen in state criminal courts. We're just moving cases, plowing through the day's calendar with plea bargains."[11]

In 2002, the Russian parliament passed a law that required Russian courts hearing criminal cases to give defendants a trial by jury if they asked for one. As part of the preparation for this major change in Russian procedure (the Soviet constitution imposed in 1917 had prohibited jury trials, leaving all findings of fact to a panel of judges and laymen, judges predominating, party members to the fore), several Russian judges were sent to the United States to study how the jury game was played. Among them was Judge Yuri V. Sukhanov, chairman of the Supreme Court in the province of Udmurtiya, sitting in its capital city of Izhevsk, where the Kalashnikov rifles are produced. He spent some months in Wyoming, where the local judges warned him that jury trials were "an expensive pleasure" used only when plea bargaining failed.[12] And Wyoming, one notes, was the state with by far the largest fraction of criminal defendants who come to trial—13.1 percent against a national average of 3.7 percent.[13]

For all their ritualistic tributes to the trial and the jury, the legislatures and the judges have legitimized rules that lead to increasing punishments of those defendants who won't plead guilty in a bargain, choose to take their chances on trial, and lose, as the great majority of them will. The executive branch in the form of the prosecuting attorney has exclusive power to decide what charges will be brought against a defendant. The prosecutor has a great deal of influence on the decision to permit a defendant to post bail and live his life before trial, or remain under lock and key while his prosecution is being organized. The state thus starts the bargaining with horrifying advantages. Given a choice between a possible sentence after trial that will essentially end his life as a free man and a bargained sentence that may not give him jail time or at worst will keep him behind bars only for some months—and with advice from a state-assigned, state-remunerated lawyer, who has to get to the next case, that this choice is the best you're gonna do—even an innocent defendant, actually guilty of no more than being in the wrong place at the wrong time, may decide to accept his bad luck and try to get on with his life.

"Whenever a defendant pleads guilty," Steve Bogira reports from a Chicago criminal courtroom, "most parties are satisfied, even if the defendant happens to be innocent. It's a conviction for the prosecutor and a dispo [disposition] for the judge, a fee for the private defense lawyer or one fewer case for the PD [public defender]. The defendant is relieved he didn't get something worse."[14] The judge gets a "dispo"; he comes into the process to affix the necessary stamp, not to participate.

Despite the chatter about trials and juries, the best chance for an American to go free after an arrest is still what Lyndon Johnson's Commission on Law Enforcement and the Administration of Justice called "an entirely proper conviction by policemen that the invocation of criminal sanctions is too drastic a response to many offenses."[15] There is nothing mechanical or cut-and-dried about the interrelations of the citizenry, the police, the prosecutors, and the courts. How you get arrested, why you get arrested, and what happens to you after you get arrested are all questions that provoke different answers in different places. At their best, judges in criminal courts do protect the accused from disappearance into the banality of first impressions, but the wheel has been built so they are essentially cogs. Most of the important judgments are made by others.

For someone who has been "booked" by the police, the best chance to go free is a prosecutor's decision that the cops got the wrong person or that the crime isn't worth her time. Roughly one-quarter of all "criminal filings" are dismissed on motion from the prosecution. Of the criminal cases that survive both the police processes and the more formal scrutiny by prosecutors, the overwhelming majority are closed when the "suspect" enters a guilty plea, usually swearing in open court (falsely) that he or she has been promised nothing in return for a plea. Not infrequently, the bargain is brand-new, negotiated between the prosecutor and the defendant's court-appointed counsel in the corridors while they wait for his case to be called.

Judges in the courts of limited criminal jurisdiction, which hear cases involving lesser crimes and "misdemeanors," spend a high fraction of their time reading to people who say they wish to plead guilty a list—always the same list in every courtroom in that state, required by some statute—of the rights they are sacrificing by admitting their guilt. Large principles of civil rights and civil liberties can be and are left in the corners of the system. When 96 percent of criminal cases are decided by dismissal of the charges or a plea bargain, after all, it is not necessarily important that *Mapp v. Ohio* excludes from the courtroom evidence gathered in violation of the prohibition against arbitrary search and seizure. It does not matter that the police are prepared to lie, or that the forensic lab has not done the work on the fingerprints or the blood sample.

Trial as the protection for the innocent is much overrated in the folklore. Of the 4 percent of criminal cases in the United States that are resolved by a trial, roughly one-seventh produce an acquittal. Of the fifteen cities analyzed in 1998 for the National Center for State Courts and the State Justice Institute, two (Oakland and Fort Worth) reported *no* acquittals in a year's work. Six others (Portland, Oregon; Santa Clara, California; Des Moines, Iowa; Baltimore, Maryland; Omaha, Nebraska; and Austin, Texas) showed an acquittal rate of less than one percent of the cases brought.[16] The more horrible the crime (and the more drastic the penalty), the more likely it is that a defendant who will be convicted is in fact innocent of the charges.

Recent years have brought us informed and responsible estimates of the dimensions of the problem from the Innocence Projects that started at the Benjamin N. Cardozo School of Law in New York City in 1992 and have now spread through the country (several of the most effective being at journalism schools rather than law schools); those sources estimate that as many as one-quarter of death-row residents are not guilty of the crime for which they will—ceteris paribus—be executed. No serious-minded person can defend the circus the American culture makes of these trials. But against all the evidence, we continue to proclaim that in America a defendant enjoys "the presumption of innocence."

3

Alexis de Tocqueville in the 1840s thought that the use of public trials to settle civil disputes was one of the glories of American governance, and the use of juries in such cases was a source of status for judges and a foundation stone of political life. "[T]he civil jury," he wrote, "serves to communicate the spirit of the judges to the minds of all the citizens; and this spirit, with the habits that attend it, is the soundest preparation for free institutions. It imbues all classes with a respect for the thing judged and with the notion of right. . . . [I]n civil causes . . . the judge appears as a disinterested arbiter between the conflicting passions of the parties. The jurors look up to him with confidence and listen to him with respect, for in this instance, his intellect entirely governs theirs. It is the judge who sums up the various arguments which have wearied their memory, and who guides them through the devious course of the proceedings . . . I think that the practical intelligence and political good sense of the Americans are mainly attributable to the long use that they have made of the jury in civil cases."[17]

The Seventh Amendment in the Bill of Rights guarantees that "in suits at common law, where the value in controversy shall exceed twenty dollars, the right of trial by jury shall be preserved." Today, Constitution or no Constitution, Tocqueville or no Tocqueville, the use of a jury in federal civil disputes has virtually disappeared, except for personal inquiry cases. This is not necessarily important, because sixty times as many civil cases are filed on the state level as in the federal courts, but civil trials on the state level are almost as endangered a species as criminal trials. According to a 1992 study by the Court Statistics Project of the National Center for State Courts, recently updated with little change, only 3.7 percent of all tort filings (automobile accidents, product liability, medical malpractice) were resolved in a trial, and only 2.8 percent of contract cases came to trial at all. About 15 percent of the tort trials and about 70 percent of the contract trials were "bench trials," without the participation of a jury, so the descendants of Tocqueville's civil jurors heard one case for every thirty tort filings and less than one for every hundred contract disputes that came to court. And most of the tort cases before a jury were horrors, with witnesses lying, lawyers playing mind games, and professional rehearsed "expert testimony" bought and sold for the occasion.

What is supposed to justify this stuff today is the legal profession's philosophical insistence that the most certain path to truth can be found in the unrestricted advocacy of opposing positions. Rules of procedure and rules of evidence presumably act as a refiner's fire, making sure that only the relevant arguments are pursued. But this is nonsense. As Roscoe Pound, then dean of the Harvard Law School, wrote in 1921: "Technical procedure is neither a necessary check on the magistrate in the interest of liberty nor a device to advance justice. It is a remnant of the mechanical modes of trial in the beginnings of our law, developed in the eighteenth century in an age of formal over-refinement, fostered and even further developed in the pioneer or rural American communities of the last century, and turned to new uses in the standing warfare between professional plaintiffs' lawyers and habitual defendants."[18]

Sixteen years earlier, when he was still dean of the Nebraska Law School, Pound had scornfully denounced what he called "the sporting theory of justice" as part of his now-famous talk to the annual convention of the American Bar Association, "The Causes of Popular Dissatisfaction with the Administration of Justice." The talk was not well received when new, but two generations later the ABA held a conference to celebrate the seventieth anniversary of Pound's speech. A new Roscoe Pound could give the same talk today, and will.

The worst rhetorical haze surrounds the words "rule of law," a shibboleth that gains access to many let's-pretend discussions. "It is clear that laws do not rule," wrote the British political philosopher T. D. Weldon in his 1950s book *The Vocabulary of Politics*. "Logically, they are quite different from commands. . . . People impose laws on themselves and on other people. It is therefore odd that there should be a prevalent view that the Rule of Law is something which some people have but other people do not have, like motor cars and telephones. What does it mean then to be without the Rule of Law? Is it to have no laws at all? That is not possible. . . .

"Strictly speaking there is nothing difficult or impressive about 'the Rule of Law.' It is merely a convenient way of referring to the fact that associations have rules and unless those rules are pretty generally kept and enforced the associating breaks down and the activity which it was designed to promote becomes impracticable."[19]

"The same types of matters," Charles Wyzanski wrote in 1965, "are handled quite differently in different constitutional states: in one state by courts, in another by executives; in one after hearing, in another summarily; in one by accusatory methods with severe limitations upon the prosecution, in another by investigatory methods founded upon full disclosure. Indeed all that one seems able to spell out of the rule of law concept, when looked at universally, is first, that the state recognizes a presumption that an individual has the right to have his person or property free from interference by any officer of the government unless that officer can justify his interference by reference to a general law, and second, that the state provides some machinery for the vindication of that right before an independent tribunal in all cases where a crime is charged and sometimes in other cases involving serious interferences with persons or their property. To go beyond this is to indulge in readily disproved fictions."[20]

Judge Posner tries to save the phrase, defining it to mean that the laws of a society must "be general, generally prospective, reasonably clear, and administered rationally and impartially. The rule of law is a normative notion rather than a description of what all law has in common, but it is misleadingly named; it seems to imply that a society without it is lawless, whereas a society that lacks the rule of law is merely not a liberal society."[21] But it's tricky to talk about norms, because the implication is always that the norm, this object of admiration, actually exists. As Yale law professor Jerry Mashaw put it a generation ago, "Because 'ought' implies 'can,' the norma-tive presumes the empirical."[22] It is a false presumption: The norm does not exist. There is no "can" there.

There may be a way to salvage "rule of law," to clean up the moral high ground now littered with the detritus of ex-ploded justifications created by the Bush Justice Department to defend imprisonment without trial, the torture of "high value" prisoners and the impunity of high-ranking officers. Crusaders for civil society in China have demanded what translators from the Chinese describe as "rule *by* law." The implication in that phrase is that governments' actions will be taken in the light of day with reference as required to specific documents, that governments will seek to achieve their ends by invoking or if necessary openly adopting for future use "law" that legitimizes what they do. Certainly there is a clear difference between the potentially hidden presumptions in "rule of law" and the public activities of "rule by law."

For the moment, there *is* a useful phrase, most closely asso-ciated with the name of Milton Katz, the man who made the Marshall Plan work (he was number two to both Paul Hoff-man and Averell Harriman with the rank of ambassador, and designed the European Payments Union through which the nations of devastated Europe could trade with one another). When he was associate director of the Ford Foundation and a professor at the Harvard Law School, he taught the need for a "legal order," which does not speak of "rule" but carries the connotation that people in their personal and commercial lives can know within the useful bounds of statistical likeli-hood what behavior will be protected by the institutions of government, and what behavior will be punished.

Within a legal order, one can reasonably say, as Justice Holmes did, that "the prophecies of what the courts will do in fact, and nothing more pretentious, are what I mean by the law."[23] Roscoe Pound improved on that with an amendment that the *premises* for such predictions are what the law professor means by law. In the absence of a legal order, one cannot prophesy the law. Civil liberties and civil rights if any become accidental. Economies cannot operate efficiently. Not only loans and investments but simple purchases and sales are at the mercy of political interference. Economic development will be at best retarded and at worst impossible (see Africa, and India in the days of the "license raj," when bureaucrats were empowered to suck cash from enterprise at every corner).

The virtue of the legal order is that it can be changed only in full sight, by publicized action. Erwin Griswold, former dean of the Harvard Law School, former solicitor general of the United States, noted in 1976 that "most justice in the United States is administered not in courts but in law offices."[24] The glory of the American legal system was expressed in Benjamin Cardozo's great statement from the 1910s: "Life may be lived, conduct may be ordered, it *is* lived and ordered, for unnumbered human beings without bringing them within the field where the law can be misread. . . . Their conduct never touches the borderline, the penumbra, where controversy begins. They go from birth to death, their action restrained at every turn by the power of the state, and not once do they appeal to judges to mark the boundaries between right and wrong. I am unwilling to withhold the name of law from rules which exercise this compulsion over the fortunes of mankind." Even where there is a "legal order," of course, it speaks merely to process. But results tend to be constrained by the bound-aries of process, so that lawyers can assert the likelihood of similar outcomes on similar facts.

Henry M. Hart Jr. and Albert M. Sacks in their great mimeographed textbook for first-year students at Harvard Law School wrote that "the central idea of law [is] *the principle of institutional settlement*." And we must of course start there. But the statement says little about how the principle is served. "Institutional settlement" has a sound of satisfaction, which misleads. The reality is that the system forces settlements into a time frame. The judge is a major player because he makes the decisions, all sorts of them, motions, objections, the ad-missibility of evidence and witnesses and argument. It is the second requirement of a judge (the first is attentive honesty) that he or she enjoys making decisions.

Simon H. Rifkind, special master for the Supreme Court in the division of the downstream waters of the Colorado, chairman of the Jewish Theological Seminary, power behind the scenes in New York City for two generations, left the fed-eral bench for private practice in 1947 because he couldn't raise children in New York on a judge's salary, but all his many days he liked to be called Judge. He spoke at the 1976 Pound conference to oppose the already burgeoning and now main-stream belief (it has been officially adopted by the Confer-ence of [State Supreme Court] Chief Justices) that courts should get into the business of "problem solving." "Hereto-fore," Judge Rifkind said, "the accepted model of the Ameri-can court was that of an institution devoted to the resolution of disputes. The object of the judicial intervention was to bring that dispute to an end by determining whether the plaintiff or the defendant prevailed. . . . The adversary process is a well-honed tool for use in such a contest. One of its greatest assets is a convention—the convention that one or the other party has the burden of proof with respect to particular issues. It is the allocation of the burden of proof that makes it possible to resolve all disputes and to leave none in limbo. If the party which bears the burden of proof fails, the other side prevails."

Assigning the burden of proof was for centuries a function of legal form. The lawyers representing the contestants entered "pleadings" and "responses"; it was the acceptance or rejection of these points—dictated normally not by the facts of the case (assumed to be as asserted for the purpose of pleading and response) but by the citations of legislation or previous court opinions—that determined whether the issues were "justiciable," capable of resolution by evidence, and whether the plaintiff had "standing to sue."

The decision as to the burden of proof will often determine the result of the case. Abner Mikva, now an avuncular, amused, and amusing figure at the University of Chicago Law School, who served in all three branches of government—as a state legislator and congressman, an appellate judge, and counsel to President Bill Clinton—notes the progress of a charge of patent infringement. If the owner of the patent brings suit to force someone to stop using his idea or product without a license, the burden of proof is on him. If the user sues to block enforcement of the patent, the burden of proof changes sides. And the result of the case may be determined by the formal consideration. What the judge will do in fact may be a function of which side invokes the power of the court. We are still within a legal order, and we are still in a world where a lawyer can hope to predict for his client what will happen if he brings an action at law—but by no stretch of the imagination do we have a "rule of law." Mikva himself now works mostly as an arbitrator, making judgments in a realm where each case is its own law. And the two sides may indeed be looking to solve their problems.

Because so much myth clusters around the activity of lawyers and courts, we lose the sense that this activity has a purpose beyond itself and the money that changes hands. Except in sports and politics, as we shall note when we consider the law and economics movement, real life rarely generates total victory or complete defeat. Settlement itself *is* the purpose of the law, and in the context of settlement the goal should not be to maximize but—in the lingo of the social sciences—to satisfice. Even in prosecutions under the criminal law, civilized process requires considerations of the circumstances. The adversarial approach to law, cherishing myth, makes satisfaction seem a safe harbor for wimps. The lawyers control the information that can be used for decision; the judge is largely constrained to let them fight, and is not equipped to make a more definitive contribution. Too much of what goes into settlements is hidden from public view. Too often the problem is not solved and reemerges.

This, to jump ahead many tens of thousands of words, is where we will wind up: The advocates of "problem-solving courts" are right. The thing can be done, by specially trained and informed judges applying their own expertise to the evidence in specialized courts. If we are to get there safely, there is much to do, and it cannot be done quickly.

3 THE ORIGIN OF THE SPECIES: HISTORICAL PRECEDENTS

There is no happiness, there is no liberty, there is no enjoyment of life, un-
less a man can say, when he rises in the morning, "I shall be subject to the
decision of no unwise judge today."

—Daniel Webster, 1831

S ETTING UP THE COURT SYSTEM WAS THE
very first thing the Congress did, the first item of business to come before the Senate. The Judiciary Act of
1789 was the first bill to be passed, sent to the president, and
signed by him, on September 24 of that year. Article III of the
Constitution required the creation of a Supreme Court to
hear "cases and controversies" relating to federal law, treaties
with foreign countries, the relations of the newly united
states, claims involving ships at sea, and disputes between citizens of different states. (The jurisdiction authorized by the
Constitution also included disputes between a state and citizens of another state; an infuriated, recently empowered political establishment put the kibosh on that one in the

Eleventh Amendment, which William Rehnquist's Supreme Court recently resurrected). The Constitution also authorized the creation of "such inferior courts as Congress may from time to time ordain and establish."

Although mythology and publicity speak of three equal branches of government, structurally on both the state and federal level the courts depend on the legislatures for much of their jurisdiction and nearly all of their resources. At the start, the expenses of the federal courts were paid through the State Department, then through Treasury, and into the mid-twentieth century by the Justice Department, which is the most frequent litigator in the federal courts. Not until 1939 did Congress set up a separate Administrative Office of the U.S. Courts, within the judicial branch, to handle budgets and funds. It is worth noting that under the original law the director of this office, which now has about a thousand employees, was appointed by the Supreme Court as a group, but amendments in 1990 (urged by Chief Justice Rehnquist) placed the appointing power in the hands of the chief justice alone, after "consultation" with the Judicial Conference.

The appellate jurisdiction of the U.S. Supreme Court is authorized "with such exceptions, and under such Regulations as the Congress shall make."[1] In 1868, after a Mississippi newspaper editor had challenged his conviction by a military commission for inciting former Confederates to rebel against the continuation of martial law, Congress passed a bill that deprived the Court of authority to hear appeals of claims to habeas corpus in wartime, and the Court ruled (unanimously) that it no longer had jurisdiction. In September 2004, the House of Representatives voted to deprive the Supreme

Court of power to hear appeals against state laws or constitutional amendments that prohibited "gay marriage." Congress, in a petulant mood about decisions in the Warren Court, removed the justices from the ranks of the federal employees who would receive a pay increase in 1966. And it can always probe into how the courts are conducting their business. "The authority to legislate," writes Russell R. Wheeler, longtime deputy director of the Federal Judicial Center, "creates the authority to oversee."[2]

If they wish, state legislatures and Congress can push around their respective court systems. The number of judicial districts and the staffing of the courts are determined by legislation; salaries of the court staffs and the judges themselves are set by the legislature (though many trial courts have slush funds from fees that the judges and clerks can use to make up shortfalls or mischief in legislative budgets). In some states, the power of the courts to set their own rules of procedure is circumscribed by legislation, and changes in the federal rules must be sent to Congress, which can veto them, before they are adopted. The Canadian political scientist Carl Baar and the American Robert W. Tobin have argued that the state courts did not even begin to become truly independent until well after World War II. In Massachusetts, by the testimony of its Chief Justice Margaret Marshall (not herself intimidated, as her rulings on single-sex marriage demonstrate), there are ninety-one judicial districts, each a separate line in the state budget; if a legislator doesn't like a decision in a courtroom in his district, he can cut the cleaning budget in that court and nobody says boo.[3]

The structure to be created in 1789 by the new Congress

had to be imposed, of course, alongside existing court systems that had been separately established by the British colonial authorities in each of the separate states. The Judiciary Act created thirteen federal "districts" for federal courts and decreed that each should be entirely within the boundaries of one state, that the judge in the district must live in that state, and that in considering cases the judge should follow that state's rules of procedure *and the precedents in state interpretations of existing judge-made common law.* The thirteen districts, incidentally, were not the thirteen states, because North Carolina and Rhode Island had not yet ratified the Constitution; the two replacements were Maine and Kentucky, not yet separated from Massachusetts and Virginia but too far from Boston and Richmond to take their legal business to their state capital.)

The state legislatures were not happy that national judges might usurp their courts simply because litigants lived in different states. New Hampshire proposed that "all suits at common law between citizens of different states must be commenced in the state courts."[4] Though the new act did not require it (and the Constitution's insistence on "advice and consent" necessarily applied only to the Supreme Court, the only court specified in the document), George Washington submitted the names of his nominees as district judge to the Senate for confirmation. The first Supreme Court as the first Congress invented it was to consist of six justices. They would meet, rarely, in the nation's capital. Though the Constitution assured that their salaries could not be reduced, in the absence of specific appropriation by the Congress they had no funds to hire helpers of any kind or pay their expenses. When the

Capitol was finished, the Supreme Court was awarded a room in the basement where cases could be argued (no sunlight: this in an age when illumination was by oil lamp). Its housing was upgraded in 1864 to a lovely auditorium with bright skylights in the dome, which had been the Senate chambers (these nineteenth-century chambers have been beautifully restored and are now part of the museum of the Capitol).

The Court did not have a building of its own for 146 years after the passage of the Judiciary Act. In 1925, Chief Justice William Howard Taft wrote to Senator Reed Smoot: "Most of the Judges are obliged to have their offices and official studies in their own houses or apartments. As Chief Justice, I have no office at the Capitol and must use the Conference Room and Library of the Court to meet any persons who come to see me at the Capital, either officially or otherwise. Justice [Harlan Fiske] Stone, [appointed only a few weeks before] is most embarrassed now by the inability to secure a decent room for himself at the Capitol where he can have his Law Clerk and Secretary do his work. I have pleaded with the Committee of the Senate having control of this matter, and have not been able to secure a proper office for him. . . ."[5] In his book Chief Justice Rehnquist pointed out that most of the justices who were on the bench in 1935 when the new Supreme Court Building opened did not use their chambers because they were used to working at home. Taft did not live to see the completion of that enormous building beside the Library of Congress, now completely occupied by the nine justices and their helpers.

Most of the work of the Supreme Court justices in the early days involved trying cases in their other capacity as "circuit judges." Both the English court system and most of the colonial court systems had been built on the proposition that the judge came to the location of the case, "rode circuit" from one town to another, to perform his functions. Every county seat had its county courthouse or a room that could be used for such purposes, but the judge was usually a visitor, on the bench maybe one week in six. For federal purposes, under the Judiciary Act, the country was divided into three "circuits," with pairs of the justices assigned to the circuits nearest their homes. In the first years of the Republic, the Supreme Court sat as such only two weeks a year—plus twenty-eight weeks on circuit for each individual justice. The "circuit court" in each district, which heard cases too important to be left to the mercies of a single district judge, consisted of the district judge in that state plus one or both of the Supreme Court justices assigned to this circuit and traveling in it. Today's thirteen Circuit Courts of Appeals are not descendants of this arrangement; they were established in separate legislation beginning in 1891, and they handle virtually nothing but appeals from the district courts and (in some matters) state courts, and from the decisions of federal administrative agencies and their administrative law judges.

The vestigial remnant of the old circuit system is that each Supreme Court justice today serves as a hearer of emergency appeals from one or more regional circuits to stay some action (most commonly an execution) until the Court has time to decide whether to hear the appeal. Even today, though most of them live in Washington, the justices are guaranteed to be in the building only fourteen weeks a year, for the seven two-week sessions in which they all sit on the slightly hexagonal bench they share, hear oral argument of cases, and announce decisions. All Article III federal judges can sit in district courts and hear cases, if they are needed for that purpose—or if they ask for the assignment. When he sat on the Supreme Court, Justice Tom Clark insisted on hearing a trial or two every year. Malicious gossip among federal judges says he was the most likely of all federal trial judges to suffer reversal in the courts of appeals.

For many judges, it's still a peripatetic occupation. Most of the time, judges are treated within the courthouses as lords of creation, but the laws require that trials be held at places convenient to the litigants, not the judges. New Jersey is a single district with federal courtrooms in three cities, and a federal judge in New Jersey must expect to sit during the year not only on his home bench but also in courtrooms in Newark, Trenton, or Camden. Most judges in state appellate courts don't live where the court sits. In New York, the appellate division has four homes: in Manhattan, Brooklyn, and two upstate cities. The judges who sit in Albany may and do live anywhere upstate, traveling monthly to Albany for a week of hearing cases.

Federal circuit courts hear appeals in three-judge panels. They meet in the morning to hear oral argument and then in the afternoons to pick winners. Usually, each side gets fifteen minutes, with up to half an hour for "complex cases." Each circuit has its own schedule of how often panels meet. The range is from twenty-eight days (seven four-day weeks) in the Fifth Circuit (Atlanta) to fifty days (ten five-day weeks) in the First Circuit (Boston). The briefs have been in the judges' hands for sixty days, placed there by the administrators and clerks. In the afternoons of the hearings days, they sit together, discuss, and vote on the cases they have just heard and on recent submissions they agree to decide without hearing oral argument. Thereafter, in most circuits, they communicate by fax or e-mail, to make sure no one judge will talk about the case with another one, conceivably ganging up on the third member of the panel. District judges can be and frequently are co-opted by appellate courts—on the invitation of the chief judge of that appellate court—to sit on the three-judge appellate panels, and their vote counts. They, too, often travel to their week on the appellate panel.

A litigant who doesn't like the ruling he gets from a three-judge panel can appeal to the appeals court sitting en banc (in theory, en banc means all the active judges, though circuits with more than fifteen judges are permitted by law to choose a smaller number as a panel for the whole; the Ninth Circuit, with twenty-eight authorized judges, will assign fifteen to a panel). When the appeals court sits en banc its personnel includes neither the co-opted district judges nor the "senior judges," over seventy of whom do sit in the three-judge panels. Such appeals to the whole court, by the way, are not often heard. Announcing the move to fifteen judges per panel, Chief Judge Mary M. Schroeder of the Ninth Circuit reported that of 852 such requests for rehearing in 2004, only 22 were granted.

The Judiciary Act also made provision for a clerk of each district court, and a clerk for the Supreme Court. Among the rules for the new federal courts laid down by the Congress was a requirement that each clerk inform the clerks of all other judges when a case was decided. The first session of the Supreme Court was scheduled for February 1, 1790—in New

York City, of course, because the federal government, such as it was, sat there–but it had to be postponed a day because only one of the six justices showed up. Congress appropriated money to pay the judges and the clerks their salaries. The clerks were permitted to assess fees for their work, and often enough they kept the fees: in the early nineteenth century, many clerks took home more money than the judges. In the late nineteenth century, when immigrants were being accepted into citizenship by the hundreds on payment of $3, it was not unknown for the judges' clerks to do the swearing ceremony and keep the money.

2

Alexis de Tocqueville, writing in the 1840s for a European audience, explained that the new United States had not sacrificed the idea of aristocracy. Aristocracy everywhere, he argued, was essentially the group that had nothing to gain from innovation, and there was such a group in the United States. Lawyers, he wrote, "form the highest political class and the most cultivated portion of society. . . . The courts of justice are the visible organs by which the legal profession is enabled to control the democracy. . . . If I were asked where I place the American aristocracy, I should reply without hesitation that it is not among the rich, who are united by no common tie, but that it occupies the judicial bench and the bar."[6]

And this primacy of the legal profession was especially important in America, Tocqueville added, because "scarcely any

political question arises in the United States that is not resolved, sooner or later, into a judicial question."[7] Everyone in
America has access to the courts. This was different from the
English system, which derived from a time when a royal writ
was necessary to summon a defendant to court.[8] Indeed, in
Britain a hundred years after the American Revolution it was
still necessary for a plaintiff to procure a writ from a bureaucracy that related to the crown before courts would hear a
case. A political issue that could not get a hearing in Parliament probably also could not get a hearing from the issuer of
writs.

In the American system of government, for as long as there
has been a national government, Congress and the president
have had (and have taken) the opportunity to do nothing
about an issue or a problem confronting the country, but
lawyers referring to a Constitution can often find a way to
present the matter as "justiciable." Henry Hart and Albert
Sacks wrote half a century ago in their mimeographed textbook for Harvard Law School freshmen that "emerging problems of social maladjustment tend always to be submitted first
to the courts. . . . Legislatures and administrative agencies
tend always to make law by way not of original solutions of
social problems but by alteration of the solutions first laid
down by the courts." Alexander Hamilton famously wrote in
The Federalist that the courts would be "the least dangerous
branch, having neither force nor will," but he did not envision
the practical situation of a later time. The courts must be
open and must decide the case. An appellate court can punt,
referring a matter back to the district judge for further con-

sideration (the Supreme Court does this a lot), but the district judge has gotta rule on the dispute.

This is obviously true in the state courts, many of which have a "general jurisdiction." But even the federal courts, which have a limited jurisdiction (they can hear only cases that plead the Constitution or federal legislation as the foundation of their suit), must spring into action if the right buttons are pushed. As early as 1816, Chief Justice John Marshall wrote that "the judiciary cannot, as the legislature may, avoid a measure because it approaches the confines of the constitution. We cannot pass it by because it is doubtful. With whatever doubts, with whatever difficulties, a case may be attended, we must decide it if it be brought before us. We have no more right to decline the exercise of jurisdiction which is given than to usurp that which is not given. The one or the other would be treason to the constitution."[9] This has got the Court in terrible trouble on occasion. *Roe v. Wade* is the biggest example in recent times—a decision rendered almost three years after the case was argued, asserting a pregnant woman's right to an abortion she had undergone before she sued, where the Court inserted itself into a political debate that would have gone pretty much the way the case went if the justices had stayed out of it—Ronald Reagan as governor of California had already signed into law a permissive abortion bill. (I shall argue later that though I was among those who disliked the result, the Supreme Court could not have stayed out of the 2000 Florida election brouhaha.) *Dred Scott* is perhaps the best example from history; George W. Bush cited it when he was asked a question about the courts in the 2004 presidential debates. The fact that the courts are there and available to all is a prime characteristic of American political life, and calls attention to itself with some frequency.

3

Spreading west through the continent, the communities of farmers and merchants, preachers and builders, organized their towns around a courthouse square and their political lives (not to mention their entertainment) around the peripatetic work patterns of the "circuit judge" who came to town for a week or so every month or two months and took care of the crimes and disputes of the community. A hundred and forty years after Marshall's comment that the court must hear the cases it can hear, retired federal judge and successful corporate lawyer Simon H. Rifkind called the courts "the problem solvers of our society: Shall we prosecute a war, or make peace? What is life; when does death begin? How should we operate prisons and hospitals? No problem seems to be beyond the desire of the American people to entrust to the courts."[10]

The Canadian law professor W. A. Bogart makes an even larger "list of issues in the USA remitted to courts . . . housing, medical care, contraceptives and abortion, voting, privacy, bussing, affirmative action, pornography, defendants' rights (or lack thereof) are but a few. At the same time, the thrall of judges has cast a wide net, sweeping into it other kinds of lawsuits such as tort litigation [personal injury] with its claimed capacity to regulate all manner of social and economic issues."[11] Thomas F. Burke, a research scholar of health issues at the University of California, notes shrewdly that resort to the courts is built into the constitutional system as part of the Founders' concerns about centralized power: "[C]ourts offer activists a way to address social problems without seeming to augment the power of the state."[12]

"Judge" is one of the handful of honorific titles that people keep all their lives, like president, senator, governor, general, ambassador. People stand up when the judge walks into his courtroom, and again when he leaves—and in most places it is *his* courtroom, maintained by taxpayers, permanently staffed at public expense by clerks and police, bailiffs and court reporters, reserved for his exclusive use. He wears a robe, and his desk is elevated several steps above the rest of the courtroom. If he seeks evidence of his own importance, he need merely look around him. Tocqueville was impressed: "In the recreations of private life," Tocqueville wrote, "as well as in the turmoil of public business, in public and in the turmoil of legislative assemblies, the American judge is constantly surrounded by men who are accustomed to regard his intelligence as superior to their own."[13] Critics speak of a disease of "robitis," defined by a Midwest judge as annoyance when you walk into your son's high school gymnasium for a basketball game and the audience does not rise. Judge Alex Kozinski of the Ninth Circuit Court of Appeals notes drily that "judging is a job where self-indulgence is a serious occupational hazard."[14]

Philip Habib, a Lebanese-American from Brooklyn, the

first career foreign-service officer ever to be deputy secretary of state, once explained that former ambassadors still like to be called ambassador because "when an ambassador walks the corridors of his embassy, *evereebody* kisses his ass." The same goes for the judge in his courtroom. Bernard Botein, who served as a New York State trial judge before becoming chief judge of an appellate division, remembered the last day of the first trial over which he presided, when he stayed in his chambers a while to look up a point of law in connection with the charge he was about to give the jury, and as he entered the anteroom to his courtroom apologized to the clerk helping him don his robe: "I'm pretty late. I'll apologize to the jurors and counsel for keeping them waiting."

"Judge," said the clerk, "I hope you won't think I'm speaking out of turn. But when you've been here as long as I have, you'll know that no matter what time the judge enters the courtroom, it's ten o'clock."[15]

Robert W. Tobin of the National Center for State Courts lists some examples of lordly behavior by judges:

- A North Carolina judge issued an order from the bench to a city official to close off traffic on a street adjacent to the courthouse, because the auto noise was distracting the jurors. . . . The city sealed off a block of a street in the downtown area of a major city.
- A judge in an Alabama court placed his seat near a window so that he could spit his tobacco outside. The sheriff obligingly set up barricades on the sidewalk to protect pedestrians.

- A judge in Ohio once called Eastern Airlines on behalf of a court consultant to order that the consultant's plane be held until he arrived and then advised the consultant to stop worrying about it because everything was taken care of. [But Eastern did ignore the phone call.]
- A rural judge in Louisiana jailed a ferry boat operator for adhering to the ferry schedule even though he had been summoned by bullhorn to return to the dock to pick up the judge.[16]

From 1920 to 1939, when an embarrassed Supreme Court overruled its previous decision, federal judges were exempt from income tax, because the Constitution said a judge's salary could not be reduced, and the Court had ruled that compelling federal judges to pay income tax was in effect a reduction in salary. (Congress irritably passed a law to assure that the pay of *new* judges would be taxable, and the Court declared that law, too, unconstitutional.) In the 1970s a group of federal judges sued to force Congress to raise their salaries, because inflation had eroded the purchasing power of their paychecks. In 2003, Supreme Court justice Stephen Breyer expressed annoyance at his inability to get the necessary fourth vote from his brethren to hear an appeal from a circuit court that had held that Congress did not violate the Constitution when it specifically excluded Supreme Court justices from an otherwise across-the-board automatic federal cost-of-living pay raise. (He may have been right, too.) The state constitution of West Virginia prohibits the legislature from cutting the budget requests of the state court system.

Individual judges who find their courtroom or chambers a pigsty can order the place cleaned and the bill sent to the county or state—and the burden of proof that the money should not be supplied rests on the recipients of the mandate to pay.[17] In 1991, the chief judge of New York's highest court brought suit against the governor of the state to force a higher budget for the court system, and the governor, feeling trapped in his own state's court system, went to the federal courts to try to stop the proceedings.[18] A compromise was achieved, giving the courts most of what they said they needed. In 1996, the supreme court of Pennsylvania issued an order to the other branches of the state government to fund trial courts, and the money was found by the legislature. In 2002, the Kansas Supreme Court took matters into its own hands: When the state legislature cut the budget for the state courts, it imposed an "emergency fee" on litigants to fill in the receipts side of the ledger.[19] In 2005, North Carolina chief justice I. Beverly Lake warned an audience of lawyers that in the face of a cut from $383 million to $310 million in the state's appropriation for the courts, North Carolina courts might delay all civil cases until the backlog of criminal cases was cleared out.[20]

Bruce Jackson, Harvard junior fellow and Ph.D. turned spokesman for the convicted, notes that "the worst procedural offense one may commit in a court is not lying about one's guilt but insulting the judge or interfering with the normal workings of the court itself. . . . [C]ontempt of court . . . is the only crime in our criminal code in which the person of-fended is immediately permitted to act as prosecutor, jury and judge. It is also the only crime that can be purged by the offender saying, 'I'm sorry, I didn't mean it, I'll do what you wish.' "[21] Historically, public criticism of a judge has been punished by that judge on his own motion, without submitting the matter to a grand jury for indictment, and denying the accused the right to counsel, let alone a jury trial.

As late as 1940, a Missouri judge relying on Blackstone's *Commentaries* (enshrined in the Missouri 1820 constitution as the compendium of English common law) ruled that a cartoon in the *St. Louis Post-Dispatch* that ridiculed judicial rulings involving the Democratic machine was "constructive contempt" that could be punished by time in jail as well as a fine. Actually, the British law professor Sir John Fox had already shown that Blackstone had got it wrong, relying on a trivial case that had not been taken into the British canons. The Missouri Supreme Court pondered the question for ten months, then freed the newspaper and its cartoonist only on the argument that the criticism had come after the case had been decided and could not be considered a disruption of the trial.[22]

And there is a bit of mystique. "One of the things that laymen, even lawyers, do not understand," Felix Frankfurter said after becoming a Supreme Court justice, "is indicated by the question you hear so often: 'Does a man become any different when he puts on a gown?' I say, 'If he's any good, he does.'" The great tension in judicial process is between the rich who want law—the "rule of law," consistency, precedent, stability, validation in effect of their own wealth and power—and the poor who want justice, the "fair" resolution of the particular case. And dignity, especially dignity. Judges were lawyers before they became judges—it is in most states the only route,

though there is nothing in the federal Constitution that prohibits a president from appointing a nonlawyer to the bench—
and their clients were those who could afford legal services.
Trial lawyers who represent plaintiffs in personal-injury cases
use their substantial excess financial resources to pay for judicial campaigns in states where judges are elected, and public
defenders as well as prosecutors are beginning to show up in
the judicial lists. But most judges tend to be from either the
netherworld of political clubs or the top-of-the-world country club community. (More than half of the judges appointed
by Presidents Bill Clinton and George W. Bush in his first
term were millionaires.) Corporate lawyers who become
judges sometimes change their worldview dramatically when
the experience of presiding over cases introduces them to human misery, and to the often miserable lawyers who handle
the legal business of the poor. But in the appellate courts, of
course, judges are far removed from the real world.

Europe knew nothing like that. In Europe, magistrates
are civil servants, protected from lèse-majesté but no different from other government employees. They enforced a
written law, or a monarch's wish. In England, law judges
spoke for a "common law" to be deduced from precedent in
similar matters, but they were subject to overrule by courts
of chancery, presumably agencies of justice, which answered
to the king. (Three American states—Arkansas, Mississippi,
and Tennessee—still have such "equity jurisdictions," and,
Robert Tobin writes, "You can get in big trouble in these
three states by suggesting that a separate chancery court
does not make much sense.")[23] One of the complaints in the

Declaration of Independence is that George III "has made Judges dependent on his Will alone."

The Constitution established the independence of the (federal) judiciary by granting appointments for life, and prohibiting the reduction of a judge's salary or the dismissal of judges by any road other than impeachment. Theoretically, the appointment stands only so long as the judge can claim good behavior, but only the House of Representatives as proposers of impeachment and the Senate as jurors in an impeachment trial can decide that a federal judge who shot a lawyer in his courtroom or a wife in their bedroom has forfeited claims to good behavior; otherwise the convicted murderer will continue to be a federal judge and draw his salary while in jail. In 1984, Judge Walter L. Nixon Jr., a federal judge in Mississippi by appointment of Lyndon B. Johnson, was convicted of lying to a federal grand jury about alleged payments to him to help the son of an oilman who had been indicted for drug trafficking. He refused to resign, was impeached by the House of Representatives by a vote of 197–0, and then sued to prevent the Senate from hearing his impeachment through a committee rather than on the floor of the Senate itself. He lost that one, too, but in the years from 1984 to 1989, while he served his five-year sentence in the federal penitentiary, he received $286,500 in salary as a federal judge.[24]

The highest-ranking federal judge ever to go to prison was Martin Manton, who had sold his votes as chief judge of the Second Circuit Court of Appeals (where his companions were a horrified Learned Hand, his cousin Augustus Hand, and

Yale law school dean Thomas Swan). Appealing his conviction, Manton argued that "from a broad viewpoint, it serves no public policy for a high judicial officer to be convicted of a judicial crime. It tends to destroy the confidence of the people in the courts."[25] Though the states are less protective of their judges, and indeed subject the great majority of them to the indignity of periodic reelection, it is interesting to note that in the summer of 2002 a sixty-year-old Brooklyn judge in New York State's court of general jurisdiction pleaded guilty to demanding a cut before he would approve the fee of a lawyer who had won a large damage award for a three-year-old girl. He was convicted and sentenced to jail for at least three years and was permitted to retain his pension of $97,000 a year, for life.[26]

Assemblages of jurors go back to England in 1166, and the "assize of novel disseisin." At the end of a generation of civil wars, marauding bandits were taking over farm properties, ejecting the occupants, and lording it over the victims. In the new court, a jury of twelve was charged with answering the single question, "Were these people forced off the land they had occupied?" The defense that the occupiers really owned the land was not permitted, and the case had to be heard on the day it was called, no postponements. If the jury ruled that the new possessors had taken it by force, the king could and would expel them. Pollock and Maitland in their classic *History of English Law* report that within fifty years ordinary farmers were successfully appealing to the royal courts against the baronets and even barons who had expropriated them.[27] The World Bank's Richard Messick notes that this assize "marks the beginning of the civil action in England. For the first time plaintiffs could secure relief in a national court. It is the beginning, too, of the system of using juries to decide questions of fact." And this was, as Messick points out, a sophisticated system, for questions of ownership were adjudicated without juries in a separate court. The unbundling of "ownership" and "possession," one of the great intellectual accomplishments in English law, began here.[28] It could not have been done in antiquity without a jury to validate it, but that doesn't defend the civil jury today.

Judge Kenneth W. Starr insists that Supreme Court justices "focus closely on the specific facts of the case."[29] But the decision to hear a case (and the Supreme Court hears about one ten-thousandth of one percent of all the lawsuits brought each year in the United States) has nothing to do with factual questions. Facts are accepted as given by the lower court, and the assumption is that any errors in fact have been corrected in the earlier appeals process. "A petition for a writ of certiorari [i.e., acceptance of jurisdiction for an appeal] is rarely granted," the Court notes in its rules, "when the asserted error consists of erroneous factual findings." How would the Supreme Court know the facts? It hasn't seen the place, the product, the persons; it has merely heard and read the lawyers' presentations, which seek advantage, not truth. Today, as sixty-plus years ago when Judge Jerome Frank wrote it, those looking for justice will do much better in the trial court than on appeal. The trial judge has wiggle room.

In Bernard Botein's lovely formulation, "A judge first searches the facts, then searches the law, then searches his soul."[30] Living, as noted, in the partial vacuum of the printed record, the Supreme Court must want desperately to make wiggle room for itself (as the Warren Court did in the 1950s and 1960s, struggling to remedy what had been an accepted racial injustice in America). Even then, it cannot search the facts, and must make do with the law and the souls of the nine justices. Though one can stretch the argument too far, there is a sense in which the appellate judges don't care whether the convict is guilty or not. Sometimes this is a shame.

4

So much is conventional and necessary, but far from sufficient and maybe not true. Certainly, there is another, less romantic way to see the status and evolution of the American judiciary. Even in Tocqueville's time, lawyers were an aristocracy by self-appointment, and like Lord Melbourne when he received the Order of the Garter, they could claim special pleasure in their recognition as an aristocracy because "there is no damned merit to it." Some colonial lawyers had British training, apprenticeship in one of the Inns of Court, and they and their friends were effective antagonists for George III in the years before the American Revolution. But anyone could be a lawyer, and most lawyers were far from learned. There were no law schools or bar exams. Men who wanted to be lawyers apprenticed themselves to someone who already called himself a lawyer, and after three years the journeyman might anoint his apprentice by introducing him to a judge who would then permit this new-minted lawyer to practice before him.

It is not clear that judges were regarded as the aristocracy of lawyers. At the Constitutional Convention, Benjamin Franklin (who almost forty years earlier had served as a justice of the peace in Philadelphia) urged that judges be selected by vote of the lawyers in the district, because they would choose the best of their group to get rid of the competition. (He said the Scots already did something of the sort.) In British precedent, the judges held royal commissions, and every one of the original thirteen states entered the Union with constitutional provisions that judges would be either appointed by the governor or (like U.S. senators, as the federal constitution was originally written) elected by the legislatures.

Then as now, legislatures could be quite irresponsible in judicial matters. Henry Friendly, writing then with the authority of the immediate past presidency of the *Harvard Law Review* rather than as the federal appellate judge he became, noted that in Connecticut in the early nineteenth century "the members of the Council appointed all the judges and then did not hesitate to appear as advocates before them. . . . On other occasions they appointed themselves judges of the lower courts and then reviewed their own decisions. One Jonathan Brace, who was a member of the Council from 1802 to 1818, was also a judge of the county court from 1809 to 1821, judge of the probate court from 1809 to 1824, state's attorney for Hartford from 1807 to 1809, and judge of the city court from 1799 to 1815. While this record might be hard to duplicate," Friendly remarks, "it illustrates the abuses to which the system gave rise."[31]

The first justice appointed to the Supreme Court by George Washington wore a British barrister's wig to court, and others dressed in red robes with ermine trim. Deciding cases, each of the six Justices (on the rare occasions when the entire court was present) wrote and read aloud his own opinion in the British manner. It was not until John Marshall became chief justice in 1801 that it became universal practice for Supreme Court judges to wear plain black robes. (A couple of centuries later, Chief Justice William Rehnquist had *his* robes decorated with gold stripes at the end of the sleeves, certifying—correctly—that he was the *chief* justice and a bigger shot than his brethren.) And it was Marshall who established the custom of one justice pronouncing the decision of the Court. It could be argued that the main reason the Supreme Court achieved centrality in American governance is that early in its history one man—and that man greatly admired—served as chief justice for forty years, through the administrations of eight presidents.

At the end of the eighteenth century, more democratic attitudes gained force, and starting with Vermont when it split off from New York, the new states chose their judges by popular election. By 1840, twelve years into the Jackson era in American politics, the election of judges, county by county, was the norm in most states. Georgetown law professor Roy Schotland, who has been working as executive secretary of the Conference of Chief Justices to hold off the barbarians of the political advertising racket, says that in fact the pressure to elect rather than appoint judges was not part of a Jacksonian spoils system, but rather a way to preserve the judiciary from governors and legislators who would put cronies, hacks, or fanatics (or, as Friendly notes, themselves) on the bench. Centralizing the authority in the hands of the governors and nationally in presidents raised problems of its own. Though it was not until Richard Nixon that presidents sought ideological (as distinct from merely political) allies for judicial nominations (Herbert Hoover with the enthusiastic concurrence of a Republican chairman of the Senate Judiciary Committee nominated Benjamin Cardozo, a New York Jew and scion of a Tammany Hall family; Harry Truman gave the first vacancy in his term to Republican senator Harold Burton), judicial nominations by presidents and governors were too likely to be rewards for political activity. The lawyers of the mid-nineteenth century felt that an electorate was more likely to heed professional views of judicial candidates than governors with narrow constituencies to please.

Tocqueville himself was depressed by the developments of the 1830s: "Some state constitutions make the members of the judiciary elective, and they are even subjected to frequent re-elections. I venture to predict that these innovations will sooner or later be attended with fatal consequences; and that it will be found out at some future period that by thus lessening the independence of the judiciary, they have attacked not only the judicial power, but the democratic republic itself."[32] It is not yet determined whether he was wrong or merely premature; we shall look at the problem in depth in chapter 9. At the turn of the second millennium, 87 percent of all state trial and appellate judges in the United States were either elected to their office or subject to "retention elections" after their appointment. State supreme courts were more likely to be appointed by governors, but ordinary people cared a lot less about supreme courts.

Cardozo's insistence that the same matters should be decided the same way in different places was even more difficult to enforce in the America of the early nineteenth century than it is today (and it's impossible today). The roads were bad, the telegraph was still in the mists of time, and the trial courtroom was like the teacher's classroom in the egg-crate school: Nobody on the outside knew what was going on. Law *was* different not only from state to state but also from county to county within the states, and even from courtroom to courtroom within the county. Most courts were county courts in county courthouses. The county paid the sheriff, the bailiff, the clerks, the prosecutor, and the judge. At best, the judges were part of what the public thought of as a court-house gang, not a label that carries high prestige. There was a populist tradition,[33] especially in the South, that distrusted both judges and lawyers. Among the symbols of that tradition was a dislike for judges wearing any robes. In Alabama as late as the 1970s, judges who would be standing for reelection sat in business suits, until Chief Justice Howell Heflin (later to be a U.S. senator) made robing part of his effort to build the dignity of the Alabama courts. When they began wearing robes, the Alabama justices arranged that the clothing would be paid for—waste not, want not—out of a federal grant under the Law Enforcement Assistance Administration program.

Robert Tobin notes that the relationship of the county and the local judge was more complicated than anything in the philosophy of the law school professors. Tobin visited Alabama in the 1970s, during Heflin's fight to reform the system, and went to meet with Judge Jack Wallace of Barbour County, brother of then governor and still star segregationist George Wallace: "Judge Wallace was a genial man and an astute observer of the Alabama scene. His relationship to the governor gave him a certain cachet of which he was aware, but he observed that many people in the circuit would come to him about personal problems even if he were not related to the governor. When I arrived for our interview, the benches outside his office were filled with people who were clearly not among the affluent members of the community. Poor people depended on the judge to protect them or help them, not just because they elected him, but because they viewed the judicial role in broader terms than mere adjudication of disputes. People came to the judge with tales of family woes, and needs, requests for intercession with various agencies, and a variety of other social problems. . . . Residents of dying counties and dying county seats know that the end is near when judges stop coming around. Judicial presence is an important symbol of civic viability. . . ."[34]

Texas, Tobin writes, still "provides a good example of autonomous general jurisdiction courts. To this day, judges of the general jurisdiction court of Texas (the district court) are constituted as individual judges of a particular district. There are 394 separate districts. . . . Each court has a separate number and is regarded as a separate court. If you walk down the hall of a courthouse with several different district judges, there will be a sign posted indicating the number of the court. The numbers indicate the order in which the district courts were created, so in one courthouse you may see widely separated court numbers."[35] Texas also has three separate statewide courts of criminal jurisdiction, depending on the crime alleged, and an entirely separate court of criminal appeals: the Texas Supreme Court does not hear criminal cases.

Tobin tells another story of Alabama, where "there were a

number of courts created by special legislation applying to only one county. The residence requirements for divorce differed by county, as did the age at which a person ceased legally to be a juvenile. One special law to create a court abolished all courts of comparable jurisdiction in the county. What had occurred was that the attorneys in this county did not like the local judge and had the legislature create another court with a judge of their choosing. No one seemed to realize that the existing court had been abolished, and it continued to function."[36] Not many counties had enough legal business for a full-time judge; some judges held other jobs, some rode circuit, sitting in three or four courthouses a month. Often enough, each judge made his own rules for the cases in his court.

Even today in most states the local courts have the right to establish some local rules of procedure. The Internet carries "The Protocol and Practice of Persons Appearing in the Court of Judge Michael O. Wilkinson" in the Superior Court of Arizona, Maricopa County (Phoenix): "Long boilerplate motions cranked out on the word processor are ignored. Oral argument is rarely necessary but often requested. I read the motion. I don't need it read to me. . . . I am always amazed when counsel cannot resolve discovery disputes. . . . I will take phone calls to settle disputes, but it better be important. . . ." When New York State set up a "commercial division" with seven especially well-regarded judges to help the state system retain business that lawyers had been taking to the federal courts, the individual judges were given authority to write their own rules for the filing of motions and the issuance of various orders in their own courts. The clerks tell the lawyers which judges want things done which way.

Tocqueville might credit the civil jury as the source of special respect for the judiciary, but the jury trial was seen by most Americans in the nineteenth century as a way for ordinary people to prevent judicial tyranny. Then as now, lawyers had little reluctance to work on juries to gain results contrary to law, what a later time would call "jury nullification." Juries were and are always susceptible to arguments that relate to this case and not to the consistency of the law: Whatever its applicability to a world of judges and stare decisis, Cardozo's hope of achieving identical results for identical facts obviously runs afoul of any civil jury system. This battling for hearts and minds did not diminish the conviviality of the group of lawyers and the judge taking his week in this place on circuit. It was all part of the game. But the physical circumstance of the county courthouse and the social traditions of trial-based law made for a somewhat raffish approach to the law, not for popular reverence of judges or lawyers.

Tobin writes compendiously of the condition of American courts right after World War II: "Many judges were elected and were beholden to those who supported them, very commonly lawyers who appeared before them. . . . Politics rather than merit pervaded the whole system and extended into court support divisions, some of which were appendages of urban political machines. . . . Trial courts, even those of general jurisdiction, were deeply intertwined with complex local government structures and manifested all the intricate organizational subdivisions of this structure. . . . Because many judges had no real support staff, traveled on a circuit, were part-time, were not attorneys, or lacked any significant administrative authority, they were not in a position to run their own courts. Lawyers willingly filled the void. Prosecutors controlled criminal calendars, and civil attorneys controlled the civil calendar. All the judge had to do was show up."[37]

5

Measuring the stature of the judicial branch, Tocqueville, like modern commentators, stressed the fact (unique in the world for the better part of two hundred years, though the European Union has now followed suit) that judges in the United States can declare "unconstitutional" and therefore void the laws and regulations enacted by a legislature with the consent of the executive. One of the great political science questions of the early twentieth century was the locus of sovereignty in a polity where there was no sovereign. Unlike a king, a president was greatly constrained—he could not even appoint ambassadors to represent him abroad without the consent of the Senate—but he was of course the head of state. Woodrow Wilson while a professor at Princeton (he changed his mind when he became president) thought sovereignty in the United States resided in the Congress, especially the House of Representatives, where all money bills had to originate. John Jay, the first chief justice (he resigned to become governor of New York), thought that the revolution and the Constitution had transferred sovereignty from the British throne to "the people of the United States," with some residual sovereignty for the citizens of the individual states. Common sense and analogy to royalty placed sovereignty in the office of the president. Harold Laski, British leftist, chairman of the Labour

Party, first head of the London School of Economics, and faithful correspondent of Justice Holmes, put it in the Supreme Court, and there it has stayed. (Laski also, it should be noted, thought both Britain and the United States had a good deal to learn, especially in criminal cases, from the procedures in the Soviet Union. Indeed, he wrote in 1935 and reprinted in a book in 1940, "the whole world will go to school to Russia in the next generation."[38]) The Supreme Court, writes Judge Kenneth W. Starr of Whitewater fame, is "first among equals."[39]

This power in the courts, of course, makes the United States much less a democracy than its propagandists have always insisted it was. In the blunt statement of Robert H. Jackson, the last Supreme Court justice to rise from a background that did not include law school (born in the small town of Jamesport, New York, he became a lawyer by the apprenticeship route): "Judicial power to nullify a law duly passed by the representative process is a restriction upon the power of the majority to govern the country."[40]

Indeed, it is worse than Jackson argued. Though final adjudication of such political matters rests in the hands of a court of last resort in each of the fifty states for violations of a state constitution, and at the Supreme Court for violations of the U.S. Constitution, there are many situations where a single trial judge can temporarily enjoin political authority from enforcing a law or in general carrying out its wishes. (For many years—until the Great Depression of the 1930s discredited the business leadership of the country—judges routinely issued injunctions ordering people striking their employer to go back to work. As illustrated in the New York transit strike at Christmastime 2005, it is still the device of choice to enforce laws that prohibit strikes by public employees.) And unless the object of an injunction can get a higher-level court to intervene, the judge's "stay"—the command you give a dog—becomes what an unfortunate vice president of the United States once called "controlling authority." While the suit is in progress, you can't cut the trees in the habitat of the spotted owl.

It is sophistry to rest the argument for this power, as John Marshall did, on the supposed fact that the Constitution was adopted by the people while the laws are written merely by legislators. In his Holmes lectures of 1958, Judge Learned Hand argued that the Supreme Court's authority to void acts of Congress had been accomplished by a coup de main,[41] but there can be no doubt that James Madison, then a congressman shepherding the Bill of Rights through its adoption process, intended the relationship to work out that way. The problem is, he thought judicial power was necessary not to express the people's will as written in the Constitution but to frustrate the will of the majority when legitimate minority interests would otherwise be sacrificed. For liberty to thrive, he argued, it was necessary for ultimate control to rest with a nonrepresentative governmental body.[42]

When the Supreme Court issues orders on the authority of the Constitution, there is no appeal—at least, for a while. As early as 1793, the barely organized Supreme Court refused to give Secretary of State Thomas Jefferson an advisory opinion President Washington had requested, because advice did not have to be taken, and the Court was not to be second-guessed. This is a luxurious status. Justice Jackson once reminded his brethren that they were not final because they were infallible; they were infallible because they were final. With the passage of time, finality fades. Perhaps the most important power a Constitution gives a Supreme Court is the appeal to the document as a greater authority than precedent, the Court's own prior decisions. "There can be no authoritative interpretation of the Constitution," Edward H. Levi wrote while still dean of the University of Chicago Law School (he later became Gerald Ford's attorney general). "The constitution in its general provisions embodies the conflicting ideals of the community. Who is to say what these ideals mean in any definite way? Certainly not the framers, for they did their work when the words were put down. The words are ambiguous. Nor can it be the Court, for the Court cannot bind itself in this manner; an appeal can always be made back to the Constitution."

The power of the Supreme Court to declare federal laws unconstitutional was first asserted by Chief Justice Marshall in 1803, under circumstances still a little embarrassing for historians and especially law professors. The case involved a William Marbury, a loyal Federalist appointed a justice of the peace in the District of Columbia by President John Adams, in one of some forty commissions Adams signed in the last hours of his presidency. These commissions required a seal from the secretary of state before they actually awarded the jobs, and the secretary of state, John Marshall—already appointed chief justice and hearing cases but continuing to serve in the Adams cabinet in its last months—had in fact sealed Marbury's appointment. But there was a slip twixt the cup and the lip. These commissions were supposed to be delivered to their recipients by *James* Marshall, President Adams's senior administrative assistant and John's brother (himself appointed in this last-minute rush to a seat on one of the new circuit courts created by a lame-duck Congress in the Judiciary Act of 1801 to take the burden of hearing cases off the shoulders of the Supreme Court justices and to assure that the federal courts would retain a Federalist attitude after Thomas Jefferson and his Republicans took power). And somehow James Marshall had failed to make the deliveries.

Taking office, Jefferson's attorney general, who was also holding a place as secretary of state until James Madison could dissolve other ties and join the Jefferson cabinet, found some dozens of commissions, fully sealed, on his predecessor's desk. He asked what he should do with them, and Jefferson (who planned and soon got the repeal of the 1801 Act), told him to keep them, thus preventing three dozen Adams appointees from taking office. Marbury sued—it was a political case: Marbury was a rich land speculator who did not need the part-time JP job (there is to this day a Hotel Marbury in Washington, on land he once owned)—and it started at the top, in the Supreme Court, because the Judiciary Act of 1789, which established the Court, gave it power to issue writs of mandamus (orders to do what the Court said) to both private litigants and governments.

It is not clear that Madison would have delivered the commissions if Marshall had ordered him to do so: Thirty-three years later, Marshall ordered Andrew Jackson's White House and the state government of Georgia to honor the country's treaty with the Choctaw Indians, who were expelled anyway, from their homelands to Oklahoma. But Marshall found a way to assert his authority without attempting to exercise it.

He agreed that Marbury should have his commission, but said he lacked authority to compel its delivery. The Constitution listed the matters that triggered the "original jurisdiction" of the new Supreme Court—the cases it could hear from their beginning rather than on appeal—and mandamus was not among them. The first Judiciary Act purported to expand the Court's jurisdiction, but the Constitution (adopted not merely by a legislature but by the people, as in "We the people of the United States") stood senior to any legislation. Legislation that violated the Constitution was void from the beginning, and no court could enforce it or use it. The role of the Supreme Court was not to make law but to determine what the law *is*. When the law is inherited from the British common law or has been created by a legislature, the legislature can change it. But the powers of the legislature are also circumscribed by the Constitution that established the Court, the Congress and the presidency alike, and when the Court says a law violates the Constitution, that law is toast.

This was not, by the way, the first time an English-speaking court had asserted its power to throw out legislation. In 1609, as part of his continuous contentious dialogue with King James I, Lord Coke had proclaimed that "when an Act of Parliament is against common right and reason, or repugnant, or impossible to be performed, the common law will control it and adjudge such act to be void."[43] And it should be noted that the assertion of this power did not make the court a crusader for the rights enshrined in the first ten amendments to the Constitution. One of the few things that Thomas Jefferson and John Marshall agreed on was that the Bill of Rights did not apply to actions by the states. Writing to Abigail Adams about his pardon for broadsheet publishers who had viciously pilloried her husband and been convicted under the Alien and Sedition Acts, Thomas Jefferson noted his belief that the acts violated the Constitution and he could not enforce a law that violated the Constitution. But the absence of presidential power did not "remove all restraint from the overwhelming torrent of slander which is confounding all vice and virtue, all truth and falsehood in the US. The power to do that is fully possessed by the several state legislatures. It was reserved to them, and was denied to the general government, by the constitution according to our construction of it. While we deny that Congress have a right to control the freedom of the press, we have ever asserted the right of the states, and their exclusive right, to do so." Marshall in 1833, in *Barron v. Baltimore*, professed himself unable to intervene in state matters simply because the state was violating one of the first ten amendments. As late as 1922, the Court noted in an opinion that "the Constitution of the United States imposes upon the states no obligation to confer upon those within their jurisdiction either the right of free speech or the right of silence."

"The relation of the United States and the Courts of the United States to the states and the Courts of the states," Justice Holmes once wrote, denying an appeal by Sacco and Vanzetti alleging violations of their federal rights by the state of Massachusetts, "is a very delicate matter that has occupied the thoughts of statesmen and judges for a hundred years and can not be disposed of by a summary statement that justice requires me to cut red tape and intervene." And Sacco and Vanzetti were duly executed.

In 1947, Justice Hugo L. Black claimed that in passing the

Fourteenth Amendment after the Civil War, Congress intended to apply the Bill of Rights to the states, and though he was wrong on the history and deceptive in his argument, he got three other justices to agree. And though the hallmark of the Rehnquist Supreme Court was restriction on federal powers and restoration of states' rights, the world has gone Justice Black's way. Today it is unimaginable that a state should assert a power to censor publications or broadcasts, deny defendants counsel, subject defendants to double jeopardy for the same crime, or set its own standards for search and seizure. Or—as the State of Illinois did in the nineteenth century, with the specific approval of the U.S. Supreme Court—forbid women to practice law.

In Tocqueville's time, the court loomed nowhere near so large. Marshall had established the supremacy of the Supreme Court over the Congress in Marbury, but he never again declared an act of Congress unconstitutional. The Court did not throw out another piece of federal legislation for half a century, until Chief Justice Roger Taney, a Southerner out of President Andrew Jackson's cabinet, declared the Missouri Compromise beyond the powers of Congress. As a practical matter, this meant that Dred Scott would remain his master's slave wherever he might go in the United States, subject to arrest and shipment back home, and that no state or federal law could emancipate a slave as long as the state of his residence as a slave continued to maintain slavery. Ever.

The Constitution can be amended only through cumbersome procedures, though twice the procedure did work fast: in 1804, to close a strange loophole that had permitted candidates for vice president to work on members of the electoral college to substitute their name for that of the presidential candidate on the same ticket (Aaron Burr had tried this trick on Thomas Jefferson), and before that, in 1798, to permit the states to fend off lawsuits by creditors. This Eleventh Amendment is now much cherished by the majority on the Supreme Court, especially Justice Clarence Thomas, as a springboard for diminishing the power of the federal government.

The Eleventh Amendment is worth a detour, as the Michelin people put it, because the current Court in awarding its stars of significance has given it such a raft of recommendations.[44] The case that stimulated the amendment involved a suit by the executor of an estate that included a claim against the state of Georgia for supplies provided during the Revolutionary War. He hired Edmond Randolph, who was also Washington's attorney general, to sue Georgia for the money. (There was then no rule prohibiting the attorney general from serving private clients while holding public office.) Article III of the Constitution provides that the federal "judicial Power" extended to "Controversies . . . between a State and Citizens of another State." Georgia refused to make an appearance before the Supreme Court, but filed a "remonstrance" declaring its sovereign immunity to suit. On a 4–1 vote, the Court sided with Randolph, and Georgia settled the claim. But virtually all the states were debtors in the aftermath of the war, some of the creditors were English, and the political leaders of the states, only recently independent entities, did not like the idea that they could be sued. The Eleventh Amendment went through Congress and the states like a dose of salts. It says quite simply that "the Judicial Power of the United States shall not be construed" to cover suits against a state by citizens of another state." There is no mention of "sovereignty." Indeed, one of the justices who read an opinion in *Chisholm v. Georgia*, himself a signer of the Constitution, argued that there was no such thing as "sovereignty" in the United States, while the chief justice, John Jay, one of the authors of *The Federalist*, wrote that in his view in America—this is what the revolution had been about—the citizen was as sovereign as the state.

Recent decisions by the Supreme Court involving the Eleventh Amendment demonstrate how little the Court is in fact bound by logic or experience once it has the bit in its teeth. Arguing that the Eleventh Amendment forbade the Federal Maritime Commission from requiring the South Carolina State Ports Authority to give docking space to a ship, Justice Clarence Thomas ruled in 2002 that as a state agency the Ports Authority had sovereign immunity from orders of a federal agency—as a state university had immunity from suit when inadequate safety precautions had led to the rape of a student, and a publishing house owned by a state university could violate copyright with impunity. "Instead of explicitly memorializing the full breadth of the sovereign immunity retained by the States when the Constitution was ratified," Justice Thomas wrote, "Congress chose in the text of the Eleventh Amendment only to address the specific provisions of the Constitution that had raised concerns during the ratification debates and formed the basis of the *Chisholm* decision. . . . We have understood the Eleventh Amendment to stand not so much for what it says, but for the resupposition of our constitutional structure which it confirms." Yet no one has been more enthusiastic than Justice Thomas in support of

Justice Scalia's doctrine that the specific language of the Constitution and the laws, not intentions or "presuppositions," should control decisions by the courts.

Commenting, Judge John T. Noonan of the Ninth Circuit Court of Appeals (San Francisco) writes, "A doctrine that has swelled beyond bounds, a doctrine that cannot be consistently applied or reconciled with the federal system, state immunity from suit suffers from one further, final difficulty for a doctrine of the law. It is unjust. Why should a state not pay its just debts, why should it be saved from compensating for the harm it tortiously causes? Why should it be subject to federal patent law, federal copyright law, and federal prohibitions of discrimination in employment and not be accountable for the patent or copyright it invades, not accountable for its discriminatory acts as an employer? No reason in the constitution or in the nature of things or in the acts of Congress supplies an answer. The states are permitted to act unjustly only because the highest court in the land has, by its own will, moved the middle ground and narrowed the nation's power."[45]

In a wistful book called *The Hollow Hope*, Gerald N. Rosenberg, who teaches both political science and law at the University of Chicago, noted the limits on what the Supreme Court could achieve in school desegregation and other issues dear to the hearts of liberals in the period 1953–2000. The next decade or so may see the limits on what the Court can achieve in a more mischievous mode. Just as a sort of jurisprudential vulgarity crept into the later years of the Warren Court (much of it, indeed, in efforts to extend federal authority to areas where it had not been exercised before), a sort of frivolous brutality marked many of the opinions of the later

Rehnquist court. Tocqueville would be shocked; it is unclear whether today's commentators should be amused or horrified. Judge Noonan, a former law professor, a good Republican, a serious Catholic, and a Reagan appointee to the Ninth Circuit, has cast a strong vote for horrified. We shall look at these matters again on our way out.

4 IN PRACTICE: THERAPY COURT IN BROOKLYN

THE COURTROOM OF THE NEW YORK court system's Second Appellate Division is a chaste but elegant, very clean space with classical columns on the second floor of Brooklyn's Borough Hall. This winter late afternoon its anteroom was lined by metal tables with paper tablecloths, punchbowls full of yellow and pink nonalcoholic punch, plastic cups, paper plates for the platters of cookies. Balloons rose from the railings. Several middle-aged African-American ladies in their Sunday best guided visitors to the coatracks, and then into the courtroom, where nearly all the three hundred or so seats were occupied by a mostly (though not entirely) dark and Hispanic crowd of low-income New Yorkers, new "graduates" of the country's biggest drug program, their families, and friends.

Above the well of the court and behind the raised desk the five swivel chairs were occupied by judges out of their robes.

In the center sat the chief judge of the New York Court of Appeals, Judith Kaye, a trim, rather stiff woman in a red-and-black tweed suit with dark hair in curls, who was pleased to be where she was and showed it with a persistent smile. On one side of her sat the senior administrative judge of the Brooklyn criminal courts; on the other a somewhat younger woman with auburn hair down to her shoulders and an extravagant smile that could have been used for a toothpaste ad—Jo Ann Ferdinand, judge of the Brooklyn Treatment Court. The borough president of Brooklyn was there, as were a deputy commissioner of police and a state senator. The eight clerks and police who work every day in the treatment court were also in the well, in uniform but not at work, joining the celebration. One of the policemen called the names of the graduates as they came up to get their rewards, and shook hands with them, sometimes with a wisecrack about some problem from their time in the program. Shaking his head as he shook hands with one of the young men, the police sergeant said, "We had some bad times together."

The honorees were several dozen drug addicts whose conviction on charges of (nonviolent) drug-related crime had been suspended to permit them to take court-supervised daily treatment of their addiction—mostly on an outpatient basis but sometimes in residences. "I am here," Judge Kaye said earnestly, handing out diplomas, "to pay tribute to the graduates who have changed their lives." Graduation meant that the conviction was expunged from the record, and the charges were dismissed. Three of the graduates, chosen by their peers, read brief statements: "I had streetlike behavior that I couldn't get rid of. Now I am on the road to recovery, which is a long one and it is bumpy." "At the time of my second sanction, Judge Ferdinand told me to grow up. Judge Ferdinand is my guardian angel."

During the course of their treatment, these graduates had to come to Judge Ferdinand's ninth-floor courtroom in the Brooklyn criminal courts building—at first twice a week, later once a week, then once every other week, and eventually as infrequently as once a month—and report to the judge on how they were doing. Before entering the courtroom, they had submitted a urine sample to the "case managers" in a ground-floor office associated with the court. One of the eight "case managers," men for men and women for women, accompanied the (hopefully ex) addict to the bathroom and supervised the production of the urine sample. The results of that test were immediately available to Judge Ferdinand on her computer screen. When the subject appeared before her, the judge knew whether he or she was "clean" or "dirty."

People who are clean get congratulated, by name. If they have been clean for ninety days, they get a certificate in a hard binder, which the judge hands them with a handshake from the bench while the audience of fellow drug users and their families applaud. About fifty cases are processed every day. Clean for 120 days, people move on to a new phase of treatment in which they are required to report less often and their treatment begins to stress "educational, vocational, and employment objectives." Many addicts are school dropouts; the court encourages them to get a General Equivalency Diploma, and there is another congratulatory scene when that goal is achieved. Length of time in "Phase II" is dictated by "criminal justice issues": Misdemeanor offenders can complete it in two months, first felony-offenders in four, and multiple felony-offenders in eight. In the third phase, which involves another four to six months, "participants endeavor to reintegrate with their communities and develop independent day-to-day living strategies."[1]

All courtrooms are separated societies, where the people who work with each other every day live in their own world, and the litigants, the accused, and the witnesses are strangers. The Brooklyn Treatment Court is an extreme example of isolation—from its first days in 1996, it has known only the one judge, and one Legal Aid attorney represented the "participants" for six years. The police and the clerks receive special training in drug addiction and treatment; their tenure is also measured in years. But what this means in Judge Ferdinand's courtroom is that everyone knows the people passing through. She greets everyone by name, and (thanks to what has been entered in the computer) she knows who's been naughty or nice at the treatment center, and she remembers important details. One visitor to the courtroom noted that Judge Ferdinand asked an adolescent boy why his grandmother, who had brought him to court on other occasions, wasn't there today—and she listened to the explanation. A young lady got up to testify to her pleasure in starting job training. "You should do very well," said Judge Ferdinand. "You wrote such a good paper about why you wanted to be a nurse."

No small part of the treatment is that the judge, always the same person, a familiar human being, seems to care about the participant. The touchy-feely aspects, however, are only for those making progress. Anyone who does not follow through at the treatment centers, or turns up dirty, will be sanctioned. The lightest sanction, very common (the judge expects backsliding in the early phase even from people who will succeed), is an order to write an essay of at least 250 words about why the treatment program should be followed. A little heavier is two days early morning to late afternoon in the "penalty box," which is where a jury would sit in this courtroom if there were juries, watching others get their congratulations and rebukes. Every so often, Judge Ferdinand will ask someone in the penalty box to comment on the people she has rewarded or disciplined that day. Heavier sanctions may include assignment to a residential detox treatment center rather than an outpatient program—and from one to twenty-eight days in jail; and eventually dismissal from the program, with imposition of the original jail sentence for those who repeatedly break the rules. More than 500 participants in the first five years, a quarter of the total, flunked out of treatment and were given jail terms.

Everyone arrested in Brooklyn for a felony charge of drug sale or possession is brought to the Treatment Court. People accused of violent crimes are not eligible. After a look at the rap sheet and a clinical evaluation of the accused (which includes a TB test and a health screening by people from the New York University School of Nursing), the defense attorney assigned to the case and the assistant district attorney review a treatment plan proposed by the case managers. To qualify for treatment, the accused must plead guilty; if he or she completes the treatment plan (which is stricter and longer for recidivists and for those accused of more serious crimes), the plea is vacated, the charge dismissed, and the record sealed. Almost 90 percent of those offered treatment instead of jail take the offer. If they turn it down and they are indicted, they are offered a second chance, but they will have to plead to a higher class of felony and will face a longer jail sentence if the treatment fails.

This is a deeply depressed community. At the time of their entry into the Treatment Court program, 84 percent of all participants were neither employed nor in school, 59 percent lacked a high school diploma, and 28 percent were or had been homeless. "The median length of time people in my court have been addicts," Judge Ferdinand told a conference at Fordham Law School in 2002, "is eighteen years—and 50 percent of them have never gone to treatment." Almost by definition, drug addicts are recidivists. In New York State, 34 percent of drug addicts released from jail are arrested again within a year, and 56 percent are rearrested within three years. For graduates of the Treatment Court, the comparable numbers are 7 percent and 28 percent.

Jo Ann Ferdinand's chambers are like any judge's chambers, complete with overstuffed leather-covered armchairs and the old Spy lithographs from the old *Vanity Fair*, of English barristers in their dignity. Judge Ferdinand started off in the courts as a Legal Aid lawyer, went to city government to work for the Sanitation Department, and then in 1986 she became a judge in the city's criminal courts. In 1993 she was assigned to Brooklyn. Two years later, she was elevated to the Supreme Court (the court of general jurisdiction in New York State) to permit her to sit on felonies, murders, and robberies. "Mixed in," she says, "were drug cases. I believed that if people ask for help, and they're not violent, you give them a chance. Then if they relapsed, I would send them to jail. I'd given them a chance, and they'd failed. And a few years later, they'd be back before me again. Then I heard about the Miami Drug Court, which was the first in the country, and the first time somebody describes it to you, if you've sat in a criminal court, it just makes sense.

"They come here the day after they're arrested, and the Legal Aid lawyer has the typical negotiation with the DA. There are a finite number of factors. If it's a buy, where's the money? Where are the drugs? They work out the plea, and the lawyer sits down with the client. It's not a good deal for the defendant unless his goal is to get treatment.

"Our goal is the same," says Judge Ferdinand, warming to her work. "We all want these people to succeed. Most addicts don't want to be addicts, but that doesn't mean they don't want to use drugs. They want to use drugs, but they don't want to be addicts. Most female addicts have had trauma; drugs are a form of self-medication, because life is so miserable. When they tell you they want to stop, what they're saying is, 'I want my job back, I want my house back, I want my children back. But I still want to use drugs.'

"Testing is very important. But we don't test to catch people dirty—we test to catch them clean. People don't believe they *can* kick it. The first clean test, we make a big fuss about it. No doubt this is coercive, and more coercion gets more results. Somebody with a first offense, a misdemeanor, facing ninety days in jail, may not stay with a program that requires a year in a residential center and then a year as an outpatient. Someone with a prior felony, facing three years, stays with the program. 'Predicate felons,' people with prior felony convictions—83 percent of them finish the program.

"The job of the judge is to make decisions. In this court for the first time, I've been able to say, This is the right decision. This is a place where people say, Can you help?, and you really can help. There's a boy in court for the first time, and he says, Can I go home and get my stuff, and you look in the room and there's his mother, she's shaking her head. When her son is led away, she cries—but she understands."

Judge Kaye in 2000 got the Conference of State Supreme Court Justices to endorse the idea of "problem-solving courts," and Judge Ferdinand's court is exhibit A. Drug treatment courts have now been launched in all forty-nine counties of New York State. At the end of 2001, the General Accounting Office found 791 drug courts across the country, and while it did not much like the quality of data collection buttressing the program, it did permit the Department of Justice to cite an American University study claiming that "78 percent of drug court graduates have retrained or obtained employment; more than 3,500 drug court parents have regained custody of their children and more than 4,500 became current in child support payments while participating in drug courts . . . and drug courts report saving over 9,000 jail or prison days."[2] In 2003, the California Judicial Council reported on two studies, one of which claimed an average cost saving of $200,000 per year per drug defendant in four counties when caseloads were processed through special drug courts reluctant to send nonviolent offenders to prison rather than through the normal criminal process in which a busy judge asks merely why are you here and how soon can we get you out of here. The other study found that recidivism dropped by 85 percent in a cadre of 1,945 randomly chosen defendants who were facing a second stretch in prison but could avoid it by putting their fate in the hands of drug specialists.[3] In 2006, a UCLA research team upped the savings estimate to $800 million in the first five years of the new millennium.[4]

Other courts with a "problem-solving" bias have been launched to handle mental health problems, domestic violence, and other family matters. Brooklyn's criminal court has added a psychologist and six social workers to the staff in its arraignment part. Judge Martin Karopkin estimates that a fifth of the people who pass through his arraignment part are mentally ill. The program sends people to a residential facility that is not a jail and that slowly reintroduces them to the community. About 70 percent have stayed in the facility for the full length of their mandate, and 90 percent of those have emerged to a more or less normal life and have not been called before the court again.

"Many cases," says Bruce Winnick, professor of law at Miami University in Florida and founder of what he has called therapeutic jurisprudence, "do not deal with disputed issues of fact. The court functions as a psychosocial agency. The judge says, 'I'm not a social worker.' I say, 'Yes, you are. You can be a good social worker or a lousy social worker.'" No small part of the appeal of an institution like the Brooklyn Treatment Court is that it saves the state money. Ann Sovern of the Brooklyn district attorney's office says that the six hundred graduates of the Treatment Court cost the state $22 million less than it would have cost to keep them on Riker's Island in the city jail or upstate in a state prison.

There is no federal equivalent of the therapeutic drug court, and as of the fall of 2004 no less than 54 percent of inmates of federal jails were there for drug offenses. Senior Judge Donald P. Lay, former chief judge of the Eighth Circuit Court of Appeals (Minneapolis/St. Paul) wrote a cri de coeur in *The New York Times:* "Statistics show that drug courts are a success, yet Congress persists in mandating ever-stiffer penalties for federal offenders who need treatment more than punishment. . . . Mandatory minimum sentences, enacted by Congress, have contributed to the rising costs of imprisonment and crowding in federal prisons. In federal drug cases, defendants could face a minimum of five to ten years in prison, while a similar offense in some state courts would allow a court, depending on the circumstances, to place the defendant on probation. . . . To make matters worse, a bill has been proposed in the Senate that would set mandatory sentence of ten years for a first drug conviction and mandatory life imprisonment for a second."[5]

New York City also has several "community courts" which take the process out of the big courthouses and place it in local facilities. Midtown Community Court, in the West Fifties near Broadway, deals with "quality of life" crimes—graffiti, panhandling, prostitution, shoplifting—by assigning people *immediately* to tasks, cleaning streets or buildings, mowing lawns, et cetera, for a day or two. A committee of residents and small business owners meets with the court personnel once a quarter to discuss what the court should do; the meeting is sealed, and no people other than committee members are permitted to witness it.

Not everybody thinks these courts work. Judge Morris Hoffman, supervising judge of the Denver courts, gives talks on "The Rehabilitative Ideal and the Depressing Reality." In Denver, he says, the start of the drug court on July 4, 1994, "stimulated an expansion of drug filings. The police and the prosecutors were out trolling for patients, and the number of cases tripled. About three weeks into the drug court we realized it was so busy, it couldn't do any trials. When drug defendants asked for a trial, we had to find a judge who would accept it, and the judges became reluctant to take cases. The trials were bad, the lawyers were bad, there were serious search-and-seizure issues. Ninety percent of the cases we see are for $20, $10, $5 drug transactions.

"In Denver we sent twice as many drug users to prison *after* the drug court than we did before. By 1997, we had to exclude people with two prior convictions and illegal immigrants, and as a result the hard-core addicts didn't get any treatment. Our federal grant expired: The federal government is like a heroin dealer, they give you grants to start programs and then take them away. In 1997 researchers for the University of Denver looked at comparative results. Recidivism was down from 58 percent to 53 percent. In Dade County [Miami], recidivism was up from 32 percent to 33 percent."

Steve Bogira in Chicago claims for his city the first drug court in the nation, in 1951, and the invention of night drug courts, in 1989. They did not, by his account, offer much in the line of treatment, and they added enormously to Chicago's capacity to process drug cases. "The drug courts," he writes, "are a prime example of how crime magically swells to fill the criminal courts' capacity to handle it. Before the night courts opened, police officers who found only a user amount of drugs on a person often let him go with a gruff warning, knowing that the preliminary hearing judges at Twenty-sixth Street were tossing out petty cases because the trial court dockets were overwhelmed. The drug courts made this triage unnecessary."[6]

"Problem-solving" courts presume a problem; traditional courts, at least theoretically, presume innocence. The problem-solving court becomes kin to plea bargaining: You can't get your problem solved unless you plead. Public defenders, especially of the politically left persuasion, are appalled and infuriated by the change, which seems to leave little role for advocacy. Judge Kaye meets the objection head-on: "In many of today's cases, the traditional approach yields unsatisfying results. The addict arrested for drug dealing is adjudicated, does time, then goes right back to dealing on the street. The battered wife obtains a protective order, goes home, and is beaten again. Every legal right of the litigants is protected, all procedures followed, yet we aren't making a dent in the underlying problem. Not good for the parties involved. Not good for the community. Not good for the courts."[7]

In fact, of course, plea bargaining is the normal course of adjudication in American courts. At least the therapeutic court approaches the bargaining table with something more positive to offer than a reduction in sentence.

Carl Baar, a Canadian political scientist, has pointed out

that changes in the court system originally designed to help losers—juvenile courts, women's courts (to rescue prostitutes, quite popular in the early twentieth century), small claims courts, family courts—have eventually become bureaucracies where the loss of rights persists long after the claim to therapeutic benefit has been dropped. What Baar calls "diagnostic adjudication" is something different from both the Anglo-American contest between adversaries and the continental European inquiry. Diagnostic adjudication is institutionally unstable, and converts through the adoption of rules and procedures presumably designed to help the subject into "decisional adjudication"—and the worst of both worlds. Drug courts, he argues, should be seen as "juvenile courts for adults"—a chilling and by no means implausible prospect. But much of his case rests on his assertion that "It is not among the purposes of courts to serve as a recruiting office for treatment programs."[8]

But in reality the courts are recruitment agencies for treatment programs. Benjamin Cardozo wrote in 1921, when he was a judge on the New York Court of Appeals, "The final cause of law is the welfare of society. The rule that misses its aim cannot permanently justify its existence. . . . [Judges] must let the welfare of society fix the path, its direction, and distance."[9]

5 DECISIONS, DECISIONS, DECISIONS

To the learned lawyer, and especially to the really learned judge, law is a part of himself, a part of his actual thought and existence. . . . Such a man solving a legal problem presented to him does not say, Such and such a solution seems reasonable or reaches a practical result; he says, It is law.

—Joseph Beale[1]

The judge cannot rest content with the luscious luxury of philosophical speculation that "there are at least two sides to this important question." He must take sides and render decisions involving the tangled, troubled and sometimes bloody samples of the stuff of life.

—Sheldon Glueck[2]

Life is the art of drawing sufficient conclusions (or inferences) from insufficient premises.

—Samuel Butler[3]

WHAT A JUDGE DOES FOR A LIVING IS, HE makes decisions. This is the burden our thirty-some thousand judges share, whether they sit in the slum of a traffic court or the marble palace of a federal courthouse, whether they hear divorce cases or personal injury cases, product liabilities, patents, contracts, murders, wills. Eugen Ehrlich in the nineteenth century noted that the best guarantee of justice was the personality of the judge. Because we don't train people to be judges and communications between courtrooms are mostly accidental, our only standards for judicial performance are those created by the administrators, whose political status makes them compliant. The system can work at all only if the judicial personality includes a taste for decision making. It is the promise that their work will fulfill the huge demand for decisions that links all judges into a common profession. It requires talent, not genius. "Judges," Justice Holmes once wrote, "know how to decide a good deal sooner than they know why."[4]

Some years ago in New York, a lawyer who had always wanted to be a judge and had cultivated the right politicians was appointed to fill a vacancy on the federal bench, and was assigned to a motion part, where the lawyers for litigants attempt to determine how forthcoming trials will be structured. A lot of money was involved in the first case he heard. Counsel had briefed a rather arcane issue on both sides, and the new judge read their briefs with great pleasure. He congratulated the lawyers in open court on the quality of their arguments and thanked them for the enlightenment he had gleaned from them. They waited to hear which side had won the argument, until finally the new judge realized that he was supposed to choose, and he couldn't do it. As time passed, many cases that came before him were thrown into a desk drawer for his further consideration. Federal judges serve for life, so there was no way to deal with such a situation.

Two years passed before the apparatus of the federal courts found a way to reject him as a foreign body and compel him to resign.

One does not have to be a decisive person to be a decisive judge. Frederica Brenneman, a Connecticut judge for three decades who now handles only child custody cases (and whose daughter is the authoritative if personally overinvolved family court judge in the TV series *Judging Amy*), says that in her personal life she agonizes over decisions: "If I'm giving a dinner party I usually serve both fish and meat because I can't make up my mind." But on the bench, she rules with pleasure and a firm hand.

Someone once asked Louis Brandeis, a giant of the Supreme Court from the Wilson administration through the early Roosevelt years, how certain he thought a judge should be before he made a decision. "Fifty-one percent," Brandeis snapped back.[5]

But it's not easy, especially on trial. "When a trial lawyer becomes a trial judge," says Judge Warren D. Wolfson of the Illinois appellate court, "the earth moves. Nothing in the trial lawyer's training or experience prepares him for the role of neutral arbiter. Everything looks different and sounds different. It is not just that he has acquired the power to decide. The real change is the realization that now he has to be right as often as possible."[6] It is a different experience. Trial lawyers learn early in their work never to shoot from the hip—never to ask a question unless they know the answer they will receive. Judges must shoot from the hip all day long, supporting this argument by this lawyer or that argument by the other lawyer—and if they are to be good judges, they have to get it right "as often as possible." And if you're only 51 percent sure, of course, you're likely to get it wrong pretty often.

Harold Tyler, a district judge and later deputy attorney general, remembered that when he was first appointed he went to Edward Dimock, a judge of long experience, to ask for advice. Dimock said, "At the beginning you'll find yourself distressed because you have to make decisions you aren't competent to make. After a few years, you'll get used to it."

The pressure is even greater on the appellate court judge, because his opinions make law for a swath of the country. A trial judge who gets it badly wrong makes a mistake in the individual case. His wrong decision is not likely to influence a lot of other judges (indeed, they may never know about it), and may well be overturned on appeal. On the appellate level, says Patricia Wald, longtime chief judge of the District of Columbia Circuit Court of Appeals, "we as judges have to live with a decision. It becomes a precedent. A rotten judgment makes rotten law—and it can happen because a lawyer makes an incompetent presentation of a case." Henry Friendly, who served on the Second Circuit (New York), wrote that the first thing a new appellate judge notes is "the enormous change in the effect of the simple act of signing his name. He does something he has done thousands of times without any great consequences attaching to it; then suddenly, at least if his signature is accompanied by a colleagues', 'the whole power of the state will be put forth, if necessary,' to carry out his will."[7]

When she decides a case, the judge often must issue an opinion that gives her reasoning on the way to the decision. (And there is more to it than that: Law professor Richard Wasserstrom intelligently differentiates between the "process of discovery" when she makes up her mind and the "process of justification" that defends the result, and is, as discussed earlier, a constant source of peril.[8] Only the justification, which is the less important part of the process, becomes part of the opinion.) Here too the demands are far beyond anything asked of the trial lawyer, because the facts must be absolutely right, and there will be no comfort for the judge if reliance on "facts" as stated by counsel turns out to be a mistake. The *Judicial Writing Manual* published by the Federal Judicial Center warns bleakly, "There is no substitute for checking fact references against the record. No matter how good the lawyers, the judge may find on the record facts differ from the way they are stated in the briefs."[9] The trial lawyer has a repertory of ways to brush off misstatements of fact; the judge is defenseless against critics. "My first six months on the bench," says federal judge Richard Owens, almost thirty years a judge now, eighty years old but wearing cowboy boots in his chambers in the spectacular new federal courthouse in lower Manhattan, "I thought someone would come into my courtroom in a white coat and say, 'Come with me.'" It was Owens, no longer disturbed by such fears, who beat away the objections of Frank Quattrone's lawyers and asked a jury to decide only whether or not the former securities analyst induced people to buy dubious stock in order to get his firm the underwriting business. (The Second Circuit Court of Appeals then sent the case back to be tried again, by a different judge, and Quattrone was set free.)

The taxonomy of judicial systems breaks courts by categories—some states (notably California, Illinois, and Minnesota) have courts of "general jurisdiction," where the same judges at least in theory handle all sorts of matters vicious and benign, criminal and civil, family and corporate, large and small; others divide the business into as many as *thirteen* (New York) specialized subjects. Colorado has its water court. The larger the community, obviously, the greater the opportunity to assign different offenses and disagreements to different courts with different judges.

The universal and unavoidable distinction is between the trial court, where the litigants are in the courtroom, the witnesses are in the courtroom, the public may be in attendance, and the judge has to rule rapid-fire, and then, often enough, pick the winner and the loser—and the appeals court, where the judges are cloistered, must live "in the partial vacuum of the printed record," can take their time, discuss with each other, and rule pretty much at their leisure. Justice Alan Page of the Minnesota Supreme Court is a large black man who first came to public attention as an All-Pro tackle for the Minnesota Vikings (and keeps on the wall behind his desk a large sign that reads COLORED WAITING ROOM). He says, "I probably could do what a trial judge does—but I wouldn't want to. It requires a different mind set. I like to think about things." Learned Hand as a trial judge in 1909 could not stop worrying about the uncontrollable rush of business.[10]

Appellate court judges live in nice surroundings, and the people they see every day are nice people, with whom they share a profession. Most American trial court judges live in a world of monsters, of people ordinary folks would rather believe did not exist. Visiting an arraignment part where people are brought (from holding pens behind the courtroom, to which they have been delivered from local jails) is a trip to hell. With some, not many exceptions, these are our losers, slack-jawed, shambling, chained together often enough on their trips from jail to court and back, unable to defend themselves and unable to understand fully what is said by the underpaid cadre of lawyers who will be made available at public expense for their defense. The judges who are good at this sort of thing (which does not necessarily mean they like it) may process hundreds of cases in a morning.

In family or juvenile court, in a drug court, or in the special courts spreading around the country to handle the increasing willingness of women to bring their husbands to court for "domestic violence," judges are confronted with truths very few in this society are willing to face. George Marlowe, now a judge in the Appellate Division in New York (and the chairman of the committee of judges that provides advice on ethics to their community), remembers nine awful years as a family court judge. God had intended him to be a cheerful fat man, but put him in the wrong place. "I was forty-two years old," he says. "I had a naive notion that if I listened carefully and closely, I would know what to do. Finally I accepted that there are usually three alternatives, and all of them are bad. You try for the least bad."

Though much more authoritative than most, judges also don't win all the time. Except for those on the U.S. Supreme Court, they must expect to be overruled every so often. Mostly they don't like it at all, but it comes with the territory. Indeed, judicial decision making while on trial is hedged about with so many rules of evidence and rules of procedure that actual judgment must sometimes be laid aside. Learned Hand, in 1921, in a speech to the City Association of the Bar in New York, bemoaned the status of the trial judge, "strait-jacketed and gagged and told to walk this slack rope today and climb that pinnacle tomorrow. . . . With all his sins upon him," Hand added, "his self-importance, his ignorance, his bad manners, his impatience, he is all you have got, and I believe he will produce better results if you give him a little more room to roam about."[11] Things are not as bad now as they were then. In those days, the very idea of a "pretrial conference" where the judge behind closed doors compels the lawyers to stipulate the issues to be settled by a trial (and to get at least some of those issues out of the way here and now) would have been considered egregious malpractice.

In a multijudge appellate court, of course, a judge may find that his decision is not in fact the decision of his court, because others have voted the other way. Indeed, it could be argued that the great difference between the trial judge and the appellate judge is that to get the second vote in a three-judge panel, the appellate judge has to convince somebody else that she is right while the trial judge, day by day, is a god in his own courtroom. (Like children in a classroom, the lawyers ask his permission before coming to the front of the room.) Good appellate judges really have to *listen*, not only to what happens in court but to each other. Judge Harry T. Edwards of the D.C. Circuit has emphasized the role of "collegiality" in the decision process of the intermediate appellate courts. He had come onto that court to fill a chair that had been occupied by David T. Bazelon, and relations among the judges were mostly hostile, Bazelon being a great and much publicized liberal who did not believe other people's points of view were worth considering. In those days, Judge Edwards wrote, "[J]udges of similar political persuasions too often sided with one another . . . merely out of partisan loyalty. . . . The point was that you were not supposed to 'break ranks' if a colleague asked for your allegiance. . . . When a court is bereft of collegiality, judges become distrustful of one another's motivations; they are less receptive to ideas about pending cases and to comments on circulating opinions; and they stubbornly cling to their first impressions of an issue. . . .

"On a collegial court, the overarching mission of a panel is to figure out where a particular case fits within the law of the circuit. . . . Judges also think carefully about writing too much on an issue and about deciding issues that are not before the panel. Our mutual aim is to avoid these things. . . . If one's reasoning or writing admits of ambiguities that one did not intend or legal consequences that one did not foresee, these can be cured through the give-and-take of collegial deliberation. When such flaws are addressed during the drafting of the opinion for the court, dissenting and concurring opinions are rarely required."[12]

Edwards notes that dissents from decisions on the D.C. Circuit dropped considerably after the change in atmosphere. The public loves dissents, and some by Justice Holmes have a place in American literature. Their place in law is not so certain. Roger Traynor, for many years chief justice of California, thought that dissents should be reserved for special occasions. "Paradoxically," he wrote, "the well-reasoned dissent, aimed at winning the day in the future, enhances the present certainty of the majority opinion, now imbedded in the concrete of resistance to the published arguments that beat against it. . . . Like many another judge, I have had to learn to give up dissenting while holding fast to a conviction. Thus I still believe, though still against the odds, in a dissent of several years ago against the California rule that presumptions are evidence and as such can be weighed. I no longer believe that it serves any useful purposes to reiterate that dissent. It rests with the professors and practicing lawyers to revive it in commentary if they see fit, or to hasten its oblivion by criticism, or to let it wither away if they choose in the stillness of indifference."

Still, today's dissent may become tomorrow's law. Editing a collection of Justice Traynor's papers, his son (later chairman of the American Law Institute) noted that twenty-three years after Traynor had first dissented on this issue, a California Law Revision Commission published recommendations for a new evidence code including the words "A presumption is not evidence."[13] Occasionally, indeed, victory may come sooner than that, and the author of a dissent finds his written argument has in fact convinced one of the members of the majority against him to change her vote, and what was originally planned as a dissent becomes the opinion of the court (while what had originally been the opinion of the court has to be rewritten as a dissent).

Chief Justice Charles Evans Hughes wrote shortly after assuming that post that "a dissent in a court of last resort is an appeal to the brooding spirit of the law, to the intelligence of a future day."[14] As federal appellate judge Frank Coffin observes, "one who writes for the future can always hope for deferred vindication."[15] It is true, of course, and a generally accepted criticism of Chief Justice Rehnquist's Supreme Court, that a decision rendered with three concurring and two dissenting opinions may not help future litigants or those who judge their cases decide what the law is. The National Center for State Courts notes in a rather stately way "the confusion caused by publishing multiple opinions, none of which represents a majority of the court, to the parties and others who might seek to rely on the appellate ruling in the future."[16] Surely there is much less justification for a concurring opinion that states a different rationale for coming to the same conclusion as the majority, and thereby makes it much more difficult for other courts to use this case as a precedent.

More profound differences are alleged between trial judges and appellate judges. Legal historian Herbert Jacob in 1965 drew a line between "the norm enforcement functions of trial courts and the policy-making functions of appellate courts." "I'm much more powerful than an appellate judge," said the late Constance Baker Motley, a federal trial judge, former civil-rights lawyer, state senator, and borough president of Manhattan. "I can send a man to jail; he can't."

Dartmouth political scientist Lynn Mather summarizes the argument: "Trial courts do not make policy . . . because they do not declare a general rule for handling cases, because even where there is a consistent trend in their decisions, trial judges are often not aware of it, and because few trial court cases challenge an existing norm—'Only when a norm is itself challenged can the courts engage in policy-making.'"[17]

But Mather, writing from the political scientist's perspective, shrewdly notes that the courts not only provide solutions to problems, they also, and initially on the trial level, create possible solutions that open up the exploration of problems. "Hard cases," the cliché says, "make bad law." Not always: they may merely make new law, which is not necessarily bad, or reiterate old law in a demonstration of its unsuitability. What makes a case hard is that established law creates a distasteful result. The cases Hart and Sacks noted that took major social issues first to the courts were cases heard and first decided by trial judges, who merely by hearing them may have performed the crucial action in the crusade.

Thus Cardozo on privity and product liability in *McPherson v. Buick*, ruling that although Buick had not manufactured the defective wheel and had not sold the car to McPherson it was nonetheless liable when the car spun out of control. The line is direct from there to the asbestos cases of the 1980s, when the courts ruled that companies that had bought companies that had bought companies that used asbestos were responsible for the damage done to the lungs of people who had worked in these long-buried subsidiaries forty years before. In a precedent-based system, where the appeal is always to stare decisis, the judge in the court of "first impression" may exert immense influence. The Philadelphia three-judge trial court that heard the first case on obscenity on the Internet wrote the law governing such matters: When the case came to the Supreme Court, the justices essentially repeated that panel's opinion. Sympathetic judges, Mather writes, create "a prospective solution [that] makes possible the existence of a problem by proposing that some obnoxious aspect of life hitherto thought to be unalterable ('nothing can be done') might be alleviated."

Thomas F. Burke, another political scientist, argues that the use of litigation for political purposes is built into American governance. "Courts," he writes, "offer activists a way to address social problems without seeming to augment the power of the state. Litigious policies nicely match the preferences of Americans, who want state action on social issues yet are ambivalent about the typical tools of the state—bureaucratic regulation and welfare programs. . . . Through litigious policies, activists seek to surmount the fragmented, decentralized structure of American government." Moreover, "American courts are also less *responsible* than government agencies for policy outcomes, and this, too, can make them desirable for activists. Because issues come to courts in piecemeal form, judges are less likely than agency officials to consider the impact of their decisions on a governmental program or policy arena. A judge's overriding impulse is his or her own sense of legality and justice, not governmental effectiveness."[18] And because the judge must decide the case before him, he may put forward his own solution to a problem before any significant section of the public knows that there is a problem. After all, he is paid to make decisions; the fact that the question is novel does not in any way excuse him from the obligation of answering it.

The trial judge may also have more control over his life than he thinks. The pretrial conference is now more or less mandated and is often the most satisfying part of a judge's day. The judge cannot really control what happens in a courtroom, where lawyers fed by litigants write theater for the benefit of their clients, but he can damned well control what happens in his chambers. The pretrial conference was introduced to American jurisprudence by a circuit court judge in Detroit, Ira W. Jayne, who insisted in 1929 that the lawyers meet with him in his chambers before taking a lot of time needlessly on trial with stuff that was not in dispute or could not be considered by a jury. Scandalized trial lawyers took him to the Michigan supreme court, which two years later, to their amazement, made pretrial conferences compulsory in all Michigan courts, and then the U.S. Supreme Court wrote them into the Federal Rules of Civil Procedure.

One should note also that the privilege of writing the opinion of a multijudge court is not always a pleasure. Benjamin Cardozo while still chief judge in New York had occasion to observe that "the spokesman of the Court is cautious, timid, fearful of the vivid word, the heightened phrase. He dreams of an unworthy brood of scions, the spawn of careless dicta, disowned by the ratio decidendi [the reason for the decision]. . . . The result is to cramp and paralyze. One fears to say anything when the peril of misunderstanding puts a warning finger to the lips."[19] And judges can overestimate the interest and importance of many of the matters that come their way. Soon after he retired as a federal district judge, Larry Irving in San Diego was approached to become a state supreme court justice. "Why would I want to give up what I have," he asked, "to spend all my time hearing appeals from death sentences?"

Still, decision making is an art, whether practiced singly or collaboratively, through application of the common law or obedience to statute. Patricia Wald, round and brisk and very smart, was a judge of the D.C. Circuit Court of Appeals for twenty years, half of them as chief judge, mostly policing the administrative agencies. Retiring there, she became a judge on the International Court at The Hague before undertaking a study of legal systems in poor countries for George Soros's Open Society Institute. I asked her whether there was any part of being a judge that she missed, working for the foundation. She sighed a little and said, "Yes. The judging."

In 1959, Massachusetts senator Leverett Saltonstall suggested to Boston federal district judge Charles Wyzanski Jr. that he planned to urge Wyzanski's name on President Eisenhower to fill a vacancy on the First Circuit Court of Appeals. Wyzanski wrote him to ask to be excused. "The District Court," he wrote, "gives more scope to a judge's initiative and discretion. His width of choice in sentencing defendants is the classic example. But there are many other instances. In civil litigation a District Judge has a chance to help the lawyers frame the issues and develop the fact so that there may be a meaningful and complete record. He may innovate procedures promoting fairness, simplification, economy, and expedition. By instructions to juries and, in appropriate cases, by comments on the evidence he may help the jurors better to understand their high civic function. He is a teacher of parties, witnesses, petitioners for naturalization, and even casual visitors to his court. His conduct of a trial may fashion and sustain the moral principles of the community. . . .

"While it may well be true that the highest *office* for a judge is to sit in judgment on other judges' errors, it is perhaps a more challenging *task* to seek, from minute to minute, to avoid one's own errors. And the zest of that task is enhanced by the necessity of reacting orally, instead of after the reflection permitted under the appellate judge's uninterrupted schedule of reading and writing. . . ."

Wyzanski ended his letter with the comment that "the trial judge's relative loneliness brings him closer to the tragic plight of man. Was not Wallace Stevens speaking for the trial judge when he wrote:

" 'Life consists

" 'Of propositions about life. The human

" 'Reverie is a solitude in which

" 'We compose these propositions, torn by dreams'?"[20]

They don't make them like Wyzanski anymore. He was a great polymath, an honorary senior fellow in Harvard's Society of Fellows, which he described as "the center of intelligence of the center of intelligence, the best club in the world. If I were offered a choice of the Supreme Court or the Society of Fellows," he once said, "I'd take the Society of Fellows." He was a regular participant in the monthly dinners of the society, which permitted the score or so of junior fellows who would later almost without exception become world leaders of their disciplines (think the philosopher William Quine, the psychologist B. F. Skinner, the biologist James Watson, the poet Richard Wilbur, the political scientist McGeorge Bundy) to converse on equal terms with those who were already world leaders. As Harvard president A. Lawrence Lowell set up the program (after his death it was learned that he had put up the money for it from his own fortune), junior fellows got three-year appointments renewable once to work on whatever they wished, without disciplinary restriction. In addition to working, they ate and drank well—sherry first and brandy after, with good wine in between, first in the masters' chambers of Eliot House, Harvard's most elegant dormitory, and then in the top-floor suite of Holyoke Center, the walls painted by Mark Rothko, a good friend of Wassily Leontief, one of the first Nobelists in economics, who was for many years president of the society. (He left Harvard for New York University when a new president of Harvard seized the Rothko room for his own offices.) Wyzanski and I were distantly related by marriage, and Leontief had been my tutor when I was an undergraduate, so I had chances to hear Judge Wyzanski hold forth on everything from astronomy to archaeology to literature.

For Wyzanski, the society was in part an escape from the loneliness of the judge's life. When I wrote a biography of Emory Buckner, Felix Frankfurter's close friend and the U.S. district attorney who prosecuted Harding's attorney general Harry Daugherty in the 1920s, Wyzanski informed *The New York Times Book Review* that he was going to write a review of the book and they were going to print it, and both things happened. (Nice review, too.) His letter to Saltonstall is in part amusing and in part sad. It is amusing because he was well known to the Boston bar as a judge who took the management of cases away from counsel and presented matters to juries as he thought the litigants should be presenting them, regardless of the customs of American courts. Also because Wyzanski was enjoying the best of both worlds, as the judges of the

117

First Circuit called on him very often to complete—in Wyzanski's case it was to lead—appeals panels.

(The objection to having a district court judge sit as an appellate judge and hear an appeal from another judge in his district is that it's bad for morale when a district judge votes to overrule a colleague on his own bench. That wouldn't have worried Wyzanski.)

The sad part is that much of what Wyzanski considered central to his satisfaction as a trial judge has been withdrawn from the job. At the time of Wyzanski's letter, federal judges not only had wide discretion in sentencing miscreants, but could act as their own parole officers: Rule 35 of the federal rules of procedure gave them the right to reopen sentences after a criminal had served some time in jail. William Enright, who served thirty years as a federal judge in San Diego (appointed originally by Richard Nixon), had been both a prosecutor and a defense lawyer before ascending the bench, and had served on a penal reform commission. He knew the wardens and guards at the federal prison, and thought well of them. When he sentenced an offender, he would tell him he would keep an eye on him at jail. When he visited the federal prison, which he did once or twice a year, he would ask the staff how these fellows were doing. If the staff at the prison thought they saw "significant behavioral change" in the prisoner, he would interview the convict—and more than 250 times in his thirty years as a judge, he invoked Rule 35 and set the prisoner free. He gave each recipient of this favor a key, and told them at the hearing where he ordered their release that this key had got them out of the slammer, and they should hold on to it. If he had to take it back from them, they would go back to jail. "People would come to me," Judge Enright recalls, "and say, 'I framed that key and hung it over the fireplace so I wouldn't forget it.' Only a very few, a handful, came back to me because they got in trouble again."

In fairness all 'round, sentencing became anarchic in the 1960s and 1970s, and it was not only "hardliners" who were troubled by the fact that punishments for the same crime were wildly disparate between one judge, or one district, and another. Marvin E. Frankel, an intellectual judge in the Southern District of New York, wrote a book about these discrepancies subtitled *Law Without Order*. Federal criminal procedure had not been codified at all until 1946, when the Supreme Court took up an invitation from Congress to lay out the procedures for federal criminal cases. Rule 35 was part of that initial code. It is now effectively gone, together with most of the discretion federal judges used to enjoy.

Though the Supreme Court in two 2005 cases—*Blakeley* and *Booker*—restored some of the flexibility judges historically exercised in these matters, since 1984 sentencing has been largely controlled by "guidelines" imposed by the hundred-man staff of a "sentencing commission" (its recommendations, made annually in May, take effect unless slapped down by Congress before November).

Congress in 2003, in something called the "Protect" Act (like the "Patriot" Act: sometimes one wonders who writes their stuff), self-importantly instructed the attorney general to keep a record of every time a judge tries to give a less-than-minimum sentence to a convicted defendant, and to insist that all such sentences must be reviewed by the court of appeals for the circuit. In his 2003 "Year-End Report on the Federal

Judiciary," Chief Justice Rehnquist complained that such record keeping "could appear to be an unwarranted and ill-considered effort to intimidate individual judges in the performance of their judicial duties." Judge John S. Martin Jr. resigned from the federal bench in New York with the parting comment, "I no longer want to be part of our unjust criminal justice system."[21]

2

The judgments of the judge are necessarily quite different from the judgments of others. Forced to a decision, the normal human being consults the range of his experience and knowledge, what an older generation, including Dean Roscoe Pound, would refer to as his "apperceptive mass." But the judge must seek to blank out what he knew before he became the judge on this case (indeed, if he has held pretrial conferences he must forget what was said at them once the trial begins), and elaborate rituals of choice have been established to assure that jurors do not enter into their work with views (or, worse, information) that would lead them to influence their fellow jurors behind the closed doors of the jury room. In most trials involving state prosecutions under the criminal codes, juries are to "find" the facts, and judges participate by establishing the framework of law that controls the selection of facts the jury is to consider. Only those facts the lawyers for the two sides have introduced at trial are to be considered in determining a "verdict"—a truthful saying. The judge is forbidden to tell jurors what he thinks about any testimony or any piece of evidence. But this means that the presentation of the case is in the hands of lawyers who may be of very different abilities.

The late Alvin Rubin, a very distinguished but never pompous trial judge, and later a judge on the Fifth Circuit Court of Appeals, started his career as a lawyer in his native New Orleans. Shortly after he began work as a judge he confided to a visitor that the great disappointment he felt in his new job was the revelation of the low levels of competence in the bar that practiced before him. As a lawyer, he had handled only the more important civil cases, and his antagonists had been the bluebloods of the New Orleans bar. Now he had to face the fact that the narratives constructed before him for presentation to the poor jurors were often incoherent to the point of meaninglessness.

In the late 1960s, while Warren Burger was still chief judge of the D.C. Circuit Court of Appeals, the future chief justice blew his stack at his profession in a speech to the American College of Trial Lawyers. More than twenty years later, he himself gave me an offprint from the law journal that had printed the talk. He said he had asked among a number of judges "what proportion of the cases tried before them were properly presented. The highest figure ever stated was twenty-five percent; the lowest was ten percent. . . . On the most favorable view expressed, seventy-five percent of the lawyers appearing in the courtroom were deficient by reason of poor preparation, inability to frame questions properly, lack of ability to conduct a proper cross-examination, lack of ability to present expert testimony, lack of ability in the handling and presentation of documents and letters, lack of ability to frame objections adequately, lack of basic analytic ability in the framing of issues, and lack of ability to make an adequate argument to a jury. Also very high on the list of deficiencies was the lack of an understanding of basic courtroom manners and etiquette, and a seeming unawareness of many of the fundamental ethics of the profession."[22]

The incompetence of lawyers can complicate a judge's job if he permits it to do so. What should a judge do when he sees a lawyer butchering his client's case? Mostly, I suspect, he ignores it. As one judge said, "If the defendant is dumb enough to hire an incompetent lawyer, it isn't my job to save him from his mistakes." If a lawyer does not object to the introduction of evidence damaging to his client, most judges will consider it well beyond their obligations to do it for him. A statement that he cannot in any way comment on the evidence is part of the boilerplate which every judge must "charge" a jury in every state (in the state of Washington, chosen simply because it's the one I looked at, picking it out from rows of such stuff on the shelves of the library at the National Judicial College in Reno, two thick volumes are required to print the "pattern jury instructions" written into law by the legislature, which a lawyer can require a judge to read verbatim.)

What if the defendant with the bad lawyer is a criminal defendant, and the judge suspects he shouldn't be convicted, but his lawyer has failed to make the state prove its case? Then, perhaps, several experienced judges said, the judge in the case should find a way to give the jury a better case to decide. It is also of course a free kick: Prosecutors cannot appeal a verdict of not guilty, and a judge who shows bias for a defendant usually cannot be overruled. (Though he may have a very tough time with the press: In 2005, a Massachusetts judge won a $2 million verdict from the *Boston Herald* for articles, some on the front page and touted by their author on cable TV, that portrayed him as insensitive to the injuries suffered by defendants in civil cases.) But he may also ask himself why he wants to intervene. While judges can grow very tired of lying testimony by policemen and dubious analyses by the police lab—and while some of them have risen to the bench from the public defender's office rather than (much more commonly) the public prosecutor's office—it is also true that judges rarely see a criminal defendant they do not believe to be guilty. No less than Learned Hand once spoke scornfully of what he called "the myth of the innocent prisoner."

On some level, judges are always conscious of the fact that criminal justice in the United States is today essentially an administrative process, that twenty times as many defendants are excused by the prosecuting agency (usually an elected district [or county] attorney) as are freed after trial, forty times as many defendants plead guilty as part of a bargain as are convicted after trial.

And quite apart from the competence of the attorneys, jury trials are a mess. Supreme Court justice Sandra Day O'Connor noted scornfully that "jurors are allowed to do nothing but listen passively to the testimony, without any idea of what the legal issues are in the case, and without being permitted to take notes or participate in any way, finally to be read a virtually incomprehensible set of instructions and sent into the jury room to reach a verdict in a case they may not understand much better than they did before the trial began."[23]

Day by day in the real world, judges are more likely, like

the writers of newspaper editorials and the commentators on Fox News, to be agonized about the risk that a jury will acquit a guilty defendant. Federal judge Marvin Frankel once gave a dramatic example. "Often, the judge has been made explicitly aware before trial that the prosecution's assertions, though they will be contested at every step, are true. . . . A whole class of examples arises in courts where plea bargaining is practiced. The bargain, in which the judge frequently participates, starts from an understanding that the defendant has done approximately the wrong with which he is charged. In many cases, however, no deal is made. The defendant goes to trial. . . .

"A trial about two years ago involved a group of defendants charged with major dealings (multi-kilogram, hundreds of thousands of dollars) in heroin and cocaine. Important for both conspiracy and substantive counts was a suitcase that had been opened in a Toledo railroad baggage room and found to contain over five kilograms of heroin and a kilogram of cocaine. . . .

"The motion was eventually denied, because the quaint claim of retained title proved defective. . . .

"After evidentiary hearings on pretrial motions adding to a total of eleven court days, we proceeded to a nineteen-day trial. While defendants did not take the stand, the considerable talents of numerous defense counsel were bent for four weeks on destroying any suggestion by any witness that would place their clients within miles at any time of any narcotics, including, of course, the Toledo shipment. Counsel for one of the erstwhile movants opened with the observation to the jury that there would 'not be a shred of credible evidence,' but only incredible assertions from 'individuals who are the scum of the earth.' A chemist who offered the opinion, novel only to the jury, that the substances in the Toledo suitcase were heroin and cocaine was raked by cross-examination for some three hours, his experience tested, his veracity and motives questioned, the modesty of his academic rank (and the fact that he was a mere Ph.D., not an M.D.) being duly brought to his attention when it became apparent he had a tendency to irascibility.

"Altogether, a total of forty-nine witnesses appeared. The jury heard over six hours of summation and a charge requiring (or at least lasting) nearly two hours. In deliberations extending over three days, including two nights of sequestration in a hotel, the jury called for testimony and exhibits reflecting questions, inter alia, that the movant-defendants had answered adversely to themselves, under oath, many weeks before. In the end, the defendants were convicted. . . .

"How does it all look and feel to the impartial judge, regulating the contest, waiting to see whether the jury arrives at findings he knows to be correct or is successfully kept from doing so?"[24]

But sometimes a judge has to risk the acquittal of the guilty. "How can you not hate a drug dealer?" says Abner Mikva, former congressman, former federal appeals judge, former counsel to President Bill Clinton, winner in 2005 of the American Bar Association's Thurgood Marshall Award. "He's the lowest form of life, ruins his family, ruins his friends, ruins his neighborhood. It's hard to remember that this isn't a drug dealer case; it's a search-and-seizure case. But you've got to remember it."

3

Trial judges—including federal trial judges—serve their district, and their writ runs only inside that district. When litigants live in different states (or criminals have fled to another state or country), rather elaborate arrangements may be necessary to resolve "conflicts of jurisdiction." In the Judiciary Act of 1789, which set up the whole system, Congress required federal judges to apply the forms and modes of process of the courts of the states in which they served when hearing civil cases. It was accepted then that rules of law in the single federal system might well be different from courtroom to courtroom, depending on the location of the court. One notes in passing that until 1891 the salaries of federal judges also varied from state to state. Also that Congress in 1793 instituted a uniform nationwide fee schedule for cases in admiralty (a federal jurisdiction involving ships at sea), but otherwise left the "court costs" associated with a federal lawsuit to vary according to the whims of the court clerks. Who until *1919* were compensated by fees they took from the charges they imposed rather than by salary.

A decision by a trial judge is good in a specific courtroom in a specific case. Most of the time, nobody in another courtroom even knows what decisions a judge has rendered today. A courthouse is still like the egg-crate school, where each teacher lords it over his own classroom. In many courtrooms, the judge has his own amendments to the rules of civil procedure, and the clerk of the court (usually someone who has been appointed to the job by this judge and serves at his pleasure) will tell counsel how preparations for trial in this court will be somewhat different from the practice in other courts. In most cities there is a "chief judge" or an "administrative judge" who tries to keep the trains running on time, and who supervises the mostly but not entirely random assignment of judges to cases, but she—and in recent years it often is a she— does not pay much attention, is not authorized to pay attention, to the content of a judge's work. In big cities there are newspapers for the legal market (supported by the compulsory advertising component of taxes or liens, my wife having left my bed and board, the probate of wills, et cetera). These legal newspapers report decisions within a day or two, and increasingly the state courts have Web sites to which decisions are posted, but somebody has to be looking for it. If the final decision is by a jury, of course, it does not create a precedent of any kind. Juries presumably take their law from the judge's charge and deal only with the facts of the case they hear.

The great bulk of judicial decisions in a trial, whether or not there is a jury, cannot be appealed. They are "interlocutory," part of the ongoing process of the trial—decisions about what witnesses may be heard, what evidence may be introduced, what lines of argument may be pursued, what may or may not be said by the lawyer to the witness or the witness to the court. The ability to deliver very quick decisions, to shoot from the hip, is clearly necessary in the middle of a trial, for the trial must continue. It should be noted in passing that the judge is not responsible for keeping a record of such events. That's part of the task of his "working group," the clerks and legal stenographers assigned to his courtroom. These people usually but not always get it right. Over time, especially in courtrooms where the same lawyers are present, representing different clients, day after day, the working groups can become incestuous. When a judge goes bad, which does happen, the members of the working group are usually implicated. In the New York criminal courts, the personnel of each judge's working group is changed at regular intervals, to reduce temptation. As recently as twenty years ago, judges in the New York criminal courts were rotated around the city to different boroughs every six months or so, to make sure nobody got too cozy with the locals. After a messy scandal in Brooklyn's family court in 2003, the New York administrators began moving the clerks and bailiffs around in family court, too.

Lawyers may preserve their rights and those of their client by noting their disagreement with an interlocutory decision at the moment of decision—indeed, they will not be permitted to argue that a decision was a "reversible error" unless they reserve their rights at the moment the decision is made—but the appeal comes at the end of the case, and even if the judge got it wrong, the appellate court (not wishing to saddle the world with the nuisance and expense of a new trial) is likely to find "harmless error," a mistake to be sure, but not a mistake big enough to affect the result. Less than 2 percent of the appeals in criminal cases result in the reversal or modification of a guilty verdict. And in this context, one should remember that less than 4 percent of criminal prosecutions ever go to trial. Reversals of criminal convictions are the stuff of newspaper headlines and novels; they happen in fewer than eight of every ten thousand criminal prosecutions.

If the trial judge writes an opinion as part of deciding the case, other judges can cite that to defend or distinguish their own opinions (indeed, they may have to do so, because counsel in any case will buttress their arguments by reference to what happened in previous, similar cases), but the opinion of a trial judge has no formal authority outside her own courtroom. An appeal taken from the decision of a trial court will go in the federal system and in the forty states that maintain such facilities to an intermediate appellate court with a larger geographical footprint. In the ten states that don't have intermediate appellate courts, the appeal goes directly to the state supreme court.

The intermediate appellate courts usually sit in three-judge panels, and the organization of the system may vary within states. In San Francisco, the state appellate court divides into districts, each of which has a four-judge bench from which three are chosen at random to hear the case, but in Los Angeles the districts are larger and the three-judge panels are chosen from cadres of ten district appellate judges. In New York, there are four appellate divisions, one in Manhattan, one in Brooklyn, and the other two upstate; the courthouse of the Manhattan division, on Madison Square Park, is one of the most glorious rococo buildings in the country, and recently glamorously reconditioned, too. The appellate judges, who sit in panels of five (four in Manhattan) are appointed by the governor from the ranks of trial judges, and they serve in the appellate division until their fourteen-year term as an elected trial judge expires, when they may stand for reelection to the trial court and possible reappointment to the appellate division. Usually governors appoint appellate judges to fill unexpired terms in state appellate courts, usually from a group of names recommended by a panel of state dignitaries. But in

Virginia and South Carolina the legislature makes the decision—and in Louisiana and Massachusetts appellate judges themselves make the choice (in Louisiana the appellate judge appointed by the supreme court to fill out a term may not stand for election to the seat).

Generally speaking, despite the rules that call for random assignment, the chief judges and administrators of the federal appellate courts try to mix up assignments so that judges serve with the widest possible variety of other panelists. The assignments arrive in the form of the antagonists' briefs in a batch of thirty, about six weeks before the proposed hearing date (though every so often a case will be thrown at the judges with only a week to go before the date). In most though not all of the federal circuits, all members of the panel read the briefs themselves (there is no "bench memo" from the law clerks, though each judge has four clerks and they do a lot of research), then meet to decide whether they wish to hear oral argument. About half the cases are disposed of by "summary judgment" without hearing oral argument, and without opinion. Such decisions don't count as precedents. Indeed, their whole rationale is that the precedent already exists and the appellate circuit is merely confirming it.

Professor Mary Ann Glendon of the Harvard Law School severely criticizes the shrinkage of appellate opinions: "The discipline of writing out the reasons for a decision and responding to the main arguments of the losing side has proved to be one of the most effective curbs on arbitrary judicial power ever devised. (Many are the stories told by judges of how they changed their minds after they realized that an initial hunch just 'wouldn't write'."[25] Roger Traynor once observed that a decision "will not be saved from being arbitrary merely because [the judge] is disinterested."[26] In California, perhaps because of Traynor's continuing influence, all appellate decisions have opinions attached, the Supreme Court having ruled that such documents are required by the state constitution. They may be a single paragraph of boilerplate, but they're there. In Massachusetts, where the intermediate court of appeals sits in the same building as the Supreme Judicial Court, there is a staff of senior attorneys who review all opinions to make sure the case citations and the facts are correct before anything is released to the public.

To hear oral argument in the federal courts of appeal, the panels on their hearing days sit from ten in the morning to one in the afternoon, allocating from ten to forty minutes to each of the lawyers presenting a client's argument (the judges also hear an occasional pro se litigant arguing his own case). These presentations are made in open court, and the public can come listen, which they rarely do. In some circuits but not others, the panel has already held a "preconference" to discuss the case and agree on which topics the judges would like the lawyers to address. After the hearings, the panel members meet in private and discuss. In some courts, the most senior judge speaks first and the most junior speaks last; in some it's the other way round. Once the panel sees where they are going to wind up, the judge with the greatest seniority accepts the responsibility of writing the opinion. Most often, because they have already disposed of the easiest cases by summary judgment, the panelists decide to think about it a little more.

But they don't meet again on the case. After that initial conference, communications about a case are still sent in some
courts by fax messages, which each judge signs with his ini-
tials, and in others, a growing majority, by intracourt e-mail.
"If you make phone calls," says one federal appellate judge,
"you talk with only one judge; with faxes that get sent to
everyone, everything is in the open."

Sixty or ninety days after the oral argument, if the decision
on the case has not yet dropped into the clerk's in-box, the
judges on the panel in most court systems will get a memo
from the chief judge of the circuit or the chief clerk or the
circuit executive, inquiring as to the status of the case. Most
circuits have meetings of the entire bench three or four times
a year. At these meetings the circuit executive and the other
administrators crack the whip. Before his fellows, each judge
is asked *when* each of the aged cases will be decided, and when
the opinion will be available for publication.

All panel systems leave some degree of uncertainty as to
whether a different panel would have come up with a different result, a situation especially troublesome in the federal
system, where a three-judge panel may include a senior judge,
a district judge serving by temporary assignment on the appellate level, and only one circuit court of appeals judge. A
ruling on the appeal may thus be on a 2–1 vote with the only
appeals judge on the panel forming the minority, and the
value of such decisions as precedents is doubtful, even when
they are buttressed by an opinion, which is of necessity in this
situation written by someone not on the circuit court bench.
The rules are that senior judges can sit and vote in three-
judge panels, but when the court sits en banc—all the circuit

judges together—senior judges do not have a vote.

The number of slots for "active" judges on each circuit court is determined by act of Congress, and every so often Congress also changes the geographical boundaries of a circuit. The rules of borrowing and lending judges from one circuit to another are simple: No circuit that is borrowing judges can permit active judges to go out to other circuits. The D.C. Circuit when Harry Edwards was chief judge had a flat rule against borrowing judges from anywhere.

Sometimes these things turn up trickier than they look. The big "affirmative action" case involving the University of Michigan and its admissions policies came to the Sixth Circuit Court of Appeals in Cincinnati on appeal from a district court in Detroit. The petitioners, trying to stop the law school's admission program, asked the bench to go immediately to an en banc format. The court by a 5–4 vote approved the university's procedures. Judge Danny J. Boggs, one of the dissenters, argued in an appendix to the dissent that chief judge Boyce F. Martin Jr., who wrote the majority opinion, had moved slowly to circulate the papers required for considering the request for an en banc hearing, with the predictable result that two older judges who would have voted against the university had passed their seventieth birthday and could not vote when the time came to rule on the case. Judicial Watch, a right-wing activist group, brought a formal complaint based on Judge Boggs's accusations, and Judge Alice M. Batchelder found that they "raise an inference that misconduct has occurred." Judge Martin, who had not responded to the original accusation by Judge Boggs, called the Batchelder report "factually incorrect" in an interview with the *New York Times*, noting that the circuit handled more than four thousand cases a year, and that the procedures by which the clerks circulated petitions to a large bench were time-consuming. As Judge Batchelder did not recommend any action against Judge Martin or any reconsideration of the case (which had in the interim been argued before the Supreme Court), it is not clear what the purpose of her report was, except perhaps to warn litigants and their counsel not to get caught in the personality disputes of the Sixth Circuit.

Assignments of district judges and senior judges to appellate panels are by the chief judge of the federal circuit, who by law is the judge sixty-four years old or younger who has served longest on this bench and has not been chief judge before. This does not guarantee superior judgment. The problem has become increasingly severe as the federal appellate panels issue more and more decisions without explaining the reasoning behind the result—less than one-third of the federal appellate decisions are now accompanied by an opinion. Appeals from the circuit courts to the Supreme Court are not likely to bear fruit. In the 1980s the Supreme Court won from Congress almost complete control of its own docket, and in recent years has heard only about eighty-five cases a year. So the federal courts of appeals have turned increasingly to brief rehearings en banc, all the judges participating, which becomes unwieldy in a circuit like the Ninth, where twenty-eight judges are theoretically eligible to participate in the rehearing. There is much debate about judges behaving like legislators. A bench with twenty-eight judges on it *is* a legislature. In 2005, the chief judge of the Ninth Circuit established fifteen as the maximum number for an en banc hearing.

In most states and in the federal system, everybody is entitled to one appeal (consideration by the appellate court is said to be "mandatory"), which does not mean that the judges of the court will actually hear it. Appeals and the answers to them are filed in writing within a certain time of the original decision. Each judge on an appellate court has up to four law clerks, bright young things in the federal court system, usually veterans in the state court systems, where the judges really need all the help they can get. Because lawyers cost what they cost and most litigants are not rich, an increasing proportion of appeals are pro se (for oneself), and the first task of the gate-keepers of the appellate courts is to figure out what the hell the appellant wants to say. That task is given to clerks (in some states to a "commissioner" who has no other function), who write memos that circulate either to the panel that has been assigned the case or to all the judges on that bench. Though clerks may discuss cases with each other, each memo is officially the work of one of them. These memos are working papers of the court, and are not available to anyone but the judges. The decision to hear oral argument of the appeal is taken in scheduled meetings of the panel or the whole bench, depending on the state. In some courts (most significantly, the Court of Appeals for the D.C. Circuit) a single judge who wants to hear the case can put it on the calendar; in some, a majority of the group must wish to hear it. The term of art is "I'm with the docket," which means that the judge casting the vote agrees with the recommendations in the memo.

At the U.S. Supreme Court, the agreement to hear argument on a case is presented as a "writ of certiorari," summoning the court that made the decision now under appeal to send along all the records of the case. Four of the nine justices must vote to "grant certiorari." Meetings to make this decision are held in the conference room beside the chambers of the chief justice on Friday mornings, with no one in attendance but the justices themselves—no clerks, no secretaries, nobody. The justice who has been on the court the least time sits in the chair nearest the door and opens the door when anyone comes with a message, which happens rarely. At this writing, eight of the justices pool their staffs and use the same memo of law from the same clerk when considering whether to grant certiorari. Justice Stevens has his three clerks look at all the "requests for cert" and report their views only to him. Every so often the Court on the basis of briefs, without hearing oral argument, will tell one of the federal circuit courts or a state supreme court to look at an issue again, but the vast majority of appeals are simply rejected, which does not necessarily mean the Court is pleased with the result below. The law as pronounced by the circuit court is good in that circuit until the Supreme Court says it isn't, but refusal of the court to hear an appeal from a circuit court does not mean that this circuit court's decision applies beyond the boundaries of its own jurisdiction, any more than the failure to override a state supreme court's decision means that the justices agree with the state supreme court.

Arguably the most important part of the chief justice's job is that he lays out the case for all the judges when the petition to appeal is filed. William Howard Taft was a great disaster in this part of his job, meandering genially all over the lot. Harlan Fiske Stone was not much better, insisting on presenting all sorts of details that took endless time ("he really does not know how to work," Brandeis wrote savagely of Stone to Felix Frankfurter in 1930, "though he likes to be working"[27]). Warren Burger infuriated his brethren with his pompous insecurity, his need to cover his low analytic capacity by playing personal politics at all times. He is the heavy in *The Brethren*, the Bob Woodward–Scott Armstrong book about the Supreme Court, because he would not see them and tried to prevent his clerks from cooperating (which, in fairness to Woodward and Armstrong, they tell the reader themselves). For all his faults, however, Warren Burger was an extremely important and useful figure in American law because he understood the importance of training judges to do their work right and of training administrators to make the court system work effectively. (I did meet him, by the way, several times, and he was nice to me, too, because I was a friend of his friend Sol Linowitz, who had great talents for friendship.)

By contrast, Charles Evans Hughes got very quickly to the heart of the matter and earned from a reluctant Brandeis the encomium "he is mundane but intelligent . . . he has no imagination but he is a good artisan. . . . In the conferences, time is not much wasted." No small part of William Rehnquist's strength as chief justice was his greatly admired ability to take the issues in a matter up for certiorari and sketch them quickly and sometimes amusingly in ways that all in the conference considered fair and thorough. The universal testimony of the justices that everybody got along with everybody else was to a considerable degree a testimony to Rehnquist's skills in summary. One of the strongest arguments for welcoming John Roberts to the Court as Rehnquist's replacement was the evidence from his confirmation hearings that he fully understood Rehnquist's strengths (he was Rehnquist's clerk as a kid lawyer fresh from Harvard) and would seek to follow the same model.

6   IN PRACTICE: THE TAX COURT

THE U.S. TAX COURT STARTED OFF IN 1924, at a time when federal taxes were low and few people had to pay them. Nevertheless, important people got upset at deficiencies asserted by the Internal Revenue Service and at the penalties the law empowered IRS examiners to assess. Under the inherited procedures of the common law, people who wanted to protest these bills for unpaid taxes and assessments had to pony up before the federal district court could hear their appeals. For the price of a filing fee (now $60), Congress permitted taxpayers to petition against their tax bills without paying the taxes first. As a normal matter, that $60 payment protects the taxpayer against civil proceedings by the government until the dispute is resolved. These petitions would be heard by a judge of the newly created Tax Court.

Various disagreements get decided in Tax Court proceedings, including the divisions of interest in partnerships (and marriages), the role of estates, the significance of transfers of ownership, and so on. Disputes on corporate taxes and real estate deals may involve literally thousands of pages of documents and hundreds of millions of dollars of liability. Criminal proceedings, of course, are a different matter; those go to the district court like any other criminal proceedings and are handled by the staff of the district attorney with the assistance of IRS lawyers. Roughly 20,000 cases a year are filed with the Tax Court, though new wrinkles in tax shelters and IRS diligence in smoothing them out can bring spikes of cases, as many as 75,000 a year in the 1980s.

The Tax Court is an odd duck in American jurisprudence. Among the wishes of Congress (and the principles of political scientists) was the desire that taxes be assessed and collected uniformly nationwide. Thus the Tax Court is one of very few that operates everywhere. All nineteen of its judges are based in Washington (and the $60 filing fee must be paid in Washington), but petitioners can elect to have their cases heard in any of seventy cities, and the Tax Court judge will come to them once there are enough petitions to justify making the trip. The factual background of the cases tends to change as you move around the country. "In Houston and Dallas," says a veteran traveler, "you get oil and gas; Miami, you get drugs; New York, you get large corporations. And you get different lawyers, relating to the size of the claim."

In thirty of the cities, the Tax Court has its own courtrooms—wood-paneled, of course, no jury boxes, four or five benches with room for perhaps twenty people behind the railing, housed in some federal structure (not necessarily the courthouse). But the fact of a single Tax Court, where every decision must be supported by a memorandum of facts and law from the judge—and every such memo is automatically circulated to the entire group—does not guarantee uniform national interpretation of the tax laws. Apart from the possibility of human fallibility, neglect or incompetence, Tax Court decisions may be appealed to the circuit court of appeals with authority over the city where the case was heard, and the circuit court can reject the Tax Court judge's interpretation of the law. The appellate court's rule is then the law in its circuit, while the Tax Court judge's rule governs elsewhere in the country. The Supreme Court presumably settles such conflicts, but in fact the Court hates tax cases and almost never takes one.

The nineteen judges of the Tax Court are appointed by the president with the advice and consent of the Senate, just like federal district judges. Until 1974 they worked in the same building that houses the IRS (though they had a segregated entrance). Now they have their own rather dramatic brown-brick building the size of a city block with a main entrance in a glass wall that runs the full height of the building from the top of the granite stairs that slash almost the full length of the building. The glass wall reveals the circular rear wall of the courtrooms that occupy the center of the structure. This dramatic entrance at the top of the stairs is not used; visitors when they get to its locked doors, tugging, perhaps, at the suitcases they have just lugged up the thirty-odd steps, are directed back down the stairs to a tiny doorway beside the bottom of the stairs on the ground floor.

Tax Court judges are "Article I" judges—that is, their court was set up under the authority granted Congress by Article I of the Constitution, and they do not automatically have the protections federal judges enjoy under Article III. They serve fifteen-year terms, which may or may not be renewed by the president. (The term of art, says Chief Judge Joel Gerber, is that Tax Court judges "offer up their willingness to be reappointed.") If they are not reappointed or choose not to offer up, they can retire at the end of their fifteen years and retain the full salary of a Tax Court judge, which has been set at that of a member of the House of Representatives and may not be reduced in their lifetime (though Congress can increase its own pay without increasing that of the retired Tax Court judges). They must take senior status at age seventy, but can and do continue to hear cases and travel around the country. As of mid-2005, there were seven senior judges to help carry the caseload—and nine special trial judges, appointed by the chief judge, offering an optional "fast-track" procedure for petitioners whose liabilities totaled less than $50,000. Petitioners who elect the fast-track procedure give up their right to appeal. Something approaching three-quarters of the petitioners before the special trial judges represent themselves, but the IRS, of course, is always represented by counsel.

Sometimes a case involving more than $50,000 is assigned to a special trial judge to take evidence and save time for the Tax Court judge to whom the case is assigned. Until 2005, the report of the special trial judge was a nonpublic document that only the Tax Court judges were permitted to see—and that was not necessarily kept by the court. An appeals court judge noted in 2003 that he had reviewed more than 880 Tax Court decisions involving a report from the special trial judge, and every one of them had opened with the statement that the Tax Court judge was accepting the findings of the special trial judges. This turned out not to be true in a case of Burton W. Kanter, a Hollywood creator of tax shelters, whose own tax returns had been rejected as misleading by the IRS. The case was assigned to a senior judge, who ruled, supposedly on the basis of the report by the special trial judge, that Kanter and his associates had "devised a multifaceted scheme to shield kickback payments" and owed the government some millions of dollars. The 606-page opinion began with a statement that it "agrees with and accepts the opinion of the special trial judge"—but in fact it reversed the findings of the special trial judge. After the Supreme Court wondered why findings and opinions by special trial judges of the Tax Court should not be subject to the same sunshine rules that applied to other hearing examiners and administrative law judges, the Tax Court changed its policies, the reports of the special trial judges were made public, and the discrepancy in the Kanter case was revealed.[1] Appeals from Tax Court decisions may now become easier for lawyers defending their clients against the IRS.

There is no nonsense here that any lawyer—even any of the 130,000 lawyers who have taken the simple steps to be recognized for practice in the Tax Court—can be a judge. Considerable expertise and a history of work in the tax field is required. For many years, there was a formal committee consisting of the general counsel of the Treasury, the chief counsel of the Internal Revenue Service and the tax counsel of the Justice Department, who met at the White House and made recommendations to the president to fill any vacancies on the court. Political criteria appear to play a relatively minor role—the leaders of today's Tax Court are mostly judges who were appointed by Ronald Reagan and reappointed by Bill Clinton. Chief Judge Gerber says the average age of the judges has declined: "When I came in 1984, I was the only one at the table with a full head of hair; now there are a number of judges in their forties and fifties." Mostly, the judges are drawn from the counsel's office at the IRS and the counsel to the tax-writing committees of the Congress, but some judges come from private practice, mostly from smaller firms. Tax partners in big law firms enjoy a lifestyle that cannot be supported on the salary of a Tax Court judge.

Organizationally, too, the Tax Court is unique. District court judges in the federal system cherish the randomness of assignment of cases. Every judge's name is in "the wheel," every case comes up in chronological order to be assigned to the judge whose name comes out of the wheel, and only the most extraordinary and public maneuvering can change the assignment of a case to a judge. In the Tax Court, the question is geography. When a sufficient volume of petitions piles up in a city, the clerk of the Tax Court asks its judges who would like to go there. First priority goes to someone who hasn't visited there for the longest time, or has never gone as a tax judge. San Francisco and New York have a backlog of requests, as do Miami and Phoenix in the winter. If no one has volunteered for Wichita, the clerk will make an assignment.

Cases are assigned five months in advance, and the judge is sent the papers, the petitions and responses, and the supporting documentation. Thirty days before the calendar date, the judge gets a list of expert witnesses and each side's "theory of the case," says Judge David Laro, thirteen years a tax judge, relaxing after a long first day in New York, sitting in what are of course anonymous chambers for visitors (no diplomas, no photos of judges with presidents or commissioners) beside one of the two Tax Court courtrooms in the Javits Federal Building right off New York's Foley Square. "I may get involved. I may write an 'issues memorandum': How *are* you going to prove this issue? *Can* you settle this case?" The damnedest things do happen, of course. One case overheard dealt with a crook who was selling gynecologists partnerships in a farm that produced frozen cow embryos to be sent to Africa. The whole thing was a scam (the promoter's secretary later testified that she kept the office open and continued to sign her boss's name to letters after he was sent to jail), but the doctors took their losses as tax deductible. IRS counsel, bouncing up and down to object, insisted that the Federal Rules of Civil Procedure be strictly applied to opposing counsel, who kept asking witnesses whether they had done something or read something or said something, all prohibited as leading questions, until Judge Laro said wearily to petitioner's lawyer: "Questions that begin with "was' or 'did' are going to be leading questions. Questions that begin with 'where,' 'when,' what' or 'who' will probably be all right." These tax shelters, incidentally, had been claimed in 1983 and 1984; IRS was claiming interest owed to a total of about twenty times the deficiency.

A week or ten days before the calendar call, the office staff in Washington packs up the exhibits the lawyers will wish to introduce at trial and ships them off to the courtroom, where they may take quite a lot of space. The judge travels over the weekend and brings his clerk with him, and picks up a local court reporter, and that's the entire staff on site. Being inside a federal building policed by the General Services Administration, the Tax Court doesn't even have its own cops. Monday's calendar call consists mostly of setting a date when the documentation of the deal between the petitioner and the IRS will be presented to the judge for final approval—95 percent of cases docketed for the Tax Court settle before trial. Most trials are completed in a single day, but Gerber remembers one that took nine weeks, involving forty-three expert witnesses, seven thousand documents, and some hundreds of millions of dollars.

Another oddity of the Tax Court is the administrative role of the chief judge. Elsewhere in the federal system, the post of chief judge is awarded by formula, to the judge on this bench under sixty-five who has the greatest seniority in that district or circuit when the chief's post becomes vacant. The new chief judge then serves until the age of seventy, usually priding himself on not interfering with his fellows. At the Tax Court, the nineteen judges vote on who is to be their chief, and the winner serves a two-year term, to which he or she can be reelected once. Mary Ann Cohen, a Californian, appointed by Reagan and reappointed by Clinton, served two years as chief, dropped her chiefdom, and then stood successfully for reelection. There being no tradition of independence from central authority, the Tax Court has closer relations than the Article III courts with the Administrative Office of the federal courts, which means the chief judge spends most of his time not hearing cases.

Chief Judge Gerber has been particularly interested in automating the trial process in the tax courts, which are of course heavily dependent on paper. Every new document that comes into the court now is scanned and digitized—and every document in the court's archives going back to 1995 has been put into the computers. The Tax Court has a small information technology department headed by a brisk young lady named Ann Chumbley, who works closely with the AO. The court's system is the one recommended by the AO, which contributed the half-million dollars needed to prop up the floor of the computer room. Gerber remembers from his long trial sitting on the bench and feigning patience while the lawyers rummaged around in steamer trunks to find documents that had been filed under what he describes as a "Byzantine numbering system." In future complex cases, the lawyers and the judge will be able to tap out a few words and the computer will deliver the desired documents. Instead of heading out to San Francisco with huge plastic tubs of documents, the Tax Court judge will tuck a CD-ROM in his briefcase.

First, of course, you have to persuade the lawyers to use it. And one of the difficulties of being an "inferior court" is that you're restricted in the orders you can give the lawyers. The Second Circuit Court of Appeals can publish an announcement in the Federal Register that henceforth it will insist that all documents associated with appeals be submitted in digital form, but the Tax Court can't do that. Not yet, anyway.

Gerber likes to say that the Tax Court is "an experiment that worked." People like the idea that they can appeal to a neutral body whose members do not work for the IRS an assessment reflecting what they regard as an unfair exclusion of deductions they have made on their returns. By pressing its cases in a civil rather than a criminal venue, the service itself gets help in drawing a boundary (always an area, not a "line") between tax avoidance (legal) and tax evasion (criminal). Political tides do flow through the system. After the Clinton tax increase of 1993 pulled a Republican majority into Congress, there were hearings about and denunciations of allegedly high-handed behavior by IRS auditors, and the atmosphere in the tax courtroom tilted toward petitioners. In 2005, a Congress struggling with frightful deficits noted claims that two to three hundred billion dollars of taxes every year were being lost to inadequate enforcement. IRS counsel became more aggressive and the promoters of tax shelters were on the defensive. It was nontrivial that they had a court in which they could interact.

7 30,000 JUDGES, 100 MILLION CASES: THE SCOPE OF THE ENTERPRISE

If you were to design a legal system today, from scratch, you would regard the one we have as the worst imaginable.

—Chief Judge Marvin Aspen, shortly after he retired to senior status in the federal district court for Chicago (2004)

[W]e are creating a workload that is even now changing the very nature of courts, threatening to convert them from deliberative institutions to processing institutions, from a judiciary to a bureaucracy.

—Department of Justice report to Congress, 1977[1]

I N 1998, AND AGAIN IN 2003, THE NATIONAL Center for State Courts in Williamsburg, Virginia, did a study of state judicial offices came up with about 29,000 trial courts and another nine hundred or so judges who heard appeals. That counts the District of Columbia and Puerto Rico as states and part-time justices of the peace as judges. Almost as important are the 7,500 clerks and administrators of the courts, who keep the dockets, summon the jurors, and keep records of who shows up, call the lawyers to find out why they didn't show up for the trial date, plan with chief judges to allocate the work and get paid only a little less than what a trial court judge makes. Since the 1970s, when Chief Justice Warren Burger went on the warpath about the antiquated management procedures of the courts, the clerks have been supplemented by trained administrators, many of whom are not lawyers. In many states—the list includes Alaska, Arizona, California, Colorado, Illinois, Indiana, Iowa, New Jersey, New Mexico, Louisiana, New York, and Pennsylvania—the senior court administrator is paid as much as or more than a trial court judge. Administrators are almost all appointed, usually by the chief judge of the bench with which they work; but many of the clerks, like the judges, are elected or are appointed by a single judge with whom they work. Indeed, given the importance that control of the docket has in the life of a lawyer practicing in a court—and the value to banks of being chosen as a court's depositories, a decision usually made by the clerks—some of them can raise more money for their election campaigns than the judges can. In many court districts, other cadres of clerks are also responsible for the budget and for auditing the payments actually made pursuant to the budget.

Clerks are absolutely forbidden to discuss in any forum what happens in a courtroom or in a judge's chambers. "The judge-clerk relationship," writes federal judge Ruggero J. Aldisert, "is as sacred as that of priest-penitent. Indeed, to emphasize the importance of this relationship, I give new law clerks a formal message: 'I have retained you as researchers and editors, but you are also my lawyers. As lawyers, you are absolutely forbidden to disclose the intimate details of this lawyer-client relationship, of the decision-making and decision-justifying processes that take place in these chambers. This court is a family, and there will be times that I will make remarks about my family members. They will be uttered sometimes in the heat of passion, or despair. They will not be repeated beyond the chambers doors. Even if I occasionally blow off steam, remember that these judges are my colleagues and will be my friends long after you are gone from here.' "[2] This is addressed primarily to the "elbow clerks" (otherwise "law clerks") with whom the judges work very closely for a year or two, but much of it applies also to the less intimate clerks. "The administration of a court system," says Kathleen Blatz, chief justice of Minnesota's Supreme Court, "has a lot to do with justice. Administratively, we have to work with other people."

The federal circuit courts of appeal at Chief Justice Burger's insistence (for once, the Congress listened to him) have a "circuit executive" in addition to the court's clerks. The circuit executive assigns judges at random to the panels that hear the cases, and the clerks assign the cases to the panels. In some jurisdictions, "presiding" or "administrative" judges are deeply involved in this work. In December 1998 California adopted a "unified court" system to replace what were literally dozens of specialized courts in different counties, each with judges who sat only in that court. The new model was voted in on a local-option basis, the carrot being the availability of state money to replace county contributions. The last to adopt were Los Angeles, for budgetary reasons, and Kern County, where the judges hated each other. Each California district now has a "presiding judge" who is, in the words of recently retired San Diego court administrator Stephen Thornberg, "the chief manager of the court. Judges are responsible only for hearing cases and for following the personnel plan when they hire, fire, discipline, and compensate the people who work in their courtroom."

This is a big change. In the old days in many parts of California, judges appointed whomever they wished to jobs in their courtrooms, and spent the money allocated to them on their own private budget. Now personnel for the courts is centralized in the executive officer. But, says Thornberg, "it wouldn't be human for me as executive officer to say to you as judge that Suzy is going to be your courtroom clerk. So we have a civil service exam that produces a list, and the judge can take one of the top three names on the list." The winner of the job, however, goes on the payroll of the executive office of the courts, not the judge's payroll. Before unification, San Diego had suffered with five separate court systems, each with its own rules and separate information technology system. Thornberg, who had been chief clerk and had quit after twenty-three years—"My experience," he says, "was that superior court [the most prestigious of the five] was unmanageable, because there was too much activity by the judges"— came back to install the new procedures. The San Diego district court in 2003 had 151 judges working in twelve different courthouses around the immense county. Seventeen of them, by appointment of the presiding judge, heard the most important civil suits, which were assigned to them by the computer on an "Individual Calendar." If a lawyer didn't like the judge to whom his case had been assigned, he had ten days to protest.

The question of whether the court, the county, or the state pays for the maintenance of the courthouses is contentious everywhere, because the building also houses other functions: district attorneys, probation officers, sheriffs, and other county functions.

Chief Justice Rehnquist proved that an appellate judge can do quite a lot of supervision—of the Administrative Office of the Courts, the Judicial Conference, the Federal Judicial Center, all of which he chaired—while carrying a full judicial load (though perhaps it should be noted that he led the Supreme Court to reduce by more than half the number of cases they hear). In New York, the chief administrator of the state courts is a man who rose through the New York County clerk's office and left that job to become a judge in that court, and knows where every piece of the puzzle fits. Most judges, however, are too busy with their own judge work to give more than cursory attention to what may be happening in other courtrooms. Federal appeals judge Frank M. Coffin complains from Maine that the Judicial Conference regularly has more than twenty committees considering various issues, taking the time of several hundred judges.[3] The system conduces to comfort: The sort of judge who enjoys having fights with his fellow judges is not likely to get appointed as an administrative officer.

The authorized aristocracy of the business consists of 990 "Article III" federal judges (the reference is to the Constitution), 800 trial judges and 190 appellate judges, appointed by the president and confirmed by the Senate. Judges on the Court of International Trade also have "Article III status." Trial judges are appointed to "districts" that must lie entirely within a single state (the larger states all have more than one district: California, New York, and Texas have four each); the appellate judges belong to one of thirteen "circuits," the largest of which hears cases originating in a geography that runs from Tucson to Anchorage with a detour to Hawaii. The judges on this Ninth Circuit appeals court may live thousands of miles apart, and sit infrequently on the same three-judge panels. Judges on this bench must expect to take several weeks a year living in hotels far from home to hear the cases where the litigants live.

Article III federal judges continue in office "during good behavior"—in effect, they have lifetime appointments. They can be removed only through impeachment by the House followed by a trial and conviction in the Senate. The Constitution bars any reduction in their salary as long as they live. It is the strongest assertion anywhere of the "independence" of the judiciary. And no one "rates" the performance of federal judges. (The law, specifically 28 U.S.C. 476, instructs the director of the Administrative Office to publish lists of judges with motions or nonjury trials more than six months behind their original schedule—or any matter more than three years old. And the list *is* published, though ordinary mortals may not be able to find it. It is not posted on the courts' Web site.) In 1993 a National Commission on Judicial Discipline and Removal recommended that the courts develop a system for evaluating judges, and the district court in central Illinois ran a pilot program in which federal judges agreed to be evaluated in confidence by their peers and the lawyers who practice before them. But little came of it. In 1922, Chief Justice William Howard Taft expressed his hope that a new judiciary act creating what is now the Judicial Conference of trial and appellate judges from around the country would end "the absurd condition, which has heretofore prevailed, in which each district judge has had to paddle his own canoe and has done as much business as he thought proper."[4] But a federal district judge in his courtroom or in the chambers associated with that courtroom is still very much on his (increasingly her) own, even today.

Also in the census of judges are the Article I federal judges, mostly appointed by the Article III judges themselves (by vote of the district bench) to jobs created by Congress that can be eliminated by Congress. The largest category is the 600-odd bankruptcy judges. Article I judges do not have lifetime appointments, though their terms may be long (fourteen years for bankruptcy judges). "Magistrate-judges" are elected for eight-year terms by vote of the district court judges of the district they serve, handling arraignments, federal misdemeanor cases, and (with the consent of the parties) civil trials of all sizes. Among the reforms of the court system Congress enacted in the late 1990s was an increase in the size of the courtrooms where the magistrate-judges work.

Also claiming the job description of federal judge are thirteen hundred "administrative law judges," who also serve unlimited terms in the structure of one of the government's many agencies and departments (though their offices are usually not in the same building with the agency for which they work). Administrative law judges (ALJs) are supposed to carry forward the policies of their agencies, but they draw their fact-finding authority directly from the Administrative Procedures Act of 1946, which stipulates an ALJ whenever an action by an agency or department requires a "hearing on the record." Though the name "hearing examiner" still attaches to some of these jobs, they are full-time judges, probably wear robes (it's optional), and are part of the government's "Senior Executive Service" though they are not subject to "performance reviews" or any other form of criticism. There is a "chief" ALJ in each agency, chosen by the agency head or cabinet secretary, and the chief assigns cases to the judges in the group (not arbitrarily—the law says "in rotation as far as practical"), but the chief has no disciplinary power whatsoever. Some of them feel that's too bad.

"Hearings on the record" includes all denials of disability benefits under the social security laws, a category that accounts for 1,100 of the 1,300 ALJs. The words do not, oddly enough, cover the process by which benefits are denied to veterans, a task that employs about 1,600 Veterans Administration employees, who are not necessarily lawyers but have been called "judges" since 1976, when then Assistant Attorney General Antonin Scalia ruled that in an agency employing people who made judicial-type decisions, hearing examiners had a perfect right to use the word "judges" in describing themselves. AJs may be part-timers with other responsibilities, are subject to performance review, and usually can be fired for cause (though the cause at least in principle may not be their employers' dislike of their decisions).

Since September 11, 2001, the greatest growth in the federal "judiciary" has come at the Immigration and Naturalization Service, where "immigration judges" (also not necessarily lawyers) decide what should be done with strangers arriving at the ports and airports. The Bush administration has let the immigration judges know that they can be assigned to other and less desirable work if they approve too many applications for asylum. The term "judges" is not applied to the part-time cadre of insurance adjusters who are assigned by their private company employers to decide for the Department of Health and Human Services whether applicants should or should not get Medicaid reimbursements—decisions, incidentally, that cannot be appealed.

2

Only two appellate courts have nationwide jurisdiction: the Supreme Court and the Court of Appeals for the Federal Circuit, on which twelve judges hear appeals from the Court of International Trade, the Court of Federal Claims, the Merit Services Protection Board (formerly Civil Service Commission), and certain decisions by the secretaries of agriculture and commerce. About the only statement that can be made about the American judiciary as a whole ("there is no generic court system in the United States," the Bureau of Justice Statistics of the U.S. Department of Justice observed grimly[5]) is that geographical boundaries are central to the organization. Were he to return to earth, St. Thomas Aquinas would not find in America, despite its miracles of communications, any reason to change his dictum that "a judge's sentence is like a particular law regarding some particular fact."[6] The system is atomized and arbitrary, about as confusing as can be. Many states have separate civil and criminal courts. (In Texas, the separation of criminal from civil goes all the way to the top. The Texas Supreme Court deals only with civil matters, and a separate court of criminal appeals okays all those death penalties.) And there are of course many other separations—family courts (which in many states do not handle divorces), probate courts for wills and estates, landlord and tenant courts, juvenile courts, drug courts, traffic courts, and so on, including local oddities like the water courts in Colorado.

The question in many states is whether the judges who work in one kind of court can also work in others, a "unified" system, in which judges can be assigned where needed, being much more efficient administratively. This does not mean that the distinctions among the courts must be lost, or even that new specialized courts cannot be created for previously unspecialized judges. Nobody has fought harder than Chief Judge Judith Kaye of New York to establish a unified court system in which all judges are equal and anybody can handle any kind of case, but at the same time she has set up various special courts, down to a courtroom in Brooklyn to which all the city's gun offenses are sent. *Within* courts, Judge Kaye and her administrators have established specialized "parts," so that each judge hears only the same kind of case, thus reducing the number of steps the court personnel, lawyers, and so on, must take over the course of a week—and increasing the chance that rulings will be consistent and informed. In these courtrooms, judges are more specialized than they were before, so that judges who hear cases of abused and neglected children do just that all day long, all week, all year. Some judges acquire and cherish expertise: New York's experience is that judges assigned for two years to nothing but medical malpractice stay with medical malpractice.

In Oregon, *after* a recent and hard-fought simplification, there are 141 judges in municipal courts, handling traffic violations and misdemeanors, thirty justices of the peace, seven county courts that handle adoption, mental health, estates, and juvenile cases, a tax court hearing appeals of state administrative actions, 160 circuit court judges in 26 judicial districts hearing cases of greater significance and appeals from the courts of limited jurisdiction, a court of appeals with ten judges who sit in panels of three, and a supreme court with seven justices who sit en banc. New Jersey, the epicenter of court reform since the days of Chief Justice Arthur T. Vanderbilt in the 1940s, still has about five hundred municipal courts established by the authority of the municipality itself, self-supported by their fee collections, and liable to be closed down by the municipality (their functions transferred to the county) if their operations show a loss. New Jersey ranks second in the country in salaries paid to state trial court judges (Delaware is first); municipal court judges' salaries are set independently and much lower by the municipalities. But in New Jersey, the same man, usually a leader in a political party, can serve as judge for several municipalities, collecting several salaries, not to mention several pensions.

Judicial districts are determined by political authority, usually etched in stone by constitutions. Each state has its own court system, and the federal government has several. Geography rules. No federal court district can cross state lines, which means that many of the suburbs of New York,

Chicago, Philadelphia, Cincinnati, St. Louis, Kansas City, and Charlotte operate under laws potentially different from those of their central cities. And county lines in most states determine the jurisdiction of separate state courts. Because workloads do not necessarily correspond to political divisions (and shift from time to time) courts routinely borrow judges from other jurisdictions, though only federal judges can be moved across state lines. Historically, as noted, judges "rode circuit" within their district and held court in different towns in different weeks. Administrative law judges and Tax Court judges still do; many of the statutes that created their agencies specify that a case must be heard within seventy-five miles of the base location of one party or the other.

In general, judges can be appointed to the bench (or can run for judicial office) only if they reside in the district they will serve, though Herbert Stern, then only thirty-six years old, was living in New York when President Richard Nixon at the insistence of Senator Clifford Case appointed him to the federal bench in New Jersey, where he had been working as a commuting U.S. attorney. Appellate judges usually must live in the area from which their cases come—by law in the federal system. Except in Massachusetts, judges other than the lowest level justices of the peace and municipal magistrates must have law degrees. (In Maine they don't need a law degree but must be "learned in the law"; in North Carolina there are still a very few judges who were first elected before November 1, 1981, who can continue to serve although they lack a law degree.) In most states, judges must have been members of the state bar association or practitioners for periods of time ranging from two years to ten.

In the states that set a minimum age it is usually thirty, though New York requires only eighteen (from very precocious candidates, because nobody can serve who has not been a member of the state bar for ten years). Illinois has no minimum age, and any attorney licensed to practice in the state can serve. Most states have a maximum age, which is seventy, but various arrangements are made to permit judges to continue to hear cases after formal retirement. (Not in Michigan, where the state constitution forbids anyone over seventy from serving as a judge.) Federal judges serve for life, though chief judges of districts and circuits must relinquish that honor at age seventy, and any federal judge may elect to take senior status when age and duration of service add up to eighty. "Senior status" means the judge will do only what he damned well wants to do (the chief judge or administrative office can assign cases to him only with his own consent; the other side of the coin is that management may decide not to assign him any work at all). When a federal judge takes senior status, it opens a slot on his court in the federal budget, and the president with the advice and consent of the Senate appoints a new judge to that district or circuit. The senior judge, however, usually retains chambers complete with private bathroom, clerks, secretaries, and often a personal courtroom dedicated for the use of this judge, not available for trials before other judges without his consent.

Every federal judge retains full salary for life. If she retires, she continues to receive a judge's salary as of the day of retirement, but does not participate in any salary increases Congress awards to the federal judiciary. If the chief judge of their district or circuit certifies that she continues to carry at least one-quarter of a normal load, she continues to receive whatever Congress determines as the full salary of a federal judge. There are two ways to look at this situation. A few days after he moved to senior status from the job of chief judge of the federal district court in Chicago in 2003, Marvin Aspen noted that in effect he works for nothing, because his salary would be paid whether he worked or not. In 2003, the Second Circuit Court of Appeals in New York, which is deluged with immigration appeals and time-consuming appeals brought pro se, had thirteen active judges and nine senior judges, "without whom," said one of the active judges, "we couldn't function."

In theory, and mostly in fact, all judges in a district (or appellate judges in a circuit) are created equal and remain equal, but there are administrative chores that only a single judge (with lots of little or big helpers) can do for a court. Those include assigning cases and judges, budgeting (including liaison with the executive and legislative branches) and enforcing the budget, scheduling (the terms of art are "calendar" and "docket"), riding herd on output, policing obedience to the local rules of procedure, and generally evaluating the performance of the many helpers who work at the court. Evaluations of judicial performance have become quite common in state courts, with lawyers and sometimes litigants filling out questionnaires or even testifying to a commission on how their matters were handled. But most evaluations are secret, and they concentrate heavily on the speed with which matters before each judge are resolved, this being the one objective measurement.

Except in Arkansas and Mississippi, which leave everything in the hands of the clerks, every appeals court and every multijudge district has a "chief judge," or "presiding judge" (in Pennsylvania, "president judge," in Texas "local administrative district judge") who performs such functions. Sometimes he is elected by his fellows like the chairman of an academic department; sometimes he is appointed by the chief of a higher court; occasionally he is elected or appointed specifically to be the chief judge. In the federal system, as noted, the chief judge of a district (or an appellate circuit) is the judge on this bench who is under the age of sixty-five and has served longest as a member of this court. One repeats that this does not always guarantee that the right man gets the job. Given the considerable independence of every judge in his own courtroom, it is not entirely clear how important the choice of chief is for a trial bench: "There's no doubt the chief judge holds the reins of power," says Russell Wheeler, recently moved to a think tank after fourteen years as deputy director of the Federal Judicial Center, "but new chief judges often complain that the reins aren't attached to anything at the other end. The chief clerk and the chief probation officer actually have more statutory authority, but they work for the chief judge."

The chief of a federal appellate circuit both subtly and directly carries more of a leadership role. It is the chief of the appellate court, for example, who decides to invite a district judge to move up onto a three-judge appellate panel, and he decides which judge he will request. But the chief of the appellate court gets to hold the job in the same brainless way as the chief of the district, and about the only authority given him by Title 28 of the U.S. Code is precedence in entering the room at meetings of judicial groups. Except on the Supreme Court, where the chief justice receives $8,000 a year more than the associate justices (and earns it), the chief judges in federal districts and appellate circuits are paid the same salary as their colleagues on their bench.

Reporting on advocacy for change within the federal system, the Federal Judicial Center's report on *Federal Court Governance* notes rather bleakly that "some chief judges have tried unsuccessfully to direct a judge to clean up a backlog of pending motions, withdraw an administrative order creating confusion in the clerk's office, or cease behaving tyrannically in the courtroom. Such judges often tell the chief judge, in effect, 'You and I have the same commission, and I have no intention of changing my behavior.' The chief judge can either try to mobilize the entire court to confront the judge, which may not be effective, or seek help from the circuit council, which may not be well equipped to provide it."[7]

In the state court systems, the procedures for appointing chief justices of the supreme court are very varied. In Virginia, Wisconsin, and Louisiana, the chief justice is the senior supreme court justice by years of service. In Kansas, West Virginia, Pennsylvania, and Nevada, the associate justices rotate the job of chief. In Massachusetts, the governor appoints a chief justice to serve till the age of seventy; in Maine, Maryland, and New Jersey, governors appoint to indefinite terms; in New York the governor appoints to a fourteen-year term. In a plurality of states, the justices of the supreme court choose their own chief, with terms as short as two years in Florida and New Mexico, three years in Illinois. In North Dakota, the judges of the trial court also get to vote on who should be chief of the state's supreme court. A wrinkle in Washington has selection by the justices, with rotation among the state's three judicial geographically set divisions. Popular election survives in Montana, Ohio, North Carolina, Texas, Minnesota, Arkansas, and Alabama. In Indiana no politician meddles: the appointment is by a "judicial nominating commission." In South Carolina, the state legislature appoints all appellate judges and their chiefs without asking the opinions of the governor or the sitting judges.

Chief or presiding judges in the state courts are usually paid more, but not much more, than the others on their bench. On the supreme court level, Maryland pays its chief $18,000 a year more than the associates, but several states (Michigan and Illinois, Georgia and Alabama, Washington and Nebraska—there is no pattern) pay the chief and associates the same. On the trial court level, the difference between a chief and ordinary judges is usually in the range of $1,000 to $5,000. In Texas, which pays experienced judges more than neophytes, the bonus for years on the bench may push the salary of an experienced judge beyond that of a newcomer chief. A few states still give counties the authority to set judicial salaries; in Arizona, some police court judges are paid more than the justices of the state supreme court.[8]

In most state supreme courts, as in the U.S. Supreme Court, the chief justice, if he is on the majority side, assigns the writing of the court's opinion to one of his colleagues if he doesn't do it himself. If the chief is in the minority, it is usually the judge on the majority side with the greatest seniority who does the assigning, but systems vary. In Colorado, the chief justice assigns both the majority opinion and the dissent if there is to be a dissent. Both the opinion and any dissent are circulated, and colleagues comment. Sometimes the author of the opinion heeds the comments; sometimes the commentators may feel a need to file dissents or concurring opinions. In most intermediate appellate courts, "chief" or "presiding" judges do their administrative work with the left hand, delegating most administrative chores to the court clerks. Which means that the court clerks run the logistics, the docket, and a lot of the personnel decisions, leaving many judges with the feeling that the system pushes them around.

But the autonomy of the judge was never in fact the autonomy of the professional, and the intrusion of administrators and superior courts is not like the intervention of the health maintenance organization or the insurance adjuster or the general counsel. These exist in part to impose a customer perspective on professional work, and an American court sees no customers: One way or another, once the case has started, everyone in the courtroom is coerced to be there. Robert Tobin describes an effort by a court consultant to interest court employees in Total Quality Management, with its emphasis on the needs of the customer: "Before he progressed very far in his presentation, he became aware of snickers and barely suppressed laughter. Finally he paused and asked his audience what was so funny. One senior clerk said the talk seemed unreal because the people they had to deal with were 'slobs and jerks.' "[9] Tobin comments: "So much for the customer perspective."

The judge is a lord in his chambers, where his secretary and his law clerks are normally people he has appointed himself. (In Illinois after a series of scandals, judges were deprived of their previous privilege of appointing the clerks that worked in their own courtrooms.) In small towns and rural counties the judge is a key member of the courthouse gang, and participates in hiring decisions; in larger cities, the clerks and bailiffs and guards and court stenographers, probation officers and child psychologists and translators who work in his courtroom may have been hired by somebody else. (In New York, the judge gets to hire a "confidential secretary" and a law clerk, and all the rest, including the clerk of the "part" in his courtroom, come through the civil service. The part clerk in New York, by the way, is quizzed three times a day by the mainframe computer—at 11:00, 3:00, and 4:30— and must report through his desktop what is going on in that courtroom: Is there a trial in progress? Is there a jury in the box? Is there a judge on the bench? If the place is deserted, and the judge has not arranged with the court executive to reserve some reading time, the chief clerk's office will send a case over *muy pronto.*)

In some systems, there may be featherbedding. (Tobin tells a story of a Boston municipal court where there were three bailiffs, "who justified their presence by separately announcing the same case. The court was like an echo chamber."[10]) Municipal courts tend to have unionized staffs; state courts know no unions; and this difference in employee status may make it impossible to "unify" the courts. The administrative law judges who work for the social security system have formed a judges' union.

In any event, the court staff and the lawyers stand between the judge and the public. Counting the maintenance staffs in the buildings, the ratio is roughly thirty to one—thirty clerks, bailiffs, probation officers, court stenographers, legal assistants, secretaries, janitors, security providers, and so on for each judge.[11] Even the trial judge is largely insulated from those on the other side of the railing. The judge's public is what sociologists call "the courtroom work group"—the police, the clerks, the government lawyers in criminal cases, the plaintiffs' lawyers, the defense lawyers, the court stenographers, the bailiffs, the probation officers. And she is "Your Honor" to everyone. Doris Provine in her book about justices of the peace notes that these people are crucial to the judicial function, because "cooperation and routinization are the keys to moving cases efficiently through the system. The defendant [in criminal cases], by contrast, plays but a minor role in the courtroom. In one of the city courts I visited, for example, the judge turned to the defendant's lawyer, not the defendant, to ascertain the spelling of his name, and the work group became so engaged in another discussion that no one noticed when the defendant, whose fate they were discussing, dissolved into tears."[12] In this context, what professionalism means is knowledge of the routine; experience becomes the life of the law in a sense far different from that Holmes intended. And for the appellate judge, there is no public: She has to be reminded that they exist.

It should be noted (and this is the place to note it) that the courts are not doing very well with the public. In 1996, the Gallup organization found only 34 percent of Americans with "a great deal" or "quite a lot" of confidence in local courts; 66 percent "some" or "very little" confidence in the courts.[13] And this was before *Bush v. Gore*, or the same-sex marriage fiasco. As more and more judges are elected in contentious political campaigns replete with negative advertising (see chapter 9), confidence is likely to deteriorate further.

3

Among them, according to the reports of the National Council of State Courts, these thirty-some thousand judges in 2003 disposed of about 100 million cases, about 57 million of them traffic cases (and 20-plus million of those were parking cases, very few of which require the involvement of a judge). But that left 43 million—almost 1,500 per judge per year—that were not traffic cases. About 21 million of these were criminal cases, a number hugely larger than the number presented in the previous study in 1998, partly because the statisticians moved most drunk driving offenses to the criminal category, mostly because cases of "domestic violence," the most rapidly growing category in the thesaurus, were included as crimes for the first time. (It is a problem, says Judge Albert Rosenblatt of the New York Court of Appeals, "that has been swept under the rug for the last two thousand years.") Most of the rest grew out of contracts where somebody didn't perform or somebody didn't pay and the court system will compel an end to the matter. In 1996, 17 percent of winning tort plaintiffs got awards of more than $250,000 in tort cases tried by juries while 14 percent got such awards in cases tried by judges alone (judges were more likely to give high awards in medical malpractice and automobile cases; juries in all other categories).[14]

The load is very unevenly distributed, though the details

are hard to come by because different states report on different things. In the statistics published by the National Center for State Courts after its 1998 survey, the Washington, D.C., neighborhood is clearly the litigation capital of the world. The District of Columbia reported more than 20,000 civil filings per one hundred thousand population, closely followed by Maryland with almost 18,000 and Virginia with more than 14,000. No other state came close. Tennessee reported in at only 1,310 civil filings per one hundred thousand population, the bottom of the list. But the reporters cautioned: Nine-tenths of the D.C. cases were small claims and landlord-tenant, and 69 percent of Maryland's cases were tenants versus landlords. Virginia reported each motion made in a case as a separate filing. And Tennessee's data do not include cases brought in the state's courts of limited jurisdiction.

Another section of the same report shows that South Carolina with fifty-one trial judges has only 1.2 judges for every hundred thousand of adult population. In 1998, South Carolina judges carried a caseload of 3,763 cases per judge per year, more than fifteen new cases for each judge every working day; and the five-member supreme court had to dispose of 427 appeals per justice, almost three times as many cases per justice as went to any other supreme court in the country. And this is a five-justice court where everybody participates in every case, so there are more than 2,100 cases altogether, or ten per working day for the justices to decide. But South Carolina's reported totals do not count the work of fifty-two family court judges in sixteen circuits, and forty-six probate court judges (who handle mental health as well as wills and estates)—and no fewer than *six hundred* magistrates and municipal court judges, who handle small claims, misdemeanors, all traffic (up to thirty days in jail or $500 for drunk driving), and preliminary hearings on major criminal matters.

By contrast, Illinois has 865 trial judges, more than any other state in the country though it ranks only fifth in population. Moreover, all these trial judges are equal—Illinois has a "unified" court system, where there are no specialized courts and anyone on the bench may be asked to hear any case. Newcomers have a year on traffic court, and are then without any training whatever thrown onto the bench in civil cases expressing disagreements among participants in the business community of the nation's second largest financial center. Every last one of the Illinois judges was elected on a partisan ticket with the full panoply of multicandidate primaries in which voters face a choice from page after page of candidates whose names they have never encountered before. Even with 865 judges, the 1998 caseload in Illinois was 1,580 per judge. But that's all there was—"circuit court" judges, the only kind Illinois has to hear trials, have "exclusive civil jurisdiction (including administrative agency appeals), exclusive criminal jurisdiction, exclusive traffic jurisdiction, exclusive juvenile jurisdiction"—and divorces, too.

Of the 14.6 million criminal cases brought to the American court system by the police in 1998, 1.93 million (an all-time record) were felonies. Of the criminal cases that came to court, two-thirds were resolved by plea bargains, with a judge brought into the process late in the game, approving the deal or (very rarely) blocking it. (In the federal system, the attorney general can order a U.S. district attorney, who works for the Justice Department, of which the attorney general is the boss, to reject a plea negotiated by lawyers from his office. In fall 2002, Attorney General John Ashcroft caused great scandal among the federal DAs, and the judges, by rejecting deals that involved abandoning the quest for a death penalty.) Where the same judges try both civil and criminal cases, which is true in most of the country, there is pressure from the lawyers to get the criminal stuff out of the way, to leave time for the civil stuff on which the bar makes its living. But in most states the law requires that criminal cases take precedence, and there is also pressure from the judge's conscience to spend more time on the criminal cases, where a defendant's freedom is at stake.

For a good judge in a rural court of original jurisdiction—one who hears a divorce today, a product liability case and an automobile accident tomorrow, a landlord-and-tenant matter on Wednesday, a robbery on Thursday, a disputed will on Friday—the requisite skill is a combination of patience and fast reaction time. Chief Justice Kathleen Blatz of the Minnesota Supreme Court remembers that she got the state legislature to authorize a 28 percent increase in funding for trial judges in her state by telling the tale of a judge in the southwestern corner of the state who handled a much-publicized three-week murder trial—and in the same three weeks had to dispose of 257 other cases.

One of the great political battles of the last twenty years has been over control of the "case flow" in the courthouse. The heart of the effort is "differentiated case management"

(DCM), which means that very soon after the parties have filed their papers to begin the lawsuit, a judge is assigned to speak with the lawyers and make a judgment of how much time this case should take. In the old days, cases were tried, or called for trial, in the order in which they had arrived at the court. DCM requires an early judgment of whether this is a simple matter likely to be settled by the parties with minimal judicial involvement, a more complex matter that still might yield a pretrial settlement, or a complicated case likely to need court time. Then the judge and the clerk and the computer that keeps the records apply the old queue theory principle of getting the easy stuff out of the way (your computer couldn't work without it), and the participants in the easy cases are given a nearby date to finish up, the cases of intermediate difficulty are given a schedule on which the lawyers should report on their progress, and the judge in the hard case is told to set up a number of checkpoints he and counsel should observe in the months to come. The proponents of DCM find it a little easier than practitioners to accept the idea that chief judges should have full authority to short-circuit the usual random selection process and make sure that "high-profile cases" be "specially assigned to a judge with the requisite training, experience and temperament to manage the case from its inception through its conclusion."[15]

The burden on the federal courts is much smaller. Sol Wachtler, when he was chief judge in New York, liked to say that his judges resolved more cases every day than the federal system did in a year. Historically, much of their business came from "conflicts of jurisdiction" (a driver from Idaho who rented a car in St. Louis collides in Arizona with a car rented in Los Angeles driven by someone from Pennsylvania). Thirty years of deep aversion to such cases, by Chief Justice Warren Burger and then Chief Justice William Rehnquist, has pretty much driven them back to the states. There is a long history behind the allocation of business between the federal and the state courts. Urging the ratification of the Constitution in *The Federalist*, Alexander Hamilton insisted that the federal and state courts would be "ONE WHOLE. The courts of the [states] will of course be natural auxiliaries to the execution of the laws of the Union, and an appeal from them will as naturally lie to that tribunal which is destined to unite and assimilate the principles of national justice and the rules of national decisions."[16] Though he argued that the state courts would lose none of their pre-Constitution jurisdiction, Hamilton saw no problem about appeals from the decisions of multimember state supreme courts being taken (as indeed they still are) to a single federal judge.

But the fact is that the courts of each state respond to the constitution of that state, and that the Judiciary Act of 1789, which established the federal courts, provided that "the laws of the several states . . . shall be regarded as rules of decision at trials at common law, in the courts of the United States." The act was shoved aside in 1842 in the case of *Smith v. Tyson* by Supreme Court justice Joseph Story—"a man of great learning," law professor John Chipman Gray later wrote scornfully, "and of reputation for learning even greater than the learning itself . . . fond of glittering generalities."[17] Story's ruling posited a federal "common law" created by the decisions of federal judges, superseding the legislation and court decisions of the states. After the Civil War, in 1867, Congress legislated a right for nonresident litigants to move their case to the federal courts on an affidavit that they could not get justice in a state court, and in 1885 in the Pacific Railroad Removal Cases the Supreme Court held that every claim against a federally chartered corporation (except a bank) could be removed to the federal courts.[18] Felix Frankfurter commented that as late as 1875, 40 percent of all cases that went to the Supreme Court involved questions of "federal common law."

By the 1920s, a decade before the Court abandoned Story's creation, the fraction was down to 5 percent, which made it easy to revoke the antique precedent. Indeed, when Chief Justice Charles Evans Hughes presented counsel's request that the Supreme Court hear an appeal in the case of *Tompkins v. Erie Railroad* in 1938, it was with the suggestion that it offered a clear opportunity to overrule Story's decision of ninety-six years before. In the aftermath of *Smith v. Tyson*, the federal courts had arrogated to themselves the authority to overrule state courts (up to and including the state supreme courts) on interpretations of precedent from state cases as well as federal cases; in the aftermath of *Tompkins*, especially in the reigns of Chief Justices Burger and Rehnquist, interference with state court decisions by the federal bench has become much less common, for better or worse.

This tale is not entirely a story of willfulness in Washington. Forty-two of the fifty states of the Union came into being with constitutions that said that until superseded by legislation, English common law should be the guide to decisions in the state courts. The notion that the same common law could give rise to different decisions in different jurisdictions is repugnant to the legal mind, and not without reason. After we have dug through all the kitchen middens, all the ballyhoo about the institutional settlement of disputes, the purpose of the enterprise remains its guidance to citizens as to what their behavior should be. Indeed, those who believe the common shibboleth that we have a government of laws, not men, must despair when they find that cases involving the same facts are not decided the same way in two different courtrooms. Under those circumstances, it was not entirely unreasonable for the U.S. Supreme Court to decide that a national court had authority over state court rulings based on the common law, or that a "federal common law," nowhere mentioned in the Constitution or in federal legislation, should be posited by the courts. As John Marshall grandiloquently put it in *Cohens v. Virginia*, "In war we are one people. In making peace, we are one people. In all commercial regulations, we are one and the same people. . . . America has chosen to be, in many respects, and for many purposes, a nation, and for all these purposes her government is complete, to all these objects, it is competent."[19] Thus Virginia had to permit the sale within its borders of lottery tickets from the District of Columbia.

Cases arrive in the federal system today because they involve the actions of the federal government, federal legislation, or the federal Constitution (greatly expanded in its coverage by the Fourteenth Amendment, which required states to guarantee that their actions came only after "due process of law"). There are few federal crimes—fewer than

60,000 criminal cases a year are filed in federal courts, as against 23 million filed in state courts. Seventy percent of the business that comes before the federal courts is bankruptcy business, heard in separate bankruptcy courts by a separate cadre of judges who serve fourteen-year terms after appointment by vote of the judges of their circuit. (It should be noted that the district judges do not lose control of these cases after they refer them to the bankruptcy courts, and every once in a while a district judge intervenes to change the direction of a bankruptcy proceeding.) Much of the work of a federal district judge consists of trying to find federal law that applies to a case with obvious national implications when Congress has not legislated in years.

Mark Twain once wrote that "Congress is in session and no man's life or property is safe." On the state level, Tom Phillips, while chief justice of the Texas Supreme Court, told a conference at New York University that "some colleagues on my court think the independence of the judiciary is damaged every time the legislature comes into session." In truth, the relationship between legislation and judicial opinion is complex, especially because the judicial interpretation of a law stands, in a sense, by itself. "It is ironic," Justice Traynor wrote, "that the unsound interpretation of a statute should gain strength merely because it has stood unnoticed by the legislature. It is a mighty assumption that legislative silence means applause. It is much more likely to mean ignorance, or indifference.[20] In fairness, it is also true that Congress must sometimes hit the Court between the eyes with a sledgehammer to get the changes in judicial decision that Congressmen had expected from a piece of legislation. We shall look at this question in depth in chapter 14.

4

"I hate lawyers," New York mayor Michael Bloomberg said to a candidate for a ten-year appointment to New York's family court, a benefice in his gift. "They waste a lot of money. The courts are the worst wastes of time and money in the city."

"I quite agree," said the candidate, who was thereupon reappointed.

In fact, this shabbiest of courts—Brooklyn's family court moved to a new building in 2005, but the shabbiness moved with the court—is still bloody expensive for the city. So simple a case as the decision to give a parent renewed visitation rights to an abused child involves a judge, an assistant at the front of the room, two uniformed officers, a lawyer for the court, a lawyer for the children's aid agency, a "legal guardian" for the child, a lawyer for the "respondent" parent, and at least one social worker who has been visiting the child. All of these people are being paid by some governmental agency. The salary costs of the one-hour hearing—which is not the first or the last this case will have—are at least $500, and it is by no means clear under the eye of eternity that the world would not be better off if we simply gave the child the $500 and asked her to decide whether she wants to see her father. Moreover, because family court in New York does not do divorces, or crime, or landlord-tenant disputes, this family, strongly assisted by taxpayers, is probably providing lots of income elsewhere for the court system and lawyers. But the society opted many years ago to bear the costs of the orderly management of these disputes "under law," so all the efforts to control those costs boil down to making the place nasty and eliminating "frills" like court stenographers (the legally required record is made by a tape machine, when it works).

In Oregon, *all* trial judges are family court judges. While carrying their normal caseload of other matters, they are also assigned a "limited number" of family law cases. They are "responsible," writes Victor Eugene Flango of the National Center for State Courts, "for family members' domestic violence, dissolution, drug/alcohol, criminal, and children's matters."[21] Several of these would as a normal matter have their own courts. Oregon runs on a system of one judge to one family: Once this family is assigned to this judge, by a clerk who "bundles" their various problems together by checking the records of lots of courts, he has 'em, maybe for years. One expert in these matters noted grimly, "God help the family that gets stuck with the wrong judge—forever." Where Oregon has succeeded, Flango believes, is in the creation of court-related "family resource centers" that may house as many as seventeen social agencies under a single roof. "Community 'buy-in' is important . . . to have the community believe that the court is theirs." Meanwhile, the rotation of assignments makes the judges understand that the problem is theirs—and reduces the judicial burnout characteristic of family courts.

There are few good numbers on the total costs of the court system, because federal, state, county, and local government bodies all make contributions, and litigants must pay "court costs" to use the facilities. (On the lower levels of the criminal justice system, people come out of jail owing the courts a lot of money for the procedure that put them away; most of them will not, probably cannot pay.) The Bureau of Justice Statistics takes a shot: In 1999, it says, "Federal, state and local governments spent over $146 billion for civil and criminal justice, an 8 percent increase over 1998. For every resident, the three levels of government together spent $521." Of that total, the federal government spent "directly" more than $22 billion; $50 billion was spent by the states, $35 billion by counties, and $39 billion by municipalities. Most of this, of course, went to "correctional," i.e., prisons. (Two million prisoners at $40,000 each equals $80 billion per year.) The most recent numbers for courts qua courts go all the way back to 1990, when the bureau's estimate for state courts was about $8 billion, excluding the costs of maintaining the buildings and defending the indigent in criminal proceedings. This was a little more than $31 per capita in the country, masking a difference between the $13 in Arkansas (where, one notes, Bill Clinton was then governor) or $15 in Mississippi and $49 in California or $52 in New York.

To estimate the total cost of state courts qua courts, Tobin, too, could come no further than 1990, and he thought the number then was roughly $11 billion. The 1990s were a time of migration of court costs from county and local budgets to the state budgets, usually but not always with the support of the county authorities and the judges. The county authorities were of two minds because they were usually left with the maintenance of the courtrooms, and the judges feared that loss of control over their budgets would mean loss of autonomy as the state administrators followed the money. Objections diminished as the money flow increased: The late 1990s were good for court budgets as for all other government budgets. If $11 billion was accurate for 1990, something like $17 to $18 billion would probably have been right for 2001. No more and conceivably even a little less for 2005, because the recession had put a substantial crimp in state budgets, and they didn't fully recover in 2004.

Something less than $4 billion of this total went to pay the salaries and benefits of judges, and the judges and their spokesman argue strongly that much more is needed to acquire and keep a first-class judiciary. The case that judges are underpaid was very strong in the middle of the twentieth century. In 1944 Simon Rifkind was appointed a federal judge by Franklin Roosevelt as a favor to Senator Robert F. Wagner, to whom he had been highly useful. Rifkind loved being a judge, but by 1950 he had two sons to put through college and the job paid $10,000 a year. Julius C. C. Edelstein, who had also worked for Wagner early in a career that led him to the vice chancellorship of the City University of New York, remembered that Rifkind went to Wagner to complain. And Wagner said, "Son, just don't expect that you'll ever be paid as much as a United States Senator." So Rifkind went off to private practice, where he flourished for more than half a century, made a fortune, became one of the half dozen most influential men in New York. He was able to continue to do important judicial work, serving as "special master" for the Supreme Court in what was arguably, in terms of the money involved, the biggest case the Court has ever had to decide: the conflict between the states of Arizona and California over the allocation of water from the Colorado River. In early 2006, Chief Justice John Roberts pointed out that over the period of the past fifteen years, ninety-two federal judges had resigned, fifty-nine of them to go into private practice.

Two aspects of judicial salaries are especially significant. The first is that the job pays what it pays. The budget for the courts shows a judge's slot that pays precisely this amount of money, and that's what everybody on that level gets. Texas, Georgia, Connecticut, North Carolina, Nevada, and Rhode Island increase a judge's pay for every year of service, but elsewhere the beginner receives precisely the same salary as the veteran with twenty years' experience. There is of course no relationship between output, even if that could be intelligently measured, and salary. And there is no reward for training. The second aspect is the very flat distribution. In a country where the average CEO receives hundreds of times the compensation of the average shop foreman, the chief justice of the United States gets little more than double what any but a handful of low-cost states pay their traffic judges. Trial court judges in Montana and Wyoming—the worst cheapskates—get less than $90,000, but only sixteen states pay *any* judge less than $100,000, and the chief justice at this writing gets less than $200,000.[22]

By comparison with the seven-figure drawing accounts of the rainmakers in the big corporate law firms, not to mention the exorbitant share of huge awards taken by the personal-injury bar that operates on a contingent fee, there can be no question that judges are underpaid. Roy Schotland, adviser to the Conference of Chief Justices, notes that the Iowa legislature recently gave its judges a sizable raise after a study that showed that 1,070 employees of the state were paid more than its supreme court justices. Indeed, the top graduates of the top law schools, going to work for the top law firms, make more money by their second year on the job than all but a handful of federal appellate court judges and a scattering of Texas justices of the peace who keep some of the money from real estate closings. In 2004, the deans of the ten most prestigious law schools averaged a salary slightly more than double that of a federal district judge. And while state judges' salaries have been rising, they lag increasingly far behind the rewards of partners in big law firms, whose pay rose from 1990 to 2004 by four times as much as judicial salaries.[23]

It can be argued, however, that the problem here is more the overpayment of the fat-cat lawyers, not the underpayment of the judges. For a fifty-two-year-old lawyer (the average age of appointment to the bench), a federal judge's salary of $155,000 *for life* represents present value of about $215,000 a year (assuming retirement at sixty-eight), and it comes with top-quality, secure lifetime free health insurance. Especially out in what the political pundits have taught us to call the "red states," that is suitable compensation for a fifty-five-year-old man or woman who already owns his or her own house in Omaha, Nebraska, especially if the children go to state college or have already endured such rites of passage. (A state court trial judge in Omaha gets about $110,000 a year, with a defined-benefits pension worth perhaps $40,000 more.) Federal judges, moreover, may supplement their salaries by $20,000 worth of fees for "educational" services—lectures at law schools or conferences, books or articles, and so on.

Still, the procedure is bad. In the interests of judicial independence, judges' salaries should be set not by the legislature or the governor's budget but by a commission charged with this task alone, with representatives from the legal profession, the law and business schools, corporate management, and state government. Such commissions were pioneered by Jimmy Carter when he was governor of Georgia, and have since been copied by seven other states. Another fourteen states have "advisory commissions" that propose pay schedules for their courts. Six of the eight states with salary-setting commissions rank higher in national comparisons of judicial compensation than they do in comparisons of household income.

It may also be worth noting that the federal court system is partway through a building program voted by the Congress in the late 1990s. Some $2.8 *billion* has been authorized for the construction of new courthouses all over the country, and there will of course be cost overruns. The new Moynihan courthouse in New York City cost more than $350 million all by itself, and the visitor to it wonders whether there is any marble left in Vermont. The money put into the construction of new facilities for the federal judiciary would have been more than enough to double the salaries of federal judges for the next twenty years.

8 IN PRACTICE: THE COLORADO WATER COURTS

Colorado has intermediate appeals courts, and there are only two kinds of cases that go on appeal immediately to the Supreme Court, which must hear them. One is death penalty cases, and the other is appeals from decisions in the water court. Those are the only things that really interest Coloradans—death and water.

—Colorado Supreme Court Justice Gregory J. Hobbs Jr.

THOUGH CONGRESSMEN HATE TO HEAR IT, American law traced back far enough usually rests on English common law as received from the mother country in colonial days. And in the English common law, landowners own the water that flows through their property, subject to a public right of navigation if the river is navigable and the right of the landowners downstream to receive their historic flow. The landowner may make "reasonable use" of this water, or no use at all, and no outsider has rights to use that water in any way—including fishing, which the landowner may prohibit in streams where he owns the banks.

The English landowner had no obligations whatever to neighbors who might wish to irrigate their farms or gardens by using some of the water he was not using. England is a well-watered place, where farmers get enough from the heavens to cultivate their fields.

The American West was different. Zebulon Pike in the first decade of the nineteenth century and Stephen Long in the second informed the political and military leaders in Washington who had sent them that most of the land bought from France in 1803 was doomed by lack of water to be an uninhabitable desert. Still, in 1862 the Homestead Act offered every American a 160-acre property to be carved from the land owned by the federal government if he would live there and farm the land. Most such properties, of course, did not have streams running through or beside them. The year before the Homestead Act, when Colorado Territory was spun off from Kansas and Utah, the original legislature passed "an Act to Regulate the Irrigation of Lands." One provision of the act included a landowner's right to build a ditch through other men's land from his property to the nearest stream with water that no one was using. "The whole of the Front Range, is interlaced with ditches that run through people's front yards" says Colorado Supreme Court justice Greg Hobbs, himself a former water lawyer and an enthusiast on the subject. (He writes poetry about landscapes, and finds ways to slot other Western poets' work into his opinions and articles.) "People buy houses and are astonished to find they can't fill in the ditch."

As the Territorial Supreme Court put it in 1872, enunciating what later became known as the Colorado Doctrine,

IN PRACTICE: THE COLORADO WATER COURTS

"When the lands of this territory were derived from the general government, they were subject to the law of nature, which holds them barren until awakened to fertility by nourishing streams of water, and the purchasers could have no benefit from the grant without the right to irrigate them. It may be said, that all lands are held in subordination to the dominant right of others, who must necessarily pass over them to obtain a supply of water to irrigate their own lands, and this servitude arises not by grant, but by operation of law."[1]

Water in Colorado, then, was all "owned" by the public, and "water rights" were severed from other property rights. The rights to a given volume of water (measured in acre-feet, each of which is about 326,000 gallons a year) belonged to the first person who claimed ("appropriated") it and put it to "beneficial use," which could be anything from washing laundry to irrigating crops to sluicing away the undesired minerals in mining operations. The rule was that nobody could have a "water right" who wasn't using it or building structures that would use it soon: "Speculative ownership" was impermissible when the stuff was so precious. Your right covered only as much as you were using: If you cut back, someone could challenge your priority for that much of your title. And if you stopped using your water, you lost ("abandoned") your water right, and someone who had plans to use it could at least in theory claim it away for himself. Among the duties of today's "division engineers" in the state's Water Department is a decennial census of water rights to assure that all are in use, and to declare the abandonment of those not in use.

Some part of the water used by the holder of the right

would disappear or become worthless ("consumed") by the use, but much of what was taken from the streams returned to them as the water ran down the domestic drain, or the irrigation ditches leaked, or "tailwater" at the end of the ditches joined other streams or leached down into the aquifers that fed the streams. "Downstream," says first district division engineer Jim Hall in Greeley, Colorado, "the river keeps rebuilding itself"—and this "rebuilt" water, if there's enough of it, can be appropriated and used by the holders of junior rights. The question of how much a designated use consumes may be crucial, for good or ill. Recently, for example, the city of Golden wanted to have a "white-water" amusement park, and the courts saw no reason why it could not buy what would be in fact quite inexpensive rights to the water, nearly all of which, after all, would run out of the amusement park down to the farmers' irrigation ditches.

First matters. "A right junior to 1890 isn't very reliable," says Marjorie Sant, a recent law school graduate who hopes to become a water lawyer, working now as clerk to Chief Judge Roger Klein, water judge for the first district, which is the watershed of the South Platte and includes Denver. Klein is a businesslike veteran who says he applied in 1995 to the governor's judicial appointments panel to become a district judge because he was tired of practicing law and having partners—and later applied to be the water judge because he was fascinated by the subject. He recently tried a case involving a water right first approved by a judge in 1865, just before the end of the Civil War, in continuous use ever since. The purchaser of a water right buys its place in the time line. If the holder of a "prior right" for water is not receiving the water to which that prior right gives him title, he can issue a "call on the river," bumping aside others in the watershed who are taking water though their rights are junior—and the state will enforce the call.

Each water right also specifies a use for the water. If the holder or the purchaser of his right wishes to change the use of the water, says Raymond S. Liesman, a first district "water referee" for the last thirty years, he has to prove to the water court that "the river will not feel the change." Agriculture wants the water from April through October, ski resorts want the water from November to March. The water court can okay a deal by which a user at one season draws more than his priority right in return for a promise to "augment" the water available later to the holder of the senior right. This is a complicated and highly technical negotiation, involving testimony from competing hydrologists.

Colorado's seven water judges—one for each of the state's geological watersheds—are appointed annually from the roster of district judges by the Colorado Supreme Court, but in fact once a judge has become a water judge he or she is routinely reappointed every year. And a good thing, too, says Klein, who remembers with some pain his first year adjusting to the idiosyncratic body of law and science the water judge must apply. The post carries considerable prestige in the judiciary, if only because appeals from decisions by a water judge go directly to the supreme court, which in its own rulings must accept the facts as declared by the water judge. As of summer 2005, all seven of the water judges were also the chief judge in his district.

Technology matters. In the 1930s drought, farmers suffered.

In the 1950s drought, having been blessed in the interim by the Rural Electrification Administration, they pumped water from deep wells, which tapped not only some isolated aquifers that could legally be run down, but also some underground sources of the South Platte, which were protected by senior water rights. When the drought returned in the 2000s, the holders of those senior rights were ready and able to fight to keep the well diggers from pumping what should be flowing to them. Towns defeated in their attempts to retain the full allocations of more bountiful times have developed municipal water systems that separate the potable from the nonpotable waters they supply their citizens—with the approval of the water court.

"When you get an overappropriated river, like the Platte," says Judge Klein, "it makes for a lot of activity. Every case I have tried has had unique issues, problems of first impression. It's not a stagnant area of the law. And the [state] Supreme Court writes multipage opinions."

In theory, all cases involving changes in the ownership or use of water rights go to the water referee, who may be an engineer or a lawyer (the first district in Greeley has one of each). He (or she: here, too, the first district has one of each) publishes the request for a change in a "résumé" printed in the newspaper of record in each county where anyone's rights may be affected. This gives holders of other water rights time to object, and the law firms that specialize in water rights opportunity to show that they are on the ball. If anyone does object, and someone usually does, the referee may hold hearings and issue a "decree" that settles the matter unless one of the parties appeals to the judge. In larger matters, where expert engineering and hydrographic testimony must be bought and paid for, the litigants tend to run around the referee and save expense by declaring jointly in advance that they will appeal to the court any decree by the referee. When the referee job was new, the legislature tried to give the referee investigative powers like a European magistrate, but the supreme court struck down the provision. Still, the referee is part of the judge's office and—unlike the state's division water engineer, who is housed in the executive branch and must be kept at arm's length by the water judge as though he were a party to the case—the referee can discuss engineering matters with the judge.

Out in the field, controlled by the water court's decisions but working for the division engineer, are a staff of "water commissioners," some dozens in each district, who keep an eye on which users are taking what water. They check the big users every day. They are empowered to reduce the output from the pump on the well or to close the headgates at the irrigation ditch if users are taking more than their right.

Eighty percent of Colorado's water is west of the Continental Divide and 80 percent of the population and economic activity is east of it. Major efforts to water the east from the west were among the great public works projects of the New Deal. The Colorado–Big Thompson project, operated by the state's Northern Colorado Conservancy District with help from the federal Bureau of Reclamation, involved the digging of a tunnel thirteen miles long that can carry 550 cubic feet of water per second down a gentle slope from west to east. In an average year (which is not to be confused with a "normal" year, there being no such thing), C-BT will deliver about

210,000 acre-feet of water to the farmers, ranchers, manufacturers, and cities of the Front Range. Recently it has sought agreement to build more reservoirs, so that more of the runoff from the winter snowpack can be captured and kept for use later in the year. The project has the authority to borrow money, and can tax those who receive its water, over and above the charges for the water itself, to make capital investments. But it describes itself as providing "supplemental water" to eastern Colorado, and among its most influential participants and customers are more than a hundred ditch companies that rely primarily on their rights to the water in the eastern streams and wells. When the drought cut C-BT back to only a little more than 100,000 acre-feet of water in 2002–03, the long-established ditch companies used their priorities virtually to the exclusion of lesser users.

The situation was especially severe for the farmers and smaller municipalities in eastern Colorado because the courts had raised the bar on the "augmentation" plans by which the users of water from tributary wells promised to recharge the reservoirs and wells of the holders of the senior rights. Division engineers had been willing to assume that the drought would break, and approved temporary plans, but the supreme court in 2002 demanded that before water could be taken from the holders of the senior rights a long-term plan to replace that water had to be in place. Thousands of wells operated by members of the Central Colorado Conservancy District were about to be capped, unless "new water" could be found.

Great ingenuity was applied to this problem. The Colorado building boom had created large-scale demand for gravel, which was being mined from dried-out streams and basins. "If you're mining gravel," says Kim Lawrence, the water lawyer who sold the concept to the court, a casual Westerner with traditional drooping mustache, "you're in a riverbed." The builders could line these bottoms with bentonite, an impermeable clay, and water would then accumulate in the minireservoirs from rainfall, seepage higher in the banks, and deliberate storage during winter months when the farmers didn't need the water washing past the ditches. The city of Aurora near Denver needed water, paid the Conservancy District $19 million in cash to fund the project, and replaced the water from these minireservoirs with its own treated affluent, which was fine with the farmers. There were doubts about this plan for augmentation—fifty-three objectors, represented by thirty law firms, filed against it, and Judge Klein's calendar was marked with thirty days reserved to hear the case—but the case was settled before trial.

Leaving such matters to judges is by no means the only way to go. California handles water cases within its executive bureaucracy, and Nebraska allows much meddling by the legislature. (After the Colorado judges had ruled that the farmers' and ranchers' wells were depleting the South Platte, which they were, the Nebraska legislature passed a bill with a finding of fact that four wells in an island in the river were not affecting its flow. That is, of course, Nebraska's problem, the whole state being downstream from Colorado.) Even in Colorado, special water courts did not come into existence until 1969, when water law was rationalized, watershed boundaries were accepted as useful political borders in establishing jurisdictions, and water judges were separated out from the ranks of ordinary district judges to help assure that cases would be heard by people who understood the subject.

And there are some cautionary tales. The water law enforced and to a degree written by the courts deals almost exclusively with property rights to quantities: Questions of water quality are almost entirely reserved to an executive branch agency. (The only time the water court takes an interest is when the holder of a priority right uses his water in such a way as to foul the runoff. This mostly affects miners' use of water.) When the federal government demanded that the various suppliers maintain certain rates of flow in the streams to preserve endangered species of fish, the water courts had no jurisdiction.

Still, if the Conference of State Supreme Court Justices is looking for "problem-solving courts," there is much to be learned from Colorado's water courts. They do solve problems, and stimulate innovation, too, in an aspect of life and business much more challenging to political order than people who live east of the hundredth meridian are likely to realize. They draw freely and successfully on scientific expertise, and the judges, because their attention is concentrated on the one subject, understand what the scientists are saying. They remain seized of the problem after they have solved it, not because their solution failed (the tragedy of the family court judges who see the same awful people popping up in their courtrooms every month) but because nature is forever changing the problem. They have a cadre of enforcement personnel who are not on their payroll but respond to their concerns.

Whether the Colorado system would work as well if the legislation gave the court larger or less well-defined responsibilities, no visitor can even guess. Justice Hobbs makes the case gracefully: "It's our only specialty court. The best judges gravitate to that."

9 ELECTING AND SELECTING JUDGES

A judge is a lawyer who once knew a politician.

—Runic inscription

I presume the public will always be convinced that the mere elevation of any lawyer to the Bench gives him learning and wisdom, whether he had any before or not. It matters not what the profession may have thought of him before he became a Judge or while he was practicing as a lawyer. Although his opinions on the law may not have been received before he ascended the Bench, yet his opinions given from the Bench become law for the time being at least, and the layman naturally takes the judge at his face value.

—Francis L. Wellman.[1]

The only real power judges have is people's respect for them.

—Abner Mikva

MOST AMERICANS DON'T KNOW THE name of their congressman, or the chief justice of their state supreme court, or of any justice on the United States Supreme Court. In small towns and county seats, the local judge may play sufficient of a role in governance that the name is in people's heads, but in cities and suburbs trial judges are as anonymous as dentists. Except that their names have been on ballots: They have been elected to their office or have passed through the fire of a retention election.

The elected judge—and almost 90 percent of American judges pass through some sort of electoral process—is part of the price Americans pay for governance by a written constitution that gives judges the power to destroy legislation. Responding angrily to a speech in which the "corporation counsel" of New York City called its judicial selection process a "farce," a Supreme Court justice proclaimed that "the public's right to elect its judges is supreme."[2] Actually, of course, the election of judges leaves the choice of a judiciary in the hands of the leaders of the political parties, who are even more anonymous than the judges themselves, and who profit twice—once because the patronage of a judgeship is in their gift, and then because they can "recommend" to the judge they put in office their candidates for trustee, special guardian, "master," executor, receiver, depository, and other jobs that carry good fees.

Traditionally in New York a Democratic candidate for judge paid for his nomination by giving money to the party, which supposedly used it to gather signatures on petitions, wrap posters around lampposts, mail literature, arrange meetings, and so on. In fact, of course, the money went into the party's general fund. An old tale from the 1930s tells of a Brooklyn lawyer sufficiently unsophisticated to complain to Hymie Manusch, then the leader of the Democratic Party in

Kings County, that he had seen no electioneering on his behalf in return for his contribution.

Manusch, the story goes, studied him briefly and said, "Do you know the ferry from Staten Island to Brooklyn? Yes? I want you to go to that ferry, and go out to the end of the pier when the ferry's coming in. You know what you'll see?"

"No."

"You'll see all sorts of garbage—vegetables, mattresses, condoms, dead cats, bits of furniture—all pulled into the dock in the wake of the ferryboat."

"So?" said the lawyer.

Manusch looked wise. "Roosevelt," he said, "is your ferryboat."

The story gained renewed relevance in 2003, with new scandals in Brooklyn. One judge pled guilty to extorting a sizable fraction of his fee from a lawyer representing a minor, who could not collect the fee without the judge's approval. Another was booked on charges of doing favors for litigants in family court because their counsel did favors for him elsewhere. *Newsday* found a retired African-American judge who said that in the 1960s he had paid Manusch's successor Meade Esposito $35,000 for a Kings County supreme court Democratic nomination (which in Brooklyn was the same thing as election). Now eighty-six, Justice Thomas R. Jones said, "It was in accordance with the customs and practices of the day. It was not right then, and it's not right now."[3]

Another tale surfaced, of a law clerk ordered by the judge who employed him to change his memo on the law of a certain case to say precisely the opposite of what he had written, after a phone call from a lawyer who numbered the Brooklyn

Democratic leader among his lesser partners. And an angry lady who had *lost* a primary for a judge's job in Brooklyn complained that she had been told if she hired a certain consultant everything would be taken care of. The district attorney of Kings County, the official name for Brooklyn in the court business, announced that he was shocked—*shocked*—that political influence seemed to be rearing its dirty head in judicial nominations in his county, and he empaneled a grand jury to consider criminal prosecutions of various influential if not eminent people. At this writing, in early 2006, the grand jury has yet to be heard from; the district attorney has been reelected.

At best, not much was expected from this inquiry. In the twenty-first century, it's rare for anyone seeking a judgeship to do anything so crude as handing an envelope to a county leader. Tying a judicial nomination to lawyer's fee, a consultant's itemized bill, even a contribution to the party is virtually impossible. Moreover, much of what a candidate does to get the nomination of a party is perfectly respectable. Friend of a friend, a young man who did well enough in law school to start his professional career as clerk to a federal judge, then worked in the corporation counsel office for the city government, and then became a law clerk for a state court trial judge, beat himself up to get a nomination in New York County (Manhattan). "You see how much harm a bad judge can do," he says, "how much mischief an indifferent judge can do, and you think to yourself, I can do a better job than that."

The path to the supreme court bench (the trial court of general jurisdiction in New York) lies through the lesser dignity of the limited-jurisdiction civil court. By the rules of the game, a civil court judge can be appointed a temporary supreme court justice, and will often move up to the higher court when a vacancy occurs. Both civil court judges and supreme court justices are elected in New York, the civil court on both a district and a countywide basis. "You have to become known to the party," says the friend of a friend. "You help candidates on their campaigning. You go to fund-raisers. You hand out leaflets. You go to clubs and their functions, meet the district leaders, get to know your state senator and assemblyman.

"You know in the spring how many vacancies there are going to be in the civil court. There's a screening panel—the good-government groups, the legal fraternal organizations. Denny Farrell [Manhattan Democratic leader] says to the Puerto Rican American Legal Defense Fund, the Jewish Lawyers Association, the Fordham Law School alumni, 'Can you spare us one person to sit on a screening panel?' [One of the reforms that followed the Brooklyn scandal is that for the first time the identities of the members of these panels were revealed to the public. This is nontrivial: Before 2003, nobody in New York had any way to find out whether the lawyers to whom judges assigned lucrative receiverships and guardianships had participated in selecting the judge.]

"Usually there are about twenty to forty candidates. Your interview with the panel takes twenty to thirty minutes. Serving on the panel is sort of like being on a jury. You're thrown into a room, but you learn to take it seriously; you're doing something important, you're selecting a man for a job. The screening panel selects three names for each vacancy—if there are two vacancies, they choose six names. Once you're 'reported out,' you can seek Democratic support. Sometimes, it's a question of what Denny needs to balance the ticket: Does he need a woman, a Puerto Rican, an African American. If you're reported out once and you don't get it, you have a little more weight the next time."

The actual selection of a judicial candidate in New York is quite peculiar. On primary day, which is a September date in New York, small numbers of voters select delegates to "judicial conventions" that go back to the mists of the nineteenth century. Each of the state's counties has its own convention, with its own delegates. Few of those voting in the primary have any notion who these candidates are, and even in primaries where real contests at the top of the ticket draw a measurable number of voters to the polls, the total vote for delegates to the judicial convention is very small. It is rare for anyone to contest the party leader's choice of delegate to the judicial convention. The votes for judicial convention delegates are not reported in any of the city's newspapers. Two weeks after the primary, each county holds a "judicial convention"— usually in the county courthouse at lunchtime—where the elected delegates learn from the party leaders the names of the future judges they are to nominate. A *New York Times* reporter found someone at the Board of Elections who had the names of the 2002 Brooklyn delegates on his computer, and contacted a number of them—all relations of party leaders, state assemblymen, and the like. None of them had known before arriving for the "convention" who the candidates were, and none could remember a year later which candidates had been chosen.[4]

"If you win the nomination," says the friend of a friend,

"the election is automatic. Then in December there are 'inductions,' which are fucking interminable, and you go to little judges' camp to learn the procedures, and you're a judge."

The New York Times in November 2002 editorialized bitterly that it refused to give endorsements to any of the candidates for forty-two (!) judicial slots to be filled in that election in New York City alone: "To endorse particular candidates might mislead voters into thinking that they have a real say in choosing judges, which is decidedly not the case. In practice, this year's crop of judges has already been determined by the political insiders in the city's five boroughs who exercise tight control over which individuals get to run on the Democratic Party line, thereby ensuring their election in this overwhelmingly Democratic metropolis. . . . Defenders of this farcical system talk piously about voter choice and preserving democracy. But as this year's judicial elections underscore, the only thing really being preserved is clubhouse control of lucrative courthouse patronage."[5] Early in 2006, a federal court declared these proceedings to be a violation of the Voting Rights Act; the case is now under appeal.

There are in fact, believe it or not, worse ways to do these things. The involvement of what used to be called a "blue-ribbon panel" does to some extent control the choices the party leaders can make. Procedures in Queens County, next to Brooklyn, did not even require the fig leaf of the selection committee—and when the Queens Democrats decided to seek an opinion from the Queens County Bar Association regarding the qualifications of candidates, the consultation occurred *after* the party had made its choices. As the 2003 flap in

Brooklyn shows the party can have some moments of bad public relations if it puts into judicial positions too many people of low morals. But every few months brings another signal that nobody cares a hell of a lot. In early 2005 a State Commission on Judicial Conduct reported out a recommendation that a Brooklyn surrogate (probate judge: wills and estates, guardians, et cetera) had given much highly remunerative work to a friend, never investigated what the friend did to earn his fees, and approved the friend's overcharges routinely. The chairman of the committee voted only to censure the fellow, arguing that he didn't know what fees should be charged. Still, the chairman wrote, "a system in which a judge appoints a friend to a public legal position, solely determines the friend's compensation, and the compensation is hundreds of thousands of dollars per year—several times the salary, for instance, of the chief judge of the Court of Appeals—is anachronistic and cries out *for review if not reform*." (Italics added.)[6]

In Chicago, the sewer is the limit: Nobody is responsible for the people who sit on the bench. Though Illinois, like New York, has partisan elections for judges, the party does not control who is nominated. One becomes a candidate for judge by filing to run in a primary for a seat that is to be filled this year. It doesn't matter whether the seat is occupied by a judge seeking reelection or has become vacant. Same system. The filing cost is a few hundred dollars. A number of seats are available in each election. (New York City is divided into five counties;

Cook County includes all of Chicago and a lot of suburbs.) The ballot runs many pages, and the voters may be confronted with literally hundreds of names they have never seen before. The numbers are enormous: In Illinois in the 2000 election, there were 177 candidates for the legislature, and 556 candidates for judge. Street wisdom in Chicago says that three factors control the results: Women vote for women; short names outpoll long names; and Irish names have an edge over all others. A precinct captain was overheard telling a lady with bigoted racial attitudes that the Kelly she was about to vote for was in fact an African American, but she objected that the lady was going to win anyway so she might as well go with the winner. In 2000, a woman named Joyce Murphy who had been a lawyer for only four years and was rated unqualified by the Chicago Bar Association defeated a professionally prominent appellate court judge in Cook County. William Quinlan, leader of the Chicago bar, former judge and state senator, says he tells students at the University of Chicago Law School that if they have trouble finding a job on graduation they should run for judge, especially if they have an Irish name; it's easier to get a job with a big firm if you're a judge. . . .

In New York, the civil court judge has a ten-year term, and the supreme court judge has a sixteen-year term. In Chicago, a circuit judge serves six years, and an "associate judge" has a term of only four years. Even the unopposed can be beaten. A judge who wishes to continue faces a "retention election" on the expiration of the term. In a retention election, the judge does not face another candidate; instead, voters are asked whether so-and-so should be continued as a judge. When a judge quits midterm or dies, a replacement is appointed by the judges of the state supreme court, and that appointee then faces a retention election at the next general election. It should be kept in mind that the poor voter has never heard the names of any of these judges before he or she picks up the page after page of paper ballot. In the Illinois retention election, the judge continues in office only if he or she gets three-fifths of the votes cast. In 2002, six judges in retention elections in Cook County were so poorly regarded that every bar association in the county declared them incompetent and unsuited to continue on the bench. This was not done in private: The *Chicago Tribune* ran an editorial presenting the universal opinion of the Chicago bar that these bums should go. Every one of the six was retained, one of them with more than 70 percent of the vote. The situation is especially damaging because Illinois now has a modern "unified court" system. Assignment of cases to judges is by random-number tables, and even the cynical assure the visitor that nobody can fix the system, make sure certain judges do or do not get any individual matter. So the people who get elected may wind up hearing important and difficult cases.

This way of choosing or confirming judges also screws up the election process in Illinois. In the 2000 election, a higher percentage of the votes for president of the United States was thrown out in Illinois than in Florida, because the Cook County voters had made mistakes on the judicial section of the ballot. Harris County in Texas (Houston) and Cuyahoga County in Ohio (Cleveland) have comparable ballots with hundreds of names.

2

The one place where there is no serious argument about the suitability of election for judges is the justice of the peace in a rural area or a small town. Indeed, it is not absolutely required, even today, despite some years of fulminations by the State Justice Institute, that JPs must be lawyers. "There are some of these places," says William Brunson, dean of the National Judicial College in Reno, which offers a two-week course for newly elected nonlawyer justices of the peace, "where you couldn't get a lawyer to live there." People are entitled to a convenient forum for their traffic violations, shoplifting, rental housing problems, and so on—and there has to be a local place where someone accused of a more serious crime can be arraigned and bound over for the consideration of higher authorities in more professional surroundings. The JP system persists in New York and Texas, and also in Arizona, Arkansas, Delaware, Louisiana, Mississippi, Montana, Nevada, Oregon, Utah, and Wyoming. Its advantage to the state in most cases, of course, is that it pays for itself: The salary of the JP is more than covered by the fees he or she collects. In Texas, where they handle foreclosures of mortgages as well as the usual duties, JPs can be very well paid; a justice of the Texas Supreme Court says that some JPs in Dallas and Houston make more than he does.

It is not entirely clear that anyone is seriously disadvantaged by the nonlawyer judge. New Mexico did a study in the 1960s that turned up a surprising number of stumblebums, including one who took jurisdiction to divorce people on the grounds that, hell, he had married them. And some of the historical precedents are very bad: It took a U.S. Supreme Court decision in 1927 (when the Court was by no means a pioneer of social protection) to keep the state of Ohio from paying JPs only when the defendant was convicted. But the modern world looks much better. The only major study of JPs in New York—which at that time had 1,600 exemplars, mostly non-lawyers, hearing three million cases a year—was done in the 1980s by Doris Marie Provine, a professor of political science who had herself served a term as a lay judge upstate.[7] Before serving as JPs in New York, both nonlawyer and lawyer JPs had to take a five-day course; but the lawyers didn't have to pass the exam (!). Studies found virtually no difference between nonlawyer judges and lawyer judges in the number of times the judge is overruled on appeal.

Provine defends "the Jeffersonian concept of adjudication rooted in local authority," and blames some of the bad reputation lay judges have on the simple fact that they may work in their homes (or in a multipurpose town hall or a police station) with little if any help from the usual "courtroom work group" of clerks, police, and attorneys that dominates a "real" court. Alexis de Tocqueville thought well of the JP. "His office," Tocqueville wrote, "simply obliges him to execute the police regulations of society, a task in which good sense and integrity are of more avail than legal science." Provine notes simply that "America never made the judiciary into a true specialist's domain, requiring technical training geared to the responsibilities of the office. Practitioners whose education is for law practice, not adjudication, are our 'professional' judges." Training and experience as warrior litigator would seem something less than ideal as preparation for the work of a judge (Not necessarily, however. The most ferocious and unprincipled litigator I ever watched at work, a man willing to cast aspersions on opposing counsel for having taken as client such a no-goodnik as his client's opponent, became a distinguished judge noted for fairness as well as force.)

When cities first created small claims courts, housing courts, and family courts, the hope was that the work would be done mostly by the people affected by the decisions, not by lawyers. With the passage of time, these innovations were taken over by the legal profession; small claims courts became collection devices for merchants, housing courts became the vehicle for evicting the unlucky, family courts became unlicensed psychiatric clinics where the most forceful advocate often bullied the others. Lawyers speak scornfully of "cadi justice," the justice of the emir in the marketplace, but in truth these minor disputes that come to JPs are best handled informally. The point is not to tell people that this is the law that controls their behavior but rather that their behavior does or does not meet community standards. That people like this sort of thing is demonstrated by the popularity of the *Judge Judy* and *Judge Brown* television shows. The television judges wear black robes and wield a gavel, but their game is common sense.

Provine gives a simple example of common sense in the decision to set bail: "Judges must decide whether they will adhere strictly to the legal justification for bail: to achieve the defendant's return to court—or whether bail will be imposed for additional reasons. Some judges, I found, will set bail to sober up a drunken driver, or to protect a wife from an angry husband, or to clear a recreational area from noisy out-of-town revelers. In such cases, the judge may go to jail the next morning to reduce or revoke the bail. Bail may even be imposed for educational purposes. One lay justice described an incident in which he had asked a local defendant charged with drunken driving how much money he was carrying; on finding he had less than a dollar, the judge set bail at a dollar. This decision sent the defendant to jail, as the judge expected it would, because family and friends refused to get him out. A night in jail on one dollar bail, the justice reasoned, would give the defendant time to sober up and to consider just how disgusted his family was with his drinking."[8]

One does not wish to be Pollyanna about these things: Closeness to the community also means diminished independence. It is by no means clear that having JPs arraign prisoners, set initial bail, and supervise coroner's inquests, as Texas does, improves the criminal justice system. It was a JP who found that Lyndon Johnson's friend Billie Sol Estes with nineteen bullet holes in his body had committed suicide. What you gain on the swings you can lose on the roundabouts. Still, there is reason for people making decisions of a minor civil and criminal kind to be elected rather than appointed.

3

There is a nice story about Abraham Lincoln and the appointment of Samuel Miller to be an associate justice of the Supreme Court, a seat he would fill for twenty-eight years. A doctor who became a lawyer by reading the books, he is regarded by no less an authority than Chief Justice Rehnquist to have been "one of the great justices who have served upon the Court."[9] His great contribution to American jurisprudence was his insistence that the Fourteenth Amendment did not take away from the states their power to regulate commercial activities within their borders. And it was Miller who defended the judge-made common law of the western states with the comment that "the first judges did not know enough to do the wrong thing, so they did the right thing."[10] His biographer tells the story that when his friends came to the White House to urge his appointment on Lincoln, the president kept busy with other things on his desk until he finally heard the words "Supreme Court," when he said, "Oh, this is important. I thought you wanted me to appoint him a brigadier general."[11]

Judge Constance Baker Motley came out of the civil rights movement to be borough president of Manhattan, then a state senator, and (from 1965 to her death in 2005) a federal judge. She remembered the process that put her on the district court bench. There were two wars (apart from Vietnam) ongoing in New York. One pitted U.S. Senator Robert Kennedy against Mayor Robert Wagner; the other, Kennedy against President Lyndon Johnson. Kennedy had proposed Motley for a district seat; Johnson had trumped that by proposing her to the seat on the Second Circuit being vacated by Thurgood Marshall as he became solicitor general en route to the Supreme Court. Meanwhile, Motley had been elected to the New York State senate, where for several months the battle between Kennedy and Wagner made it impossible to elect a Democratic leader. Finally, Wagner made a deal with the Republicans, and Motley, who owed him (he had put the borough presidents on the city's site selection committee for municipal projects, greatly enhancing their clout), voted his way. At that point, Kennedy dropped her from his proposed list of new federal district judges—so Johnson appointed her.

4

Though Benjamin Franklin at the Constitutional Convention had recommended a rather different system (he thought the lawyers of each district should elect their judge, because they would choose the best man to eliminate the competition), all thirteen states came into the Union with judiciaries appointed by the governor or elected by the legislature. Federal judges in those days were no big deal—there were only nineteen of them, six Supreme Court Justices and thirteen district judges, the Supreme Court rooted in the Constitution, the other courts created by the Judiciary Act that was the first thing the new Congress passed in 1789. The Constitution provided that the president would "nominate and by and with the advice and consent of the Senate" would appoint new justices to the Supreme Court. The Judiciary Act did not require George Washington to consult the Senate when appointing federal district judges, but Washington did so, setting a precedent many presidents must have wished to change. One notes that presidential appointments in the American way of doing things are the end of a most peculiar process. The president nominates, then the senate confirms, and then the president appoints. The Senate Judiciary Committee does not necessarily hear the nominee (until the 1920s, no nominee to the

Supreme Court ever testified; the huge battle over Wilson's nomination of the Jew Brandeis, to call a spade a spade, occurred without the participation of Brandeis). And it is conceivable that having heard the testimony of his nominee before the Senate a president could (though none ever has) decide he'd made a mistake, and not appoint his own nominee.[12]

As American governance developed, so Supreme Court justice Robert H. Jackson wrote in 1952, "appointments to the District Court benches . . . have lawfully become senatorial patronage. This is due to the custom of senatorial courtesy, under which a senator, by making personal objections, can prevent the confirmation of any appointee to his District Bench." Jackson tells an amusing story of an effort by Franklin Roosevelt to get around this rule "by making a district judge appointment in the summer of 1938 without consulting Senators Carter Glass and Harry Byrd. . . . That man, whose name was Floyd Roberts, was admittedly a competent man to hold the position, but because of the failure of the President to consult them, Senators Glass and Byrd opposed the confirmation. It became very plain that the President could not get that man confirmed. The President was plainly defeated. It was a stalemate. He would not withdraw the nomination. The post was vacant.

"One day we were down on the President's yacht over a weekend, fishing and relaxing. The President said, 'I've got a job for you, Bob, and for Pa Watson. I want you to go down to Charlottesville, and see if you can't get Armistead M. Dobie, the Dean of the University of Virginia Law School, to accept the appointment as a district judge. I think if I send his name to the Senate, the Senators from Virginia will not dare to turn him down.' . . . [T]he contest at that point had become one of personal prestige, and the President wanted to put one over that they would not dare resist. This was when I was Solicitor General, not Attorney General. He was apparently handling the matter quite independently of Attorney General [Frank] Murphy. He said there was a vacancy coming up on the Fourth Circuit Court of Appeals, and that if Dobie accepted the appointment to the district court, we could say that the President would feel that he should be promoted to the Court of Appeals when the vacancy occurred.

"So Pa Watson and I took a White House car. . . . When we got in the vicinity, Pa Watson, in his genial southern way, said, 'Now, Bob, you handle the heavy thinking in this, and I'll go get a bottle of bourbon.' I talked with Dean Dobie while Pa took a little trip. When Pa came back, I introduced him to 'Judge' Dobie. . . . The President immediately sent his name to the Senate, and there was a prompt announcement from Senators Byrd and Glass that they would vote for his confirmation."[13]

Jackson's memories were incomplete. A footnote by John Q. Barrett, who edited the Jackson papers, reports that Roosevelt actually made a recess appointment of Roberts to a newly created western Virginia district in July 1938, sending his name to the Senate in January 1939. The Senate rejected the Roberts nomination, which arrived on the floor with negative recommendations from both the Virginia senators, by a vote of 72–9.[14] Recess appointments, which permit new judges to start serving immediately but deny them continuance in office unless confirmed within a year, are usually considered the ultimate insult to the Senate, and they are rare.

But Eisenhower appointed Earl Warren on that basis—one day he was governor of California, and the next day, having flown to Washington and sworn his oath of office, he was chief justice of the United States—and William Brennan, too, came to work before he was confirmed. In 2004, George W. Bush made recess appointments to the Circuit Courts of Appeal for four judges whom a divided Senate would not put to the vote, then promised never to do that again and withdrew a number of controversial nominations that had been pending in the Senate for some months. And then, having won reelection, resubmitted them.

Deference to the senators, of course, applied in its pure form only when the president and the Senator were of the same political party. Presidents are expected to pick judges whose views are consonant with theirs. A study of the political affiliations of judicial appointments from the 1880s to 1975 showed the percentage of Democrats appointed by Democratic presidents ranging from 92 percent (by Truman) to 99 percent (by Wilson); the percentage of Republicans appointed by Republican presidents from 86 percent (by Hoover) to 98 percent (by Harding).[15] Sheldon Goldman and Elliot Slotnick updated the numbers through Clinton, and found that Carter, Clinton, Bush I, and Clinton reached into their own party for roughly 90 percent of their district judges (221 Democrats to 12 Republicans for Clinton; 266 Republicans to 14 Democrats for Reagan). Theodore Roosevelt, accepting the recommendation of Senator Henry Cabot Lodge that he should appoint Oliver Wendell Holmes Jr. to the Supreme Court, expressed satisfaction with Lodge's assurance that Holmes was a true Republican, "safe on imperialism." Roosevelt wrote that

"I would not appoint my best beloved . . . unless he held the positions you describe."[16] These rules did not always hold—Herbert Hoover at the urging of Republican senator William Borah nominated the New York Democrat Benjamin Cardozo, and Harry Truman's first nominee to the Supreme Court was Republican senator Harold Burton—but left to their own devices most executives will appoint their own kind to the judiciary.

Once on the bench, of course, a judge might write decisions very different from those expected by the president who nominated him, and nobody could do anything about it. Federal judges were supposed to be independent, not accountable. One of the colonists' complaints about George III had been that he interfered with judicial decisions. To maintain their independence federal judges were given lifetime tenure. But as the time neared for the first democratic transfer of power in the United States, when Jefferson beat Adams in 1800, the defeated, with four months between the election and the transfer of power, sought to maintain their influence by creating new courts and packing them. "Retreating to the judiciary as a stronghold," Jefferson said.[17] Jefferson and his new Republican majority in the Congress solved the problem by repealing Adams's Judiciary Act (which Jefferson and friends called "The Law of the Midnight Judges") and abolishing its courts. They also attempted to impeach one of the Supreme Court justices, but failed.

It was in the Truman administration, 150 years later, that the American Bar Association formed what is now its standing committee on the federal judiciary. These representatives of the bar vetted judicial candidates for the administration or the Senate or both, ranking them as "exceptionally well-qualified," "well-qualified," "qualified," or "unqualified." Truman had appointed friends—Fred Vinson to be chief justice, Harold Burton, Sherman Minton, his attorney general Tom Clark—and though Clark was in fact a more significant figure than contemporaries thought, the leaders of the organized bar felt they had reason to worry about the future of the institution. Vinson not only played poker with the president, he kept on his desk a telephone that was a direct line to the White House.

Eisenhower was committed to put Earl Warren on the bench from the moment the California delegation to the 1952 Republican convention swung his way. Thereafter he relied heavily for advice on his attorney general, Herbert Brownell, a Nebraskan who had made it big in New York (he was a member of the Century Club for fifty-eight years)—and who, asked to find a solid young Catholic judge for the Supreme Court, recommended William Brennan of the New Jersey Supreme Court, then considered a conservative Democrat. Brownell was not a fan of the federal district bench; he once called its occupants "gray mice." Eisenhower was still alive when Nixon became president, and when the time came for Nixon to make his first Supreme Court appointment, Eisenhower sent an unsolicited recommendation of Brownell.

Kennedy and Johnson had to please a dramatically divided Democratic Party, and used judicial appointments as patronage (Johnson especially). Johnson's ambition to make his personal lawyer Abe Fortas chief justice was frustrated in the

Senate. With Nixon, ideological tests became central to the process, especially in appointments to the expanded circuit courts of appeal, where decisions restated or revised law over a considerable terrain. Appellate court nominations, because they affected a number of states, did not have to be cleared in advance with senators. Three Nixon nominees for the Supreme Court were either defeated or forced to withdraw. Reagan kept a campaign promise by a Supreme Court nomination of Sandra Day O'Connor from the Arizona intermediate appeals court. During the long period in the 1990s and early 2000s when the personnel of the Court was stable, O'Connor was the only person on it who had ever served as a legislator. Reagan also nominated Antonin Scalia, who refused to tell the Senate Judiciary Committee what he thought about anything (and won virtually unanimous confirmation, very odd in retrospect)—and Robert Bork, who was defeated after telling the committee what he thought about everything. The George W. Bush administration carried the Nixon plans to a higher level, submitting to the Senate for appellate court nominations only candidates whose feelings about economic regulation, abortion, civil rights, and the powers of the presidency were representative of the evangelical and big-business wings of the Republican Party. Democrats, with forty-nine votes in the Senate, fought back by preventing a vote on what they considered the more extreme cadre of the delegation. Cut down to forty-five votes in 2005, they continued the fight more modestly.

5

All thirteen states entered the Union with constitutions that provided for the election of judges by the state legislatures or appointment by governors or both together. "In every state, except Pennsylvania and Maryland, [judges] were removable by address of the two houses, followed by formal removal by the governor. In Pennsylvania and Vermont, the single house might remove."[18] Popular election of state judges—and it is in the state courts that more than 98 percent of the work of the law gets done—came later. Vermont split off from New York and entered the Union in 1793 with a constitution that called for elected judges. Georgia switched to the election of its entire judiciary in 1812, and Mississippi in 1832 led a charge that saw every new state admitted before the civil war enter with an elected judiciary. Other states held constitutional conventions in that period, and all but two—Massachusetts and New Hampshire—opted for elections.

Andrew Jackson did say that "judges should be made responsible to the party by periodic elections,"[19] but the pressure to elect judges was from the bar itself. Lawyers had seen their dominance of the legislature begin to erode (thirty-one of the fifty-five delegates to the Constitutional Convention had been lawyers, but the ratio kept going down in the state legislatures), and they wanted to assure the independence of the judiciary by giving the judges a separate source of authority. In his memo to the state supreme court justices urging intervention in the Minnesota case before the U.S. Supreme Court, the Georgetown law professor Roy Schotland presented a "history showing that state constitutional conventions did NOT choose elections to make the judiciary like the other branches, but rather to make the judiciary more independent of the other branches."

Chief Justice John Marshall had insisted that the Constitution was superior to the laws passed by the legislature because the Constitution represented the will of the people rather than just some representatives. Elected judges would have a better case that they preserved the rights of the people, and would be less subject to pressure from the executive and legislative branches. This theory never worked as advertised, because the executive and the legislature retained control of judicial budgets and the terms and conditions of judicial employment. (The courts were, as the Canadian political scientist Carl Baar demonstrated in his 1975 book of that title, *Separate but Subservient.*[20]) Even on the federal level, where the Constitution protected judges from political reprisal, the Supreme Court sat in poorly ventilated quarters in the Capitol and worked mostly in their homes because Congress did not provide them with chambers. In 1816, as part of a protest against Justice Story's assertion in *Martin v. Hunter's Lessee* of "implied powers" to overrule state laws and decisions by state courts, Congress refused to appropriate money for a court reporter to work in the Supreme Court.[21] On the state level, elected judges were indebted for their election to the same political leaders who staffed the governors' mansions and the state legislatures and dependent upon them for renomination.

Presumably, some of these dangers could be avoided by electing judges in "nonpartisan" elections, forcing voters to choose an individual rather than simply trail after the party symbol. In real life, as shown in Illinois in the primaries and in retention elections, the cure can be worse than the disease, for the voters don't know who these people are, which means that aggressive advertising in broadcast media becomes the yellow brick road to the bench. Judicial candidates could not go around making news, because almost anything they said that was newsworthy would indicate how they would vote on a matter they were supposed to approach with full impartiality. A well-known name, even if well-known on another person, can be decisive: the chief justice of the Washington Supreme Court was beaten in 1990 by a Tacoma lawyer who happened to have the same name as the anchorman on the local TV news show.

In the early years of the twentieth century, the Progressive movement made reform of judicial selection procedures one of its cardinal goals. In 1913 the newly organized American Judicature Society proposed that state court judges should be appointed by the chief justice of each state's supreme court, who would himself be elected to maintain a fig leaf of democratic control. The chief justices, of course, would consult with the state bar before making such appointments. As time passed, this was refined to "merit selection." In merit selection, a nonpartisan committee of lawyers and judges, with perhaps a sprinkling of political leaders and distinguished laymen, consider applications and nominations to a vacant judicial post, and forward to an appointing authority (usually the state governor) a list, usually as short as three approved names. The governor must then appoint from that list. This merit selection plan was advocated by the American Bar Association in 1937, and first instituted in Missouri in 1940, and it spread.

Missouri neatly encapsulates the history of American efforts to make its judicial selection process respectable without
training people for the job. The state was admitted to the
Union in 1821 with a constitution that echoed federal practice
of appointment by the chief executive and confirmation by
the state senate. By 1849, the kingly commons had carried out
their revolution and pushed through a constitutional amendment that called for elected judges and limited judicial terms
to four years (six on the supreme court). As this system played
out, judicial candidates competed in party primaries the summer before an election, and the winners, guaranteed to be
"trustworthy" from the parties' point of view, were then put
down at the bottom of each party's ticket in the fall elections.
In the 1930s, the Missouri Supreme Court appointed a judicial council, which among other things advocated the nomination of judges by party conventions summoned exclusively for
that purpose, a truly awful idea now realized in New York.

In 1937, the leaders of the Missouri bar formed an Institute for the Administration of Justice, which pushed the ABA's
merit selection plan with an additional gimmick—after a year
on the bench, the appointed judges would be subject to a retention election. This proposal got nowhere in the legislature,
but the institute, aided by the League of Women Voters,
gathered enough signatures to force a referendum on it in the
1940 election, and it carried. Gerald Dunne reports that the
donors to the referendum campaign sought to take tax deductions for charitable contributions, and were rebuffed—but
the Board of Tax Appeals permitted lawyers to take the contributions as a business expense on the grounds that the plan

would give the state better judges and better judges would make the lawyers' work easier.[22]

By 1990, thirty-three states had some form of merit selection of at least some judges (usually appellate court judges); by 2003, the number was thirty-five, the last to join being Rhode Island, which had had a system of election by the legislature. A legislature dominated by criminal defense lawyers elected a chief justice later shown to be a member of the mob, and the state decided to abandon voting in these matters, turning them over to the governor with advice from a distinguished panel of professionals. New York put up with a lot in the election of judges to its Court of Appeals, the state's highest court. Chief Judge Sol Wachtler ran television commercials of himself in a judge's robes slamming jail doors closed. Then he got in trouble with the law himself by harassing a lady who had ceased to return his affections and had to resign on his way to the hoosegow, and the rules were changed to eliminate judicial election to the Court of Appeals.

In some states appointment to vacancies is by the governor alone. In California, for example, lawyers apply to the governor for appointment as a judge, listing the ten most important cases they have tried (with the names of the opposing attorneys in those cases). The governor forwards the list to a committee of the state bar association, which is a quasi-public body in California (every practicing lawyer must belong), and the committee sends out a questionnaire, then interviews the applicants. The governor then appoints from a short list of those approved by the bar. All judges, like other public officials in California, are subject to recall elections. In some states the governor's choice has to be approved by the state senate.

There are two states—South Carolina and Virginia—in which judges are appointed by the justices of the state supreme court or the judges of the appellate court for the district where the vacancy has occurred. This is arguably the best way to get good judges, because the higher courts have to live with the work product of the lower courts and will pay attention, discouraging individual judges from pressing too hard for people who will later prove inadequate to the job. The federal "magistrate judges" are a growing corps of federal not-quite-judges who handle the scut work of the district bench (arraignment and motion parts, misdemeanor trials, civil trials initially involving less than $50,000, mediation proceedings). They are chosen by the judges of the district where they will work, for eight-year terms. The position was created in 1968 as simply "magistrate," and the title "magistrate judge" did not come until the Judicial Improvement Act of 1990. Chief Justice Warren Burger was always worried about them—he didn't want magistrates to wear robes or have their own courtrooms—but now everybody is very content, and the magistrate corps has become a significant source of appointments to the district bench.

Many states joined Missouri in requiring that after an appointed judge has sat for a year or two he or she must be subjected to a retention election: "Should Judge So-and-So be retained in office?" Retention elections, unfortunately, can be a disaster. From 1964 to 1994, they were all form and no substance—only 23 of 3,912 judges in retention elections failed to win 51 percent approving their continuance.[23] (Until 2004, Missouri never had an organized opposition to a judge up for retention.) Voters know little enough about candidates for legislative and executive office. They know nothing, literally nothing, about whether or not a judge has done a good job. In the old days, the objection was that the Chicago scene would be typical: You can't beat somebody with nobody. In recent years, the problem as been more subtle because political professionals have learned how to energize voters with single-issue campaigns.

The big event was a recall election that took down California chief justice Rose Bird and two of her associates in 1986. Appointed by Governor Jerry Brown and formerly secretary of agriculture in his administration, Bird insisted on articulating a very liberal agenda for her court, and never adjusted to the need for dignity in her job. More than $9 million was spent on the recall, and the myth was that the big-business interests done in Ms. Bird. In fact, as Roy Schotland has pointed out, 77 percent of the $6 million spent in the campaign against the justices was raised in small contributions while only 32 percent of the $3.2 million spent on their behalf came from small contributions. The largest single contribution to the recall campaign, interestingly, came from Richard Riordan, then a Los Angeles lawyer, later the Republican mayor of Los Angeles.

Hymie Manusch's ferryboat still pulls the candidates into the dock in New York, where the party controls who gets the endorsement on the ballot, and people vote for the party. Elsewhere, even in states where the party label controls the results (in Texas, more than 90 percent of all voters vote the same line for judge that they do for governor), primary contests are important—and, these days, expensive. The largest single source of funds for judicial elections is the "tort reform" movement—the effort by doctors, chambers of commerce, insurance companies, and big business in general to set limits on the awards juries can give for the "pain and suffering" of the victims of harmful products and medical malpractice, and the "punitive damages" that can be assessed beyond the compensation for actual harm. Together with the device of the class-action lawsuit, which permits plaintiffs' lawyers to solicit the power to represent anybody who ever worked in, say, a metal fabricating shop where asbestos was present, frequent large awards in such cases have become a significant cost for business (and medicine) in America.

Judicial elections have become big money as the U.S. Chamber of Commerce presses state campaigns especially against supreme court judges who have upheld high awards in personal-injury cases or have voted against the constitutionality of laws limiting recoveries by plaintiffs or their lawyers. Wal-Mart, Daimler-Chrysler, Home Depot, and the American Council of Life Insurers each contributed more than a million dollars to the national Chamber of Commerce fund for intervention in judicial elections in 2000, and the Chamber funded advertising campaigns by affiliates and sponsored subsidiaries (with cute names like Americans for Job Security and Citizens for a Strong Ohio).[24] These people may not know what they are doing. Awards in similar cases are roughly the same in the states where judges are appointed and the states where judges are elected (with the one exception that out-of-state defendants fare much worse in states that elect judges in partisan ballots).[25] But they think they know what they are doing, and in 2004 a coal company executive whose company had a case pending before the West Virginia Supreme Court did manage to get an incumbent justice defeated by contributing at least $2,260,000 to a group opposing him.

The Chamber is not always very good at influencing elections. In 2000 in Mississippi, the nine candidates for four seats on the supreme court spent among them $1.4 million. The Chamber spent another million to help four of the candidates. Two won; two (including a chief justice who had served for eighteen years) lost. These were essentially positive ads, praising the candidates the Chamber liked rather than trashing the candidates it disliked; but they still left a bad taste. The Brennan Center of the NYU Law School did a report on interest-group activity in state judicial elections in 2000, and quoted a "prominent Mississippi attorney" that "in the face of all the money expended, the danger existed that the public would 'get the impression that the leaders of the judiciary are politicians.'"[26]

It can be much worse that that. The Chamber spearheaded a campaign against Ohio Supreme Court justice Alice Robie Resnick, who had voted to throw out a tort reform law and was also vulnerable as author of an opinion requiring changes in the financing of public education. Two television commercials financed by the Chamber essentially accused her of being a crook. One showed a cascade of paper money on one side of the scales of justice while the lady holding them peeked under her blindfold to see it, with a voice-over that said Justice Resnick had accepted $750,000 in contributions to her campaign from labor unions and trial lawyers. The other accused her (falsely) of changing her vote on a wages-and-hours dispute after a contributor contacted her on the matter. The first commercial asked, "Is justice for sale in Ohio?" Observers credit this commercial—which embarrassed viewers—for Justice Resnick's win in the election. But she worried afterward about the impact of such campaigning on popular respect for the courts. What these commercials said most clearly was that "seats can be bought on courts." She then made herself a rather less attractive poster child for judicial independence by retaining her job after getting arrested for, and pleading guilty to, drunk driving.

And of course the trial-lawyer groups are also active—and active nationally—to influence state elections. A California appeals court judge remembers that when he was in private practice letters would come from the firm's Houston office that a decision had been made to contribute so and so much to two Texas judges, and the San Francisco office was expected to contribute this share of the funds. The lawyers and (especially) the environmentalists are not ashamed to use negative advertising on judges. In Michigan, a Democratic commercial showed cartoon trees shivering with fear about their prospects if the three incumbent Republican justices were reelected (they were), and a pamphlet accused an African-American Republican incumbent of opposing *Brown v. Board of Education*, which was manifestly impossible. The record in Michigan, however, was held by the Republican committee that showed the picture of a Democratic judge who had agreed with others on a panel on a light sentence for a convicted pedophile, and flashed the word "pedophile" in large letters next to his face. Queried by *USA Today*, a Republican spokesman said, "We don't call him [a pedophile]."[27]

In 2000 in Idaho a sitting supreme court justice was defeated for reelection, for the first time since 1944, after a full-page ad sponsored by a "Concerned Citizens for Family Values" ran the Sunday before election day in all the newspapers in the state: *Will partial birth abortion and same-sex marriage become legal in Idaho? Perhaps so if liberal Supreme Court Justice Cathy Silak remains on the Supreme Court.*[28] These things, of course, don't end on election day. Robert Tobin tells of a lawyer who "had had the dubious honor of being the first attorney to represent a client on a DUI [driving under the influence] charge before a judge just elected on a platform of sending drunks to jail. The frightened lawyer made a deal with the prosecutor that circumvented the awaiting judicial vengeance."[29]

Retention elections invite attack by interest groups, particularly dangerous because an attack can be launched only a few days before the election. In Nebraska in 1996, the supreme court justice who had written an opinion striking down a term-limits law lost his seat after the National Term Limits Association spent $200,000 on ads, and in Tennessee a woman justice who had voted to reverse a death sentence was beaten after the governor, who wanted a vacancy he could fill, criticized her vote late in the campaign. In 1998, an antiabortion group threatened to go after Chief Justice Ron George and Justice Ming Chin of the California Supreme Court. Chin, who had wanted to be a judge since he boarded with an Oregon judge as a boy going to high school—his father's potato farm was too far from the nearest school for him to live at home—found the experience unsettling and unpleasant, and was particularly unhappy about the fact that his friends had to raise a half million dollars to defend him, just in case. In the event, George and Chin survived easily (George has a very high reputation in the California court community: "He made unification happen," says Stephen Thornberg, recently retired chief administrative officer of San Diego County, "made state funding happen"), but the memory lingers.

The amounts of money become more and more significant. In the year 2000, twenty states had elections for supreme court justice, and the candidates spent more than $45 million, 61 percent more than had ever been spent before. In addition, "independent interest groups" spent more than $16 million in the five "most hotly contested" states: Alabama, Illinois, Michigan, Mississippi, and Ohio. In Florida, where elections for trial judge are nonpartisan and 43 of 277 seats were contested, candidates raised more than $14 million.[30] A high fraction of this money is contributed by lawyers who appear before these judges and by corporations and labor unions that expect to have cases before these judges.

And there can be no question that prominent advertising can make a huge difference in judicial campaigns, where candidates have no name recognition and are not covered by the press or the broadcast news media. In the Texas primary for supreme court justice, Republicans had to choose between a rival candidate and Alberto Gonzales (later White House counsel for George Bush, and then attorney general, and the man who said we could do what we liked with "unlawful com-

batants" from Afghanistan regardless of our obligations under the Geneva Convention). Texas permits early voting by
mail. Figures compiled by former Texas chief justice Tom
Phillips show that in the early vote, in the media markets
where Gonzales would later purchase advertising, he led by an
almost invisible 50.9 percent to 49.1 percent. In the election-
day vote, after the advertising, he led by 62.4 percent to 37.6
percent. In markets where Gonzales did not purchase advertising, he lost in the early vote by 61.7 percent to 38.3 percent, and in the election-day vote by 54.4 percent to 45.6
percent. Karl Rove, then Governor George W. Bush's political adviser in Austin and later major domo of the Bush White
House, did similar studies of primaries in 1998, 1986, and
1994, in which candidates who bought television time won
the cities where they had a push from that advertising and
lost the cities where they did not have such a push.

Chief Justice Shirley Abrahamson of Wisconsin has contributed to these debates a great quote from the 1846 constitutional convention in her state. One of the delegates was
Edward Ryan, a lawyer who later became chief justice. The judiciary, he said, "represents no man, no majority, no people. It
represents the written law of the land . . . it holds the balance,
and weighs [the] right between man and man, between . . . rich
and . . . poor, between the weak and the powerful." Nearly all
Americans would agree with these sentiments and hope they
have some relation to reality. Today, however, more than 70
percent of Americans tell pollsters they think judges will give a
more sympathetic hearing to lawyers and corporate litigants
who contributed to their campaigns. Nevertheless, an almost
equal percentage wish to continue to elect their judges. Which

means it's hopeless, for the fraction of the population that votes will be even more receptive than the general public in the poll to the argument that something precious has been given away when the people "lose their vote" for judges.

In Florida in 2000, counties and judicial districts held a referendum on changing from an elective to an appointive system for choosing trial judges. Every county voted to retain elected judges; nowhere did the proposition for change command more than 41 percent of the vote. In South Dakota a constitutional amendment mandating a change to merit selection went before the voters in 2004 with the endorsement of everybody involved in courts and law in that state, including the state legislature—and was beaten two to one. Schotland points out the true menace here, that the political evangelist James Dobson found that attacking this proposal, exploiting what he called "the depth of popular resentment of liberal court decisions," was a great way to get turnout for his meetings and on election day. Some folks in South Dakota argue that Democratic senator Tom Daschle got beat in that election because Dobson was able to pull the antijudge constituency to the polls.

There has been no requirement that judges "recuse themselves"—disqualify themselves from hearing a case—when either of the litigants or their counsel has made significant contributions to a judge's campaign. In 1998, the nine Murrays in the Ohio firm of Murray & Murray Co. donated $25,000 to each of two associate justices of the Ohio Supreme Court. They represented the parents of a young woman who had got herself killed by driving onto a grade crossing although the gates were closed and the lights were flashing. The trial closed with an award of $15 million to the bereaved parents, and the two judges who had benefited by the Murrays' largesse remained on the bench for the appeal, despite a request from defendants that they recuse themselves.

Various codes of ethics and codes of conduct have sought to control the harm that can be done by contested elections with heavy expenditures on advertising. Several states have forbidden judges to do their fund-raising themselves. Others have set maximum contributions to judicial campaigns by individuals and in some states by law firms, lumping together all the individuals in the law firm and their immediate families. The standard code of ethics approved by the American Bar Association and the Conference of Chief Justices forbids a judge to award receiverships and special guardianships to lawyers whose contributions to his or her campaign exceeds some low fraction of the total raised for the campaign. Historically, the remedy for the involvement of lawyers and judges in each other's affairs has been that the judge recuses herself from the case. But those who need the codes are likely to ignore them, and a kind of Gresham's Law comes into play: The average quality of judges available for a case drops, sometimes drastically, because ethically sensitive judges won't sit and ethically obtuse judges will.

An interesting sidebar to this story is what happens to the money if the judge doesn't spend all of it on her campaign. An American Bar Association Task Force on Lawyers' Political Contributions, chaired by the general counsel of the Ford Motor Company, reported in 1998 that such funds should be returned to the donors. Different states have different rules. Nevada allows a judge to keep a maximum of $5,000 per year of her term. Florida allows an "office account" of $6,000 per supreme court justice, $3,000 for intermediate appellate justices, and $1,500 for trial judges. In many states, the ABA notes, these leftover campaign contributions are the only source of financing for upgrading the courts' information technology resources.

6

All of this is about to get worse. Much worse. Trust me. I can see the future.

Everyone's beliefs are infected by his experience. In the 1960s, I worked closely with Rosser Reeves, who in 1952 had brought the techniques of commercial advertising to American presidential elections. Reeves, son of the Protestant Episcopal bishop of Richmond, was a Virginia Republican, then a relatively scarce species, but he had little interest in politics. If he had to spend time away from advertising, he preferred chess (he was nonplaying captain on the first American chess team that went to Russia) and sailing. But some Republican friends of his, still shell-shocked by Truman's win in 1948 and worrying that Eisenhower might not make it in 1952, asked him how he thought Eisenhower's message was coming across to the sort of voters to whom he sold Anacin and Colgate toothpaste. He said no message was coming through, because the stump speech covered all the issues, those that people cared about and those that people didn't care about, and because the speech demanded that people take more time on election matters than they were prepared to give. After a certain amount of negotiation and argle-bargle, Reeves took six weeks off from his duties at the Ted Bates agency and wrote sixty-second spots for the Republicans to air on radio and television in the last weeks of the 1952 election.

Reeves, I wrote in 1957 for my book *Madison Avenue, USA,* "asked Gallup what issues were most important with the public, and received the reply that people were most disturbed about the Korean War, corruption in Washington, taxes, and the high cost of living. Reeves prepared a few scripts and had an artist draw story boards for spots on each of these themes. He used in all the scripts the same introduction, an announcer saying, with suppressed excitement, 'Eisenhower Answers the Nation!' Then the voice of 'an ordinary citizen' would ask a question, such as, 'Mr. Eisenhower, what about the high cost of living?' And the General would reply, in this instance, 'My wife, Mamie, worries about the same thing. I tell her it's our job to change that on November fourth.'"

Scripts were submitted to the campaign, and Eisenhower blocked off September 13 as the day he would do the deed. The Republican committee wanted fifty spots, but only twenty-two had been approved when Reeves met Eisenhower for the first time at the Transfilm studios in mid-Manhattan. "The Bates makeup department prepared the candidate for the cameras. Reeves was particularly anxious to have Eisenhower appear in the spots without his glasses, but without his glasses the General was unable to read the prompt cards. The head of Bates's radio-TV department personally took a brush and hand-lettered huge prompt cards for Eisenhower to read without glasses.

"The first few spots went like the wind, and Reeves realized that Eisenhower probably could go through the planned fifty in a single day. [The questions the 'ordinary people' were to ask would of course be filmed separately—there was no tape in 1952.] So he sat down at his typewriter and wrote twenty-eight spots in a few hours, under forced draft. As he finished each spot he would take it to Milton Eisenhower [president of Johns Hopkins University and in many ways his brother's keeper], who would either okay or reject it. Sometimes Reeves, who was pulling most of Eisenhower's lines straight out of already delivered speeches, would protest against the rejection, to which the invariable answer would be, 'I don't care if he said it in Texas in June, the General isn't going to say it now.' Accepted scripts would be read quickly by the candidate, then passed on to be lettered on the prompt cards.

"Eventually, $1,500,000 [today, maybe $12 million] was spent to put these television spots on the air." They will, I wrote, "be worth a footnote in the history books someday. Part of that footnote should be a vignette of the President of the United States, who sat in a hard chair between takes, shaking his head and saying, 'To think that an old soldier should come to this.' "[31]

More experience. Four decades after the Eisenhower campaign, I spent some years in Washington as a guest scholar at the Brookings Institution, as regular as I could be at that establishment's "Friday lunch," where the movers and shakers of the Washington world come to tell us cloistered academics, off the record, what's really what. The convenor of these lunches has been for some years the political scientist cum columnist E. J. Dionne, who has a weakness for political consultants, amusing men (they were mostly men) who pulled a great deal of weight (and were paid a great deal for doing so), knew things other people didn't know, and were happy to brag about their accomplishments in a setting where everything was off the record. Nor was their field of the cloth of gold entirely American; they were happy to tell us how Fox in Mexico or Sharon in Israel or Schroeder in Germany or Gonzalvo in Bolivia could not have won without their help. Their focus was, of course, the United States, and how winning legislative or executive elections in the United States had become a matter of finding what the public could be made to perceive were your opponents' weaknesses, and drawing his or her blood with vicious television commercials.

After listening to them for a number of lunches, I came to realize that events had overtaken Mark Twain's observation that America had no native criminal class except for Congress. There was now another and more sinister criminal class: the political consultant. As the terrorists of 9/11 exploited the airline policy not to resist hijackings in the hope of saving lives, the political consultants rely on First Amendment protections of free speech to distort the personal and political lives of their clients' rivals—and, indeed, the clients themselves.

We have seen only a little employment of these techniques in judicial elections, because they have been barred by state-level laws and codes. Now we are going to see a lot more. In June 2002 the Supreme Court opened the gates of judicial elections to the barbarians of political consultancy. The laws and codes are gone. Robert Hirshon, president of the American Bar Association, said, "This is a bad decision. It will open a Pandora's Box."[32] Judge Rick Johnson of the Kentucky

Court of Appeals wrote that "judges will have a much harder time evading the demands of their interest-group funders to take sides on hot-button legal issues. . . . In California . . . former Supreme Court Justice Otto Kaus famously noted that for an elected judge to ignore the political ramifications of a decision near election time would be 'like ignoring a crocodile in your bathtub.' The *White* decision sharpens the crocodile's teeth."[33]

Republican Party of Minnesota v. White started with a lawyer named Gregory Wersal, who ran for supreme court justice and distributed literature criticizing the court for rulings in the areas of welfare, crime, and abortion, and for a general lack of common sense. The Minnesota constitution calls for election of judges, and in 1912 the legislature passed a law requiring judicial elections to be nonpartisan. In 1974, the court itself promulgated a code of judicial ethics requiring that a "candidate for judicial office, including an incumbent judge," shall not "announce his or her views on disputed legal or political issues." Someone complained about Wersal's statements to the Office of Lawyers Professional Responsibility, which handles ethics charges in Minnesota. That office refused to take action against Wersal, but he dropped out of the race anyway, fearing, he said, that a censure might hurt his legal practice.

Wersal returned to the chase in 1998, asking the ethics office whether he could make the statements he wanted to make. As the Jerome Kern song has it, they wouldn't say yes and they wouldn't say no, complaining that they didn't have the specifics. So Wersal went to federal district court asking for a declaration that the "announcement" clause in the ethics code was unconstitutional, and the case wound its way to the Supreme Court.

The prime question, of course, is the difference between elections for other offices, where anybody can say just about anything, and elections for judge. Legislators and executives can say they will work to change the law, can meet privately with friends to discuss public issues, can do favors for supporters. They have constituents. Judges are not supposed to have constituents, to do favors for supporters, to indulge in ex parte meetings with people interested in the cases they will hear. And as a long succession of Republican presidents has said, their job is not to make law but to find law.

Writing for the five-judge majority in *White*, Justice Antonin Scalia, previously known as a "textualist" who insisted that the law for each case is *there* to be found, criticized Justice Ruth Ginsburg's minority opinion for insisting that in America the judicial and legislative functions are distinct: "[C]omplete separation of the judiciary from the enterprise of 'representative government' might have some truth in those countries where judges neither make law themselves nor set aside the laws enacted by the legislature." Justice Scalia wrote, "It is not a true picture of the American system. Not only do state-court judges possess the power to 'make' common law, but they have the immense power to shape the States' constitutions as well. Which is precisely why"—note the enormous leap without a safety net—"the election of state judges became popular."[34] Even accepting Justice Scalia's Brennan-like argument that state judges are free to make what law they wish, it would not apply to most elected judges, who serve on the trial or intermediate appeal level, where their power to "make" law is severely constrained by the state supreme court and the doctrine of stare decisis.

The obvious fact is that judicial candidates unlike candidates for the legislature cannot be permitted to promise what they will do if elected—and, indeed, the ABA Code of Ethics from which Minnesota took its original rules (enacted, as Justice Scalia pointed out, by "judicial fiat") was later amended to prohibit candidates from "committing" rather than "announcing." The Minnesota code itself contains a separate clause that prohibits judicial candidates from making "pledges or promises of conduct in office other than the faithful and impartial performance of the duties of the office"—a prohibition, Justice Scalia wrote, "that is not challenged here and on which we express no view."[35] Indeed, the brief for Wersal's friends and their statements in oral argument admitted in so many words that "judges should not make explicit promises or commitments to decide particular cases in a particular manner."[36]

The argument between Justice Scalia and Justice Ginsburg, then, can be seen as a very narrow one. Justice Scalia (though he makes a little joke about what campaign promises are worth) does not claim that the First Amendment requires Minnesota to allow candidates for its courts to promise that they will work to overturn judicial rulings. Justice Ginsburg is clearly conscious of a foolish consistency that would forbid a candidate from expressing a view of a subject on which his opponent, a sitting justice, had written a long and aggressive opinion. The question, of course, is not whether candidates for judicial office *should* express their views on matters that might come before them if they won. The impropriety of expressing such views was clear to all the justices, who had been through a grilling by the Senate Judiciary Committee on their way to confirmation. The question is whether the state should forbid such impropriety. Justice Ginsburg is saying that reliance on the "promise" clause is trusting a weak brake on a slippery slope, because it can be evaded with a wink or a nod; Justice Scalia notes that even the most drastic restrictions on candidates could not possibly keep others from printing or broadcasting what this individual had said on these issues, officially or privately, in the past.

There were two concurring opinions. Justice Sandra Day O'Connor, the only person on that bench who had been through election campaigns (for the Arizona state legislature; experience again) sympathized with the desire of the Minnesota Supreme Court to maintain decorum. The fault lay with the decision so many years ago to have elected judges. Minnesota by and large has not had much trouble with judicial elections. In the year 2000, only five of the sixty-seven district judgeships were contested. Still, the problems the Code of Ethics sought to address were real. "Minnesota," Justice O'Connor wrote, "has chosen to select its judges through contested popular elections instead of through an appointment system or a combined appointment and retention election system along the lines of the Missouri Plan. In doing so the State has voluntarily taken on the risks to judicial bias. . . . If the State has a problem with judicial impartiality, it is largely one the State brought upon itself by continuing the practice of popularly electing judges."[37] It's like the advice the owl gave the centipede with a footache: If he had only two feet, like a normal creature, he'd have much less of a problem.

Asked how the centipede could *do* that, the owl replied, "I only make policy."

In *his* concurring opinion, Justice Anthony Kennedy waxed lyrical about what would come up in the wake of the ferryboat *White*: "[D]emocracy and free speech are their own correctives. The legal profession, the legal academy, the press, voluntary groups, political and civic leaders, and all interested citizens can use their own First Amendment freedoms to protest statements inconsistent with standards of judicial neutrality and judicial excellence. Indeed, if democracy is to fulfill its promise, they must do so. They must reach voters who are uninterested or uninformed or blinded by partisanship, and they must urge upon the voters a higher and stronger commitment to preserving its finest traditions. Free elections and free speech are a powerful combination: Together they may advance our understanding of the rule of law and further a commitment to its precepts."[38]

7

Outside the door, slavering, are the wolves of political consultancy, whose only criterion is winning. They are paid to win. Voters tell pollsters that they hate negative advertising, but the consultants know that nothing works like demeaning the character of your client's opponent. And their repertory includes endless ways to convince people that their candidate's opponent "started it." Judge Resnick survived on a backlash in Ohio because the people who went after her were amateurs. Nobody who knows this field of endeavor can with a straight face entertain the notion that armies of disinterested lawyers and civic goody-goods can police in some part-time idealistic way what the professional consultants do.

Roy Schotland of the Georgetown Law School, the authority on these subjects (this chapter owes much of its information to him), has expressed a hope that the Missouri Supreme Court has found a prophylactic, announcing that it will compel judges who got elected after making statements about how they would decide certain issues to recuse themselves from cases that might involve those issues. But political consultants couldn't care less whether their victorious client will lie in the crosshairs of the ethicists on the state supreme court.

Moreover, the problem obviously extends beyond the realm of elected judges. The federal appointments process is where much of this deviltry started, as we will see in chapter 13. "Why are you writing a book about judges?" said Stanley Sporkin, son of a Philadelphia judge, former general counsel of the Securities and Exchange Commission, former general counsel of the Central Intelligence Agency, a federal judge in Washington, D.C., for almost twenty years, a round-faced, belligerent man with heavy horn-rimmed glasses who always seems to be speaking around a cigar. "What's the point of that? That game is over. Now they won't make anyone a judge until they know how he's going to decide the cases. Nobody can trust the courts anymore."

10 IN PRACTICE: AT THE POVERTY LEVEL IN PHOENIX

Since Easter we have become used to a spiritual diet of Resurrection appear-
ances and hopes. But today, with the celebration of the Ascension near, we
again have feelings of separation and disappointment, or shattered dreams
and lost opportunities. . . . The uncertainty of transition compels us to lean
on the gospel words Jesus speaks directly to us: "I will see you again." If we
respond in faith and turn toward the Utmost, all else is unremembered.

—Noreen Sharp, OP, reflection for May 5, 2005[1]

I N THE EARLY 1990S, THE ARIZONA SUPREME
Court sponsored a "commission on the courts." Phoenix
had recently seen a national conference on "the future of
the courts" sponsored by the federally funded State Justice
Institute. Also in the city's recent background was a study of
the utilization of time in the Maricopa County courts done by
the American Bar Association for Gordon Griller, the professional "administrator" of those courts. The study group, including judges, lawyers, and laymen, worked for six months
and presented a rather anodyne report at a two-day conference to which various "public citizens" were invited. Griller

found himself at the same lunch table with one of these invitees, a young lady named Noreen Sharp; he listened with fascination as she told a story of organizing a residence for the use of mentally retarded or disabled people who could, with the proper support, work at jobs in the real world and return every night to their community-based home. The building had been purchased by the city of Phoenix with federal money, and was subject to all sorts of nonfunctional federal regulations. Ms. Sharpe had gone to Washington and got the regulations changed. This never happens; they don't make explosives powerful enough to burst the concrete in which such federal regulations are cast. Looking back, Griller says he regarded the young lady as "an energy source."

Unlike Griller, whose graduate degree was in public administration although he was working for the courts, Ms. Sharp was a lawyer, and had worked until recently at the large firm of O'Connor Cavanaugh. Griller noted the wedding ring on the third finger of Ms. Sharp's left hand and asked what her husband did. There was a brief pause, and Ms. Sharp explained to Griller that she did indeed have a husband, but not in the sense Griller understood the word, for she was a Catholic nun, a member of the Dominican Sisters order that included, among others, Mother Theresa. Griller suggested that if she ever became interested in working in a court system, he would be delighted to hear from her, and about a year later, he did hear from her.

The ABA study of how judges spend their time had highlighted the problems of processing the cases of people too poor to afford a lawyer, who desperately needed the services of the courts, especially in family matters—divorce, child custody, child support, visitation rights, orders of protection that told husbands to stay away from their battered wives, and so on. In 60 percent of the cases in Phoenix family court, one party or the other was not represented by lawyers; in 25 percent, both parties were unrepresented. In the ABA study, litigants handling cases pro se, took literally forty and fifty times as much judge time as lawyers handling cases for litigants. And that was after these customers of the courts had wasted a great deal of time with the clerks. Arizona is one of the states where the judges do not control the clerks.

The Arizona Supreme Court was persuaded that a California company called North Communications, proprietor of a kiosk that printed documents on demand, could mitigate the pro se problem, at least for divorces and small claims. The company had a video of satisfied customers pushing buttons to get the documents they could then file with the clerk of the court, and it had a publicity campaign prepared to promote "quick court." It was announced that between a hundred and a hundred and fifty kiosks were to be installed throughout the state. In early 1995, the system was shown off at a convention in Scottsdale. The president of the Iowa Bar Association, who attended, wrote a furious message to his membership, denouncing the kiosks as kiosks, and singling out for criticism "attorney Noreen Sharp," who had suggested that the courts in dealing with poor people take the Home Depot slogan: "You can do it; we can help." North Communications (and Ms. Sharp) did not have to worry that someone would come get them for practicing law without a license, because Arizona some years before had repealed the laws that gave the legal profession its monopoly. But its customers were inviting big trouble in their futures, the Iowa Bar president warned, if they entered into legally binding contracts without the advice of a lawyer.

In fact, Ms. Sharp at the conference was not defending the kiosks, which in her view were simply a way of delivering to people messages they could not understand or use. (Griller believes there is a warehouse somewhere in the desert where 150 of these kiosks are now stored.) Many jurisdictions have systems for getting paper to people. Los Angeles has put trucks on the street like the Good Humor company. New York has set aside a full-size courtroom in Manhattan for the distribution of legal forms, but the attendants, mostly volunteer law students, are told to be careful about giving away advice with the paper. New York has 300,000 attempts at eviction every year, and 90 percent of the tenants summoned to housing court have no representation. Judge Fern Fisher-Brandwein, deputy administrative judge with responsibility for housing, says, "We tell the clerks that they're not supposed to practice law and help the litigants. I want them to give information. We've got to have external partners. In a recent survey, people thought that if they were threatened with eviction they would be assigned a lawyer. And that's not true. We're now running Town Hall meetings around the state where judges answer questions."

Ms. Sharp had higher hopes than that. "I asked myself," she says, "what is the courts' capacity for sensitivity and growth? Being a judge is a vocation, a vocation for the delivery of justice and mercy. And there is no justice without mercy. What is *my* calling? Fairness and access to the courts. It's about *mission*, not about performance. The Supreme Court's goal was 'effective and efficient justice.' We want 'fair and timely.'"

The presiding judge of the domestic relations division in Phoenix (now simply labeled "Family Law") was Rebecca Albrecht, who had worked with the ABA on the time-and-motion study. "It was more anecdotal than statistical," she says, "but it was obviously true. People did not understand what the process was about. We had a 'motion to set a certificate of readiness,' and we were setting them six, eight months ahead. They'd come in on the day, they'd say, 'Oh, that piece of paper is home'—or, 'My neighbor could tell you he beats me.' But the neighbor isn't here. So you can refile, or proceed without the evidence. People don't think of themselves as pro se; they think of themselves as people who need a decree. They resent that the judge seems not to listen—but it's difficult for a judge to pay attention if people are talking about things not relevant to the decision the judge has to make.

"Sometimes," Judge Albrecht continues, "it was even worse. People *would* read the rules, and then find that we didn't in fact do things that way anymore. We'd changed the rules, eliminated the master calendar, for example, and never written it down. In Arizona the clerk's office maintains the records, and the clerk who works for me is not my employee, not the court's employee; he works for the chief clerk. When we started to put together the SSC [self-service center], we asked the clerks how much of their time the pro se client took. They said they had to spend half an hour or more with each self-represented litigant to get the papers filed right; they lent us a couple of clerks to finish the time-and-motion study. We decided that what we needed were forms that would give a judge the information he needed to make a ruling—and that people could understand. There was a place in our budget for a librarian, and that was Noreen Sharp." Her official title was "project director" for the domestic relations division of the Maricopa County courts.

"People," says Ms. Sharp, "want respect. They say, 'Let me speak,' and they want you to listen. We had a little grant, three-quarters of a million dollars, from the State Justice Institute; we gave back half a million of it. You don't need revenues to get things done; you need thinking and heart. I ran fifteen groups, each with ten to thirty people; anybody could come any time, everybody was always welcome to work on the design, through the first half of 1995. We began to write new forms that people could actually read. Then we got a break. They were remodeling the courthouse, and there was a whole floor vacant, and they gave it to us. That convinced people this thing was really going to happen—look how much space they have! And somebody said, 'Have you thought of putting this on the Internet?' We got a couple of IBM 484s, then the hottest, fastest things; we had more information technology capacity than the rest of the court." Bob James, the director of the Self-Service Centers since 1997, estimates that 250 volunteers were involved in structuring the forms. With these forms, says Judge Albrecht, "the rules of evidence are somewhat relaxed. But these are bench trials [i.e., no jury], and I'm not going to consider what shouldn't be considered."

"Florida, New York, Washington State," Ms. Sharp says, "hand out explanations of their legal forms to educate people.

Written by lawyers for lawyers. The fact is, you can't get people to do the education, but you can sneak some education into the forms. In October 1995, I went back to my room and in one month I wrote five hundred forms, on an eighth-grade reading level. At the end of each form, I printed 'By Order of the Court.' Some of my people said, 'How can you do that? Who's the court?' I said, 'I'm the court. Who else am I working for?' "

Eighth-grade reading level did not do it. "One of the things that surprised us, though it shouldn't have," said Colin Campbell, who was presiding judge for all of Maricopa County until midsummer 2005, "is that most people can't fill out a 1040EZ form." Maricopa County is 9,800 square miles, more territory than four northeastern states, and it grows by 80,000 to 120,000 people per year. The presiding judge has bigger problems than the self-service center, including the need to provide interpreters for no fewer than seven Indian languages plus a number of others, among them, for example, Cambodian. A separate Spanish-language court deals with cases of driving under the influence. "By underfunding the social service net," Campbell says, "they've pushed their problems into the courts. We have a mental health court, but courts should not be a mental health resource." Campbell has insisted that all judges in Maricopa County take their turn in family court, where the largest single slice of self-represented litigants is to be found. "They are easier to deal with than lawyers," he says, "because they never want to question each other; they just want to tell you their story."

It is somewhat easier to make changes in Maricopa County than elsewhere because Arizona gives its judges considerable discretion in writing rules for their own courtrooms, and is also what Griller's successor, Marcus Reinkenmeyer, calls "a strong executive state." The court administrator keeps records of the disposal rate of each of the ninety-one judges, and once a month there is a "bench meeting" where the judges discuss what's been happening. "They ask the leaders," Reinkenmeyer says, " 'How did you get so good?' Well, I dropped that form, and changed that procedure.' So they try it out." The meetings also provide feedback to the self-service center.

The description of the forms available on the Maricopa County courts Web site is impressively simple and exact: "We have many court forms to help people help themselves in court. These forms are assembled in packets, with all the forms you need for a particular process all grouped together, so you do not leave out anything. Also, the forms have instructions so you will know how many copies you need, where to take the forms, and what the next steps are. We do not help you fill out the forms, but our forms are easy for you to do, or you can ask a friend or neighbor to help you." There follows the list of purposes: "for Divorce, for Legal Separation, for Temporary Court Orders while waiting for a divorce . . . for Paternity orders . . . to make the other party Obey a Court Order. . . ."[2] As readers of the epigraph at the head of this chapter will have noted, Ms. Sharp writes clean, clear, and beautiful prose.

In the late 1990s, Ms. Sharp went off to work with attorney general, later Governor Janet Napolitano, to coordinate children's services, run a committee on the drought and its consequences, and in general do what the governor needed done. She returned to the Maricopa courts in 2004, to work on computer programs that would permit pro se litigants to do most of the paperwork of their case at home, with pop-ups to prompt responses, as much as possible on a sixth-grade reading level. Before leaving the first time, however, she put her functions into the system with an ingenious creation: "The Navigator," a person whose job is to help people find the forms that may help them. In 2004, this was Robin Hoskins, an unpretentious, eager young lady out of a TV sit-com. Not a lawyer—but she had twelve years of experience helping out in the child protection end of the criminal courts before coming to the family courts. She works with an "advisory council for the family court," which she describes as "a nice variety of folk who listen to people—parents, lawyers, police, religious."

Ms. Hoskins served 750 people her first year as Navigator, and a thousand people the second year, with the pressure mounting. "They're going to have to hire another me." People come to her because one of the clerks or judges has told them there's something wrong with their papers and they are upset. "I take walk-ins and e-mails. They're frustrated, upset about something in their case. But they're not crazed lunatics; they're like me. It's like someone who's drunk; they have to sober up before you can talk to them. It's a fantastic idea, and people appreciate it. I try to resolve whatever the issue is, find the bottom line. When I call back, I have validated them, even if I don't have the answer. You have to walk the fine line between legal advice and procedural advice. You tell them you can't help because it's a legal problem, and they say, 'Just tell me—if you were in my situation, what would you do?'"

Central to the ultimate development of this program is a

division of litigants between people whose issues permit them to find their way with a little neighborly help and people who really need lawyers. "Unbundling" is the term of art for the solution, breaking the work into pieces that will benefit a lot and pieces that will benefit little if any from attention by a lawyer. Ms. Sharp wrote an article for the magazine of the Arizona Bar Association to convince the profession that unbundling was a "win-win" situation, but it's still only the traditional pro bono and legal aid communities that have been sympathetic. At this writing, the self-service center is deeply involved with the courts in working for an "integrated" family law resource where all the information is on one computer. Norm Davis, a large and lordly judge with graying brown hair who gives an imperial touch to robes, has worked with the self-service center staff to create computerized requests for judicial intervention that work like the programs used by the professionals of tax-preparation. He says, "We've got them trained: People get the same answer now, morning or afternoon."

Meanwhile, the caseload mounts, and gets handled the way mounting caseloads are handled everywhere, by the appointment of temporary judges. As of 2004, Maricopa had thirty-eight "commissioners" appointed by the presiding judge who handle the overflow. As the county grows, the courts keep opening small regional courthouses. The courts even more than the litigants will need systems that improve the efficiency of adjudication.

11 TEACHING JUDGES TO JUDGE

The newly selected judge often lacks both the knowledge and the technique that are essential elements of the craft. . . . Even lawyers coming to the bench from a background of advocacy are unprepared to deal with problems of judicial decision making, writing, and the mechanics of the internal court operations. For the trial lawyer who becomes a trial judge, problems in many of the following areas must be faced: inferring the truth or falsity of material facts; interpretation of rules of law in a nonadversary fashion, sentencing techniques, supervision of the presentation of evidence to a jury, instruction of the jury; and supervision of the work of lower courts, administrative agencies, and offices.

—Glenn R. Winters and Robert E. Allard (1963)[1]

The development of the craft [of judging] is still a tough, painstaking, long and tedious process. It is much easier, frequently more interesting, and certainly more ego-satisfying to succumb to the role of philosopher queen or king by deciding cases through individual notions of what is right and good.

—Robert S. Thompson, law professor at University of Southern California, former California appellate court judge[2]

We still have to handle whatever comes in the door.

—Chief Justice Kathleen Blatz, Minnesota Supreme Court

DULY SWORN IN AND ESCORTED TO HIS chambers and courtroom, the new federal district judge finds himself deluged with written material sent to him by the judicial system: a "Judges Manual," descriptions of the Judicial Conference that presumably rules all the federal courts and two "monographs" on the history of the federal judicial system, a "Guide to Judiciary Policies and Procedures," a Manual for Litigation Management and Cost and Delay Reduction (352 pages, this one), a "Benchbook for U.S. District Court Judges" (244 pages), a "Resource Guide for Managing Prisoner Civil Rights Litigation" (172 pages), "Hirsch and Sheehey on Awarding Attorneys' Fees and Managing Fee Litigation" (167 pages), a "Manual for Complex Litigation" (568 pages), and a "Reference Manual on Scientific Evidence" (634 pages), a "Judicial Writing Manual" (41 pages), a "Manual on Recurring Problems in Criminal Trials" (162 pages), and an "Outline of Appellate Case Law" on the sentencing guidelines.

All these publications are from the Administrative Office of the Courts or the Federal Judicial Center, both housed (about a thousand souls for the AO, a hundred for the research-oriented Judicial Center) around the multistory circular atrium in the whitestone-and-glass Thurgood Marshall Building beside Union Station in Washington, D.C. The documents come automatically. With them comes a pamphlet that lists about a hundred other publications, DVDs, videotapes, and audiotapes about aspects of the work of the judiciary that will be sent to the new judge if she requests them. The pamphlet also suggests that districts organize their own orientation program to be offered to new judges ("Making the program mandatory may set the wrong tone"). Ideally, "mentor judges," also volunteers, should show the newcomer "critical proceedings . . . such as jury empanelment; civil and criminal motion calendars; Rule 16 (pretrial negotiation), final pretrial, and settlement conferences; suppression hearings; plea taking; and sentencing procedures . . .

"The program should give new judges a hands-on intro-duction to chambers organization and management, includ-ing, where feasible and appropriate, introduction to the use of computers. . . . The program should introduce new judges to the various departments of the court—the magistrate judges, the bankruptcy court and its judges, the clerk's office, and the chief probation and pretrial services offices—and provide an opportunity to learn where they are, who they are, and what they do. . . ." Separate orientation sessions, with different content, are given to newly appointed circuit court of appeal judges, bankruptcy judges, and magistrate judges.

During the course of his first year, the new district judge will be invited to two one-week "orientation seminars" run by the Federal Judicial Center, usually at resort hotels, though these are very much working sessions: Work starts at eight to eight thirty every morning and adjournment is at five or six o'clock, with none of the golf or tennis tournaments that highlight corporate "seminars" at the same locations. Nobody can make the new federal judge attend the seminar or any part of it, but 90 percent of the new judges do attend. The bar is always a cash bar, part of the lesson that judges don't take drinks from strangers. Some judges won't let friends pay for drinks, either.

All federal judges hear both civil and criminal trials, and

the emphasis in orientation is on the criminal side, partly because the federal bench is drawn from the cream of the American bar and there are very few criminal defense lawyers in that cream, partly because the rules (and simple fairness) demand quick trials for criminal defendants. The presentations are usually by video, followed by a discussion led by experienced judges, though every once in a while sessions open with lectures by experts—law professors, commissioners from the sentencing commission, patent lawyers, disability mavens, and so on. For example, a weeklong "Phase 1 orientation seminar" in fall 2003 in Redondo Beach, California, for newly appointed district judges, devoted its first morning to videos and discussions on civil case management and trials, with commentary by experienced judges from St. Louis and Topeka, followed by no fewer than five sessions on sentencing (plus a visit to a federal prison), one on "calendar management," one on "Administration of the Jury System and Conduct of a Jury Trial," one on financial disclosure "requirements and solutions," one on "judicial ethics issues for new judges," one on the judicial role in court governance, and one on "Selected Topics on the Federal Rules of Evidence." Also a lunch with a presentation on "Judicial Compensation and Benefits." In general, nobody is allowed into these meetings except the judges themselves, but spouses may be invited to "observe" when the subject is judicial ethics, public relations, or compensation.

The "Phase II" orientation seminar, also one week long, is more likely to be done in Washington, with a reception and dinner (and class photo) at the Supreme Court. And it is more likely to be staffed from the law schools and the practicing bar, with fewer presentations or comments by sitting judges. The topics tend to the practical. The meeting in spring 2003, for example, opened with a presentation by an NYU Law School professor on employment discrimination, followed by one on federal habeas corpus by a Washington College of Law (American University) professor, judicial ethics again by someone from the staff of lawyers who work for the Judicial Conference, intellectual property by a practicing lawyer, and "Stress Management and Collegiality" by a psychologist, a one-hour review of what magistrate judges do for the district court taught by one magistrate judge and one district judge, an hour and fifteen minutes for a bankruptcy judge, round-table discussions led by sitting judges separately on civil and criminal case management, and a two-hour presentation on opinion writing by the "Director of Career Development" at the humongous Washington law firm of Wilmer, Cutler and Pickering.

The literature prepared for these sessions—and for the workshops that the Federal Judicial Center runs in various parts of the country throughout the year—is remarkably high in quality, as learned as a law review article (without the impossible baggage of footnotes), more relevant to practical problems than judicial opinions, better written than most biographies. Founded in 1967 to provide research for the twenty-seven-judge Judicial Conference that makes procedural rules and administrative policies for all federal courts, the Judicial Center was the last organizational change directed by Earl Warren. (Reportedly he went to Lyndon Johnson and said, "You know I never wanted to chair your assassination commission; you owe me one.")

Educating judges was not the only purpose of the center; in fact, the first on its list of statutory charges is "to conduct research and study of the operation of the courts of the United States, and to stimulate and coordinate such research and study on the part of other public and private persons and agencies."[3] But the federal judiciary desperately needed education, and the center moved into the void.

In 2005, the center had about 135 employees and spent a budget of a little more than $20 million. The seven judges on the board of the center (the chief justice and the AO director serve ex officio) are selected for four-year terms from the ranks of federal judges by vote of the Judicial Conference. In the Rehnquist years its members met once annually in February in his hometown of Tucson, where the Chief liked to teach at the University of Arizona for a month during the Supreme Court break. Under Warren Burger, board meetings of the center lasted all day and late into the night, as everybody argued with everybody else and Burger participated. Under Rehnquist they tended to be quick and tied to the agenda, Rehnquist having no feeling for talk for its own sake. "Anyway," says somebody who knew him well, "he was never a trial judge, never an appeals judge; his bias is to let them take care of their own problems." Around four thirty in the afternoon a piano would materialize in the conference room and the Chief would lead the members of the board in a sing-along.

The director of the center is chosen, usually from the ranks of sitting judges, by its board under the leadership of the Chief Justice. He or she need not be a lawyer, though all but one have been. Three of the last four selections by Rehnquist's board were women. The director moves to Washington for the job, and serves usually for about four years. Longtime deputy director Russell Wheeler made the Federal Judicial Conference Center a life's work. Hired by Chief Justice Burger in 1977, Wheeler was named deputy by Rehnquist in 1991 and remained there until the summer of 2005, a relaxed, efficient academic political scientist who took a Socratic approach to the issues on which the center does research, presenting the arguments for and against details of proposals affecting the conduct of the judiciary. Several appellate judges, for example, crusaded for a cap on the number of federal judges. Wheeler and three colleagues wrote a pamphlet *Imposing a Moratorium on the Number of Federal Judges.* Arguing for: "A moratorium will allow the courts to avoid growing larger because it will force Congress to control jurisdictional expansion and restrict unnecessary access to the courts. . . ." The response: "The judicial workload should be determined by societal needs, not by reference to an arbitrary limit on the number of judges. And, as a practical matter, to assume that a moratorium would induce Congress to hold constant the federal judicial workload is to ignore the dynamics of the political process."[4]

Another pamphlet is called *Federal Court Governance: Why Congress Should—and Why Congress Should Not—Create a Full-time Executive Judge, Abolish the Judicial Conference, and Remove Circuit Judges from District Court Governance.*[5] Its Hegelian theses and antitheses even deal more or less fairly with the proposal (covertly supported by the Administrative Office of the U.S. Courts) that the Federal Judicial Center be merged into the Administrative Office, partly because the "Center occasionally offers policy suggestions and recommendations at odds with those of the Judicial Conference." For deputy director Russell Wheeler, this reflection of different attitudes and different customs in different parts of the country was one of the strengths of the center. "You're always struck by how different the courts are, by the existence of a local legal culture—different attitudes about moving cases, different levels of formality."

Three-day "workshops" for judges of the separate circuits provide a sophisticated continuing education, sometimes scheduled like private-sector conventions, with an afternoon off for golf at a resort that boasts about its golf. But the topics cover the waterfront. A Federal Judicial Center workshop at Amelia Island in Florida for the Eleventh Circuit offered lectures and discussions on what the Supreme Court was doing, on sentencing, on "being a judge," on opinion writing, on "law and literature" (optional), on "recent important decisions in employment discrimination," on redistricting cases, and on "emerging issues in habeas corpus." Sometimes these workshops are done jointly with a university—on "transnational litigation," for example, with NYU, or "intellectual property" with the University of California at Berkeley. The center has an annual date with Princeton for a very popular seminar named in honor of the late Judge Harold Medina, on "science and the humanities." An East Coast judge notes: "Being a judge is basically boring; the intellectual stimulation of this sort of thing is a reward." The federal courts have a closed-circuit nationwide television channel for their exclusive use, and a "J-Net" to be accessed only by insiders. There is much Federal Judicial Center material, from manuals to

snippets of audio, that can be retrieved by the public at www
.fjc.gov.

These seminars and workshops for district judges are the
core educational business of the Federal Judicial Center, but
it has three other orientation programs: for new appellate
court judges; bankruptcy judges; and the magistrate judges
appointed by the district judges to handle the smaller stuff in
the district courts. Increasingly, bankruptcy judges (who handle more business than all the district court judges combined)
have been invited to sit in on the orientation sessions for district judges.

2

For state court judges, there is one nationwide operation that
offers instruction to novices. The National Judicial College
began life in Boulder, Colorado, in 1963 (as the National College of State Trial Judges) with operating money from the
W. K. Kellogg Foundation of Battle Creek, Michigan. The
chairman of the founding committee was Supreme Court justice Tom C. Clark, a practical-minded Texan who had served
Harry Truman as U.S. attorney general and poker companion, was known best for his anticommunism and his bow ties,
but was not by any means the lightweight Northerners
thought he was. His large portrait in robes still dominates the
tunnel that connected the college's classroom building to the
University of Nevada Law School when the University of
Nevada still had a law school in Reno. Now that law school is
at the University of Nevada in Las Vegas, and the National

Judicial College has to find its faculty elsewhere. The Reno location was chosen originally in large part because that's where the Max C. Fleischmann Foundation was, and the foundation built the Judicial College and supported it from 1972, when the building opened, till the late 1980s, when the foundation closed up shop.

At this writing, Rhode Island and Mississippi require newly elected judges to take two weeks at the National Judicial College, but otherwise NJC must sell itself both to the judges who will be students and to the judges who will teach the courses, and who are not paid. On its own authority, the college offers various "certification" programs attesting to the completion of a number of one-week and two-week courses (there is also a four-week "general jurisdiction" course for new judges, offered when there are enough paying candidates to justify it, which doesn't happen every year). Through arrangements with the University of Nevada, Reno, the college also awards a degree, a Master of Judicial Studies, resting on the completion of those courses, and since 2001 judges who have completed that Masters have had an option to continue to a Ph.D., which the school claims as the only doctorate available to sitting judges in the United States. It is part of the marketing, not the academic environment.

Over the course of a year, the college will host about two thousand judges, most of them already on the bench. Among the two-week courses, one of the most useful and well-attended is a course for "judges without formal law school training," for justices of the peace: "Participants will assess the basics of the judicial role in every area . . . focus on the evolving role of the judge as a change agent in the community; conduct criminal hearings and trials in compliance with constitutional and statutory standards; assess the basic concepts of evidence; communicate effectively and appropriately in court and with the media; . . . know how and when to assist unrepresented litigants in criminal and civil cases; . . . identify major elements of contract claims and tort claims; . . . analyze the principles of damages and restitution in civil cases; learn the elements and defenses for specific crimes and develop a process of legal reasoning and analysis." Another course for this cadre is called, baldly, "Basic Evidence."

When last visited, the college was trying to get approvals for a degree-granting program in administrative law judging, especially for state administrative judges. One of the "General Jurisdiction" courses is for "judges who have been on the bench for more than five years who want to examine whether there is a better way to manage." Another course with the same title is offered as "a forum for sharing ideas with judges from across the country and across the world." There is a down-in-the-trenches emphasis in most of the courses. One five-day course deals with "Co-occurring Mental and Substance Abuse Disorders," another with "Civil Mediation" (offered three times a year), which goes with "Settlement Techniques for Judges" and "Designing and Implementing an Effective Court-Connected A[lternate] D[Dispute] Resolution Program."

None of this is a party, and it is not supposed to be a party. For the majority of participants, their court is paying the bills. The course catalog says grimly: "The college must ensure that the tax dollars spent on continuing education are utilized for the maximum benefit. It is therefore the policy and practice of the National Judicial College not to award a Certificate of Completion to any participant who, without excuse, fails to attend all educational sessions."[6] One notes in passing that this is a real problem in judicial education. An article some years ago in the quarterly bulletin of the National Association of Judicial Education dealt with "Ethics Issues in Judicial Education" and presented a hypothetical that the author asked his students:

"Judge X registered for a three-day program you are conducting. He paid his $350 registration fee with a personal check and was given a receipt. After attending the opening lunch, the judge is not seen by any of your faculty or staff until the closing banquet. After the concluding speech, your staff will distribute evaluation forms and completion certificates that have been prepared in advance, each bearing the program title and the name of the participant. You have heard that some counties require these certificates for reimbursing participant costs and that some judges list these certificates on their curriculum vitae. You think it likely that Judge X expects to receive a certificate. What do you tell your staff to do with the certificate with Judge X's name on it?

"RESPONSE: This case showed a general rejection of the role as truant officer, although half of the respondents would give out the certificate and half would withhold it. . . ."[7]

The National Judicial College avoids this problem by setting firm rules in advance. The "students" or their courts pay tuition of about $1,100 per course (plus a "conference fee" of about $250 to cover group meals); housing at the University Inn beside the lake on the University of Nevada campus runs less than $60 a night. Counting the occasional social worker, psychologist, and accountant, NJC uses about 350 volunteers every year to teach elements of about fifty courses. (In its annual report, NJC suggests that the value of this contributed time is more than $2 million a year, but it should be noted that the contribution is by the states that employ the judges, who continue to receive their salaries from home while teaching a week or two in Reno. The city itself is, the catalogue proclaims, "The Biggest Little City in the World . . . full of undiscovered treasures."

William J. Brunson, a youthful lawyer who looks and talks rather like a coach recruiting athletes to a small undergraduate college, is director of the NJC "academic department." He has a couple of dozen assistants, five of them "program attorneys" who help design the courses, pick the readings, write grant applications, and teach a few classes. One of them at last report was Felix Stumpf, thin but still sturdy at eighty-six years, for many years the boss of the California continuing legal education program, then the first academic director of the NJC in the 1970s, later the last dean of the law school in Reno. I had written about him in my book *The Lawyers* in 1965; he was an invaluable source of bibliography for this one, including his own book (published by the college) on the inherent powers of the court.

Because a substantial part of the budget has been funded over the years by the State Justice Institute of the U.S. Department of Justice, the college has concentrated in recent years on the work of the judge in criminal cases—"What the Supreme Court says in criminal cases affects all the states," Brunson says. "Civil cases are more local." With the emphasis on the criminal side, the NJC has begun to offer courses for district attorneys as well as judges. The program has many supporters among its alumni. Judge Paul R. Haerle of the in-termediate court of appeals in San Francisco (one of 103 judges in such courts in California) remembers with particu-lar pleasure meeting judges "from Illinois, Michigan—it's so different how you get on in different states."

Stumpf notes an interesting change in the student body over a generation: "New judges are no longer elderly lawyers who have been at it for a long time and are looking to per-form a public service as the capstone of their lives. Now it's younger people for whom being a judge is a career step." They are also no longer exclusively male. "When I came there was hardly one woman per class," Stumpf says; "now, they're fifty-fifty." The most important course—Brunson still thinks it should be at least four weeks—is the full general jurisdiction course, which includes "family law, domestic vio-lence, custody, and a lot of evidence, criminal, procedural, case management."

Newly elected or appointed judges can become annoyed when told by the administrators of their court that they must attend. "They call me," said Brunson, "and they say, 'I've been a practicing lawyer for twenty-one years. What are you going to teach me?' And I say, 'You're our best customer. What do you know about controlling lawyers? Or controlling your-self?'" NJC gets visitors from all around the world for pro-grams that include visits to American courtrooms, where the foreigners often express their surprise and pleasure at the def-erence accorded to the judge, and the college is a subcontrac-tor in a federally funded program for Russian judges, a program that supports a one-man NJC office in Moscow.

The only other national effort to bring prior training to

what happens in state courtrooms (but this very specifically does not train judges) are the programs run for the Institute of Court Management by the National Center for State Courts based in Williamsburg, Virginia, though its two- and three-day workshops are done all over the country. The center is a nice place, a large sandstone building out in the rolling hills on the edge of the famously restored town, and the people who work there are helpful. The founding father was Chief Justice Burger, who felt the well-furnished federal courts should do something for their impoverished cousins in the states. The launching conference for the center in 1971 commanded the participation of the president and attorney general (Richard Nixon and John Mitchell, one might remember) as well as the chief justice, and the first staff was housed at the Federal Judicial Center. The present headquarters building was dedicated in 1978. Like the National Judicial College, it includes two large auditorium-style classrooms with a mock courtroom at the front and rising tiers of desks looking onto it. Here judges learn also about the introduction of evidence by electronic means, the growth opportunity of the future.

The National Center for State Courts is mostly a research operation, gathering statistics about what happens in state courts around the country, but it also serves as secretariat for a gaggle of judicial organizations, the most important being the Conference of Chief Justices, the Conference of State Court Administrators, the National Association of Women Jurists, and the American Judges Association. Federal agencies provide about half the sponsorship for the statistical research that is its main function. State court systems are members of the center, and receive consulting services from center staff and outsiders organized by center staff. Robert Tobin's *Creating the Third Branch*, to which this book is so heavily indebted, was published by the center. The literature for the NCSC educational effort, which concentrates on court management, is disfigured with fashionable educationese—"distance learning" and the like—plus exhortative praise for the goals of its two-week courses without much specification of what the courses teach.

3

The American Bar Association began recommending judicial education in the 1930s, and by 1986 all states had some provisions claiming to meet that need. Most of them, Brunson says somewhat huffily, are "like an annual convention." An obvious exception is California, where Rule 970 of the California Rules of Court holds that "participation in judicial education activities is an official judicial duty." Every new judge in California must complete a one-week orientation program within six months of taking the oath, and a "judicial college" within two years. The college is a two-week residential program at the University of California at Berkeley, with every afternoon and most evenings committed to group activities (including a five-hour excursion to San Quentin, with dinner in jail). Accommodations are college-dorm: Each judge gets his or her own bedroom, but the bathroom is down the hall. If judges have to take a plane to get to Berkeley (it's a big state), the state government will pay the airfare; if they can drive, they send the expense voucher to the government of the county that provides their courthouse.

In addition, the California Center for Judicial Education and Research holds some dozens of "institutes" around the state to bring sitting judges up to speed. And there are institutes for appellate judges, where creature comforts are greater. The brochure for one such three-day institute, at the Palm Springs Marquis Hotel, leaves an afternoon free for golf, and includes a dinner at which former Secretary of State Warren Christopher is the speaker, and for which the judge is charged $40 if he wishes to attend. Still, once you sign up, you're committed: CCJER will pay the bills only "for participants who attend the entire course. . . . 'Attending the entire course' means arriving before the course begins and staying until the course officially ends. Those who do not attend an entire course will remain individually responsible for their own lodging and group meal expenses. . . ."

The judicial education venture in California is a big deal. Sixty-three people work in the center, which is based in San Francisco. The state has 400 courts with 1,800 judges, all now "superior court" judges available for assignment to any kind of case. "It is," says Karen Thorson, the brisk director of the center, "the largest judicial system in the world." A reorganization in the 1990s unified the court system by function, but as usual in America maintained the geographical distinctions: Special courses are offered in the training programs for the "Cow County Judges." In an average year, the state will have to train 100 to 115 new judges, and the one-week indoctrination program runs all year long, eight to five every day, designed by the California judges and taught by six of them "trained in the curriculum" and released from a week's work in their courts.

"The first half is the ethical component of being a judge," says Robert Lowney, a young court administrator who runs the educational division of CCJER, "'transitioning' from being an attorney to being a judge. The next half is the nuts and bolts of judicial procedure and evidence." Ms. Thorson adds, "We assist people to understand that they have to make decisions." And for every new judge, CCJER assigns a "mentor judge" to hold his or her hand in the early months and be available for consultation at all times. Inevitably, some judges on both sides of the relationship take this more seriously than others, but the administrators of the courts always take it seriously. "Lawyers," says Ms. Thorson, "are often quite surprised to learn what the responsibilities of a judge are."

Ms. Thorson and her colleagues—and California's chief administrative officer, William Vickrey, who sits at the right hand of the chief justice—consider it part of their duties to keep the state's judiciary up to speed on developments in law and technology. And social problems. The two-week judicial college is built on a pattern of dozens of electives, and the courses required can be counted on the fingers of one hand, but in addition to "Trials" and "Evidence" they are "Ethics," the responsibilities of judges and court buildings under the Americans with Disabilities Act, "Beyond the Bench: Judges as Community Leaders," and "Spoken Language Interpreters," including—it gives one to think—how a judge handles matters when one or more members of the jury are bilingual and understand what the witness has said without the services of the interpreter on whom the other jurors and the lawyers and the judge must depend.

The electives range from a course on communicable diseases to a course on calculating damages in personal-injury cases, to help judges settle them instead of trying them. There is a course on "Understanding Personalities," taught by "a judge who has received training approved by the American Psychological Association," and a more austere course on "Disordered and Disruptive Defendants." Also an elective on "Alcohol and Other Drugs and the Courts," the description of which begins with the flat statement that "the vast majority of criminal cases and a large number of family court and juvenile dependency cases arise from alcoholism or other drug abuse. . . . [A]s a result of this course, you will be able to interact with a criminal AOD defendant appropriately and make informed choices about juvenile placement, reunification, and delinquency. . . ."

All California lawyers are subject to a "minimum continuing legal education" requirement, and judges can satisfy it with a CCJER institute. They can also satisfy it, perhaps unfortunately, by ordering videotapes of presentations made at CCJER courses, and claiming to have watched them. Increasingly, these lectures and seminars are being offered in searchable CD-ROMs, as are the "California Judicial Benchguides," which are, says Lowney, "refined and refined and refined." And confidential, not to be shown to lawyers or visitors. The state also recognizes the courses of the National Judicial Center for this purpose, and administrators encourage California judges to go to Reno, especially to take courses in areas like family law, where the need for expertise is recognized. A recent list of subjects covered by the state's library of videotapes showed fifty-two entries under family law and forty-three under juvenile law. There remains some resistance to turning this program over to the social scientists, however: "The core of family and juvenile," says Thorson, "is still judicial in nature." In one area the sociologists and doctors have been granted primacy: A series of videotapes on post-traumatic stress disorder starts with an overview by a Veterans Administration doctor and thereafter is populated almost exclusively by Vietnam veterans, including one tape of veterans serving time in prison. Thorson has a long-term project for the development of "entry-level programs in specialized areas of the law" that would be required before judges sat on cases where decisions will turn on scientific evidence—or, indeed, complex legal rulings.

Like Reno, the California program receives government-sponsored visitors from courts elsewhere in the world, especially Russia and eastern Europe. One of the more elaborate visits, including a week of attendance at a CCJER course, involved a group from the Middle East, which was intrigued by the morning spent on the California code of ethics for judges. "For them," Lowney said, "it was very surprising. They wanted to know, 'How can we get something like that started?'"

4

William Vickrey, a very distinguished white-haired figure who looks more like a judge than most judges, serves as chief administrator of the California courts, and as such supervises the training programs. He has hopes of using the educational focus of his office to move the system toward a focus on the communities the courts serve. The experimental area started with Alameda County—Oakland—where judges were asked to cultivate contacts with neighborhood groups. The opportunity opened when the state went to a unified judiciary—everybody is a superior court judge, whether he sits in a family part or a traffic court or a commercial court. There remain three levels of court—justice, municipal, and superior—but the same judges work in all of them, and the presiding judge of the county can assign his judges to any of them on any day. "Judges don't want to take a year on misdemeanors," Vickrey says, "so we do 'community-focused planning.' The struggle in the courts is not only to have effective calendar management and rules of evidence, but to create the perception of fairness in the courtroom. So we make it a rule of court that part of judicial responsibility is community outreach. Put together an implementation committee, lawyers, and the public, and judges who work in different parts of the system. Our drug courts are treatment courts. We have rules statewide—anybody can find them—for complex litigation. When we train judges, we train them to be integrated into a justice system." This project started in 1998, and it will last a long time.

"We have a funny system of justice in the United States," Vickrey continues. "Some court systems have said, 'Why are you forcing us to do this? It's nuts.' A judge is supposed to be a neutral vessel, but we rely on representative methods of selecting leadership. We need a strong system for dealing with behavioral problems. We need a system of accountability that does not use elections. We need a complex litigation court to get a justice system that benefits society."

Vickrey comes out of Utah, where both judicial selection and judicial retention are highly systematized. Any judicial vacancy in Utah is referred to a selection panel, which has forty-five days to forward the names of three candidates to the state's governor, who then has thirty days to choose one name and forward it to the legislature to confirm the choice. The selection panel is staffed by the chief administrator of the court system. Trial judges in Utah serve six-year terms, and they are evaluated every two years. The administrator sends an open-ended questionnaire to a sample of lawyers chosen from people who have had matters before this judge, and the results—names carefully deleted—are forwarded to the judge in a sealed envelope. "People said judges would throw it away," Vickrey recalls, "but that's not human nature. The first time they were reviewed, those who got bad scores would come in to us and say, 'Look at *this!*' We would set up a program for them, visit their courtrooms, and the next time they'd get a hundred percent. People can improve if they're motivated to, and most judges are motivated."

Since 2003, New York State has also had a Judicial Institute, operating out of the Pace University Law School in suburban-industrial White Plains. Its anchor responsibility is the five-day "orientation program," for new judges (there were seventy-seven of them in the 2004–2005 class) who "in addition to seminars on judicial ethics and courtroom management . . . received in-depth training on legal issues specific to the courts to which they were assigned."[8]

The early work here shows the intensely practical attitudes

of Judith Kaye, chief judge of the Court of Appeals (the New York name for what other states call the supreme court). In the institute's first academic year, no fewer than 1,700 "court attorneys and law secretaries" attended two-day "Legal Update Programs to complete compulsory ethics training and review the prior year's major developments in the areas of law germane to their courts." Judge Kaye has taken an interest not only in the selection of judges and reforming the state's peculiar court structure, but also "on the less frequently examined issue of maintaining the day-to-day professionalism of judges and court staff." How much of this can be done in two-day seminars is uncertain, but Judge Kaye's commitment to enthusiasm and optimism has yielded surprising results in the development of "problem-solving courts" (see chapter 15), and she is not someone who rests on laurels.

5

The most remarkable and potentially important effort at educating judges in America is the handiwork of one man, Franklin Zweig, a Walt Whitmanesque figure with a casual manner, a perpetual slouch, a broad-brimmed hat, and a trimmed gray beard. With a law degree and a Ph.D. in biology, he is the president and sole full-time employee of ASTAR, the Advanced Science and Technology Adjudication Resource Center, based in Washington, D.C. ASTAR is a subsidiary of the Einstein Institute for Science, Health, and the Courts, of which Zweig is the president and sole full-time employee. But both organizations have very distinguished boards of directors, mostly judges, with a sprinkling of scientists and medical researchers.

In the 1970s and '80s, Zweig was science advisor to the U.S. Senate. In 1993, when Congress first voted to support the Human Genome Project, money was allocated to the National Institute of Environmental Health to report on the legal consequences of genetic developments, and Zweig was chosen to start a communications network. This funding launched the Einstein Institute, which was incorporated in 1993 and began to hold meetings in 1995. Meanwhile, Hillary Clinton introduced her 1,300-page bill to reform American health care, and the Judicial Conference of the United States—i.e., Chief Justice William Rehnquist—became concerned about the new causes of action in the courts that seemed a likely result if the draft bill passed as written. The Chief Justice engaged Zweig to keep an eye on the legislation as it moved through committee. Eventually, of course, nothing came of it, but through Zweig the federal courts had an informal means of input to the political negotiations in their effort (indeed, need) to minimize the litigation arising from a new health insurance scheme.

Central to Zweig's efforts are the growing intrusion of scientific evidence—not just DNA—into trials and public policy of the kind that produces trials, and the increasingly apparent truth that very few judges have even rudimentary competence in judging the relevance let alone the quality of scientific evidence. "I think," California appeals judge Thomas Hollenhorst told a meeting sponsored by the Einstein Institute, "that for the typical judge there was a Y in the road when they started college about whether they were going to be involved in hard science or soft science. I think that many of them fled to soft science because they didn't have the wiring to do hard science, and they've continued just to stay away from it."[9] Shirley Abrahamson, chief justice of the Wisconsin Supreme Court, told a National Academy of Science conference in Washington in late 2005 that "I am a lawyer and a judge in part because I didn't want to study science of any sort."[10]

In many trials, the key question is whether some piece of "scientific" evidence or testimony can be placed on the record. The Supreme Court with great courage has charged into the thick of this dilemma in the opinions written for *Daubert v. Merrell Dow Pharmaceuticals, Inc.*[11] This decision creates required standards for the federal courts to follow in deciding to admit or exclude "expert testimony" that one side or the other wished to introduce in a lawsuit. Academic qualifications, publication in peer-reviewed publications, receipt of grants from significant foundations and government agencies: Judges are to check it out. State appellate courts soon inserted similar concepts into their own rules of procedure. "The issue about *Daubert*," says Justice Abrahamson, "is whether it has judges in over their heads." Most judges became increasingly and painfully aware that in this area they did not know what they were doing. Judge Alex Kozinski of the Ninth Circuit Court of Appeals commented, "Our responsibility, then, unless we badly misread the Supreme Court's opinion, is to resolve disputes among respected, well-credentialed scientists about matters squarely within their expertise, in areas where there is no scientific consensus as to what is and what is not 'good science,' and occasionally to reject such expert testimony because it was not 'derived by the scientific method.'

Mindful of our position in the hierarchy of the federal judiciary, we take a deep breath and proceed with this heady task."[12] Among the options offered by *Daubert* is the right of the court to hire its own scientific expert—with the consent of the litigants. The American Association for the Advancement of Science has set up a Court-Appointed Scientific Experts (CASE) program that offers judges a choice of three recognized authorities in any matter the judge refers to the program. Judge Stephanie Domitrovich of the Sixth Judicial District in Pennsylvania is an advocate for such measures. "I need someone," she says, "who can teach me the science."[13] But lawyers don't like it; they want as little as possible between themselves and the jury. Stetson University College of Law in Gulfport, Florida, operates a National Clearinghouse for Science, Technology, and the Law, and the Grant Sawyer Center for Justice Studies at the University of Nevada in Reno has a research project on the extent to which science education is available in law schools. And the Federal Judicial Center has published two editions of its tome-size "Reference Manual." But ASTAR is far more ambitious.

"Our purpose," says Zweig, "is simply stated: to enhance the capacity of court systems to utilize scientific evidence."

Zweig found funding for meetings from the federal courts, the National Institutes of Health, the Department of Energy (concerned about judicial perception of nuclear matters), the Lawrence Livermore laboratory, the Salk Institute in California, the governments of Chile and Malawi, the United Nations Industrial Development Organization (UNIDO), and the National Center for State Courts. Between 1996 and 2004, the Einstein Institute organized forty-eight "judicial science education conferences," ranging from half days to three days to deal with different aspects of biotechnology and its role in courtrooms. "The first two and a half years," Zweig says, "we were dress-rehearsing. We had to bridge the phobia, the fear that many judges had of science, akin to judges' antipathy to statistics and statistical evidence." The fundamental teaching tool is a library of hypothetical cases developed by some three hundred scientists who speak English and have, Zweig says, learned to relate to judges on judges' terms. "Judges learn best from war stories," Zweig notes, "and they enjoy teaching war stories."

All Zweig's conferences are chaired by judges, and Zweig now has a cadre of a hundred "teaching judges," who have found that the science isn't that inaccessible and "can be related to jurisprudence." All proceedings are closed to visitors, so that judges don't have to reveal to anyone but other judges that they don't understand something. At Zweig's insistence, scientists who have been or will be expert witnesses in court are barred from participation. And none of the cases prepared for instructional purposes has a right or wrong answer: The program, Zweig says, is "nonprescriptive." Zweig estimates that the forty-eight Einstein Institute meetings touched four thousand judges—but most of them only for half a day, a glancing blow that did not begin to equip them to keep up with developments in a very fast-changing field of science.

ASTAR, which got started in 2005, is a consortium of three state court systems—Maryland, Ohio, and California—which have joined, to quote the Web site, "in a common project to identify, recruit, train, deploy, and evaluate not fewer than 700 resource judges in U.S. and foreign jurisdictions by this decade's end. . . . 'Resource judges' is the shorthand term for jurists who acquire advanced bioscience and biotechnology knowledge, along with a repertoire of related adjudication skills. . . ." The twenty-four judges already chosen in Maryland (one for each of the state's "circuits") have already been given authority to reach into the docket and remove from the jurisdiction of any other judge in the circuit any case that they feel has scientific elements for which they have acquired special capacity. Within budgetary constraints, these judges also have the power to appoint their own experts to set the parameters of testimony that will be permitted in the cases—or to suggest settlements.

The first "Judges Scientific School," with four days of work and attendance by a hundred judges from the three states, took place at the Salk Institute in La Jolla, California, in October 2005. The subject was "gene therapy and addictive disorders." The first "Judges Medical School," also four days, was held in March 2006 at the University of North Carolina School of Medicine under the patronage of the North Carolina Supreme Court. The topic of this one, with obvious relevance to lawsuits that will emerge in the future, is "Biogenetic and Environmental Triggers and Treatment of Cancer." Several participating judges have testified to its seriousness and value. Meanwhile, Zweig, the judges, and the scientists were arranging with various universities to construct two-day seminars and bibliographies that might permit sitting judges to acquire significant academic preparation in biotechnology. Two kinds of diploma are envisioned: for the completion of "Platform A," fifteen months of two-day seminars to provide a general background in the field; and of "Platform

B," more intensive knowledge of component parts like "Neuroscience and Bio-Behavioral Technologies." Five such components have been selected, and instructional material for them is in the planning phase.

Candidates for the program will be identified by judges already involved. Indeed, ASTAR expects that judges from the original three states will become the screeners and trainers of judges from other states. The target is 700 judges on Platform A nationwide by the end of 2010, 300 of them further qualified in some aspect of Platform B. At the beginning the states will specialize—Maryland in its existing business-and-technology program, Ohio in its mentoring programs for new judges, California in the management of complex litigation—but presumably they will learn from each other and expand as the institutions develop.

ASTAR has a thirteen-member board of directors, all but two of them judges, which will vet curricula with the help of scientists contracted for the purpose, and there is to be a separate board with greater participation by scientists that will evaluate student work and grant credentials. Most of the money is to come from grants from the state court systems and the federal government. Some is to be raised from foundations. States will have authority to accept grants from foundations chartered to operate within their borders, but ASTAR itself and the separate credentialing board will solicit and accept funds only from federal agencies and foundations that operate in more than one state. Foreign governments, either on their own or with grants from the United States, will pay for meetings designed to help their courts handle similar problems.

This is hugely ambitious, a gigantic leveraging of what are still very limited resources. But the need is there, and dissatisfaction with current conditions may be more widespread than observers believe. Archimedes argued that there was nothing you couldn't move with a long-enough lever. At the extensive meetings the Einstein Institute summoned in 2003–04, Zweig reports, there was good attendance at the unstructured kaffeeklatsches where judges and scientists met at breakfast tables.

12 IN PRACTICE: ADMINISTRATIVE LAW

The goal of avoiding unnecessary trials would be served by . . . leaving decisions in some matters to deciders outside the formal judiciary, such as truly independent administrative law judges and administrative agencies with well-developed and respected procedures.

—Judge Frank M. Coffin[1]

[M]any [administrative law judges] attended "prestigious" law schools and most graduated in the top quarter of their class. . . . [B]y education, training and experience, they are probably no less qualified than bankruptcy judges or magistrates, if not the federal bench. Moreover, ALJs unlike federal district judges are not chosen in a political way. . . . [I]n their respective spheres of responsibility an argument can be made that administrative deciders are equal to or even superior to federal judges. It is not heresy to suggest that administrative deciders with extensive subject matter expertise may have a decision-making edge.

—From a report by four law professors and the president of the American Automobile Association for the Administrative Conference of the United States, 1992[2]

Surely, the current system—hiring "by the numbers" into an effectively life-tenured job with no advancement potential and with no allocation of simple work to less experienced (and thus lower-paid) individuals—is a horror story of personnel management.

—Antonin Scalia (1979)[3]

THE GREAT INVENTION OF AMERICAN GOVernment in the twentieth century was the "administrative agency," created to regulate some aspect of enterprise. Its roots were in the nineteenth century, when Congress established the Interstate Commerce Commission to protect the nation's farmers from the rapacity of the railroads the farmers needed to get their grain to market. The question of the rates that the railroads should charge to store and ship grain was clearly one beyond the competence of Congress, and specialists working for an agency would be much better equipped to keep both sides in business.

For a generation thereafter, efforts to use the commerce clause of the Constitution to control business behavior were left to the lightly manned Justice Department and to private litigants, who could sue under the terms of laws like the Sherman Anti-Trust Act. State laws were hopeless—the Supreme Court was in its "liberty of contract" phase and under authority of the Fourteenth Amendment threw out almost all state laws (though there was a window of approval for such legislation after Theodore Roosevelt scared the justices in his second term). The burden thus was on the judges in the federal courts, who were few and lacked expertise and were rather inclined to sympathize with corporations, anyway. Woodrow Wilson's administration gave birth to the Federal Trade Commission as an antitrust enforcement agency, among other things. Then the Depression gave first Herbert Hoover and then Franklin Roosevelt power to experiment.

From the businessman's point of view, the administrative agency system was thoroughly unfair. The National Labor Relations Board was the most resented, because the elections the NLRB supervised could force employers to deal, and deal "in good faith," with the union organizers who had signed up their workers against the wishes of management. NLRB made rules (a legislative function) about what employers could and could not do when unions tried to organize their workforce. It had an investigative staff (an executive function) that could be summoned to inquire whether the parties to a labor dispute were bargaining in good faith. The general counsel's office could bring a complaint against a company, after which the agency's trial examiners would hear testimony and argument from friends in the agency and from opposing counsel, and would issue rulings complete with penalties to be assessed (a judicial function). All these people were on the same payroll (until 1938 many NLRB examiners were hired on a per-diem basis), were promoted or not promoted by the same bosses who ruled the other parts of the agency, ate in the same cafeteria, and indeed might move from one bureau of the agency to another, several times a year. Supervisors could edit and make significant changes in the findings of a trial examiner. Decisions in individual cases were made by the board, political appointees to limited terms, most of whom were not lawyers, and the trial examiners might be called into the board's presence to explain their decisions, which were not in any way binding.

For the first Roosevelt term, the Supreme Court busied itself declaring such agencies unconstitutional, either because the government shouldn't do things like that or because the established departments of government had no authority to delegate their powers. The president and Congress kept going to the drawing boards to achieve the desired results another way. After the landslide against Alfred Landon and the president's introduction of a bill that would have empowered him to name enough new judges to bend the bench, the Court receded. As Finley Peter Dunne's Mr. Dooley said, talking about the controversy over the law applicable to the American colony being established in the Philippines a generation earlier, "I don't know whether the Constitution follows the flag, but I do know that the Supreme Court follows the election returns." With the flag flown high in wartime, more administrative agencies were created to police the economic activity of the war effort.

After the war, urged on especially by small-business constituents for whom the record keeping was a real burden in an age before computers, an increasingly restive Congress began assaulting the growing bureaucracies at the agencies. In the case of the NLRB, its general counsel was made an office independent of the board, separately appointed by the president and confirmed by the Senate. And in 1946, the last Congress elected with Franklin Roosevelt passed an Administrative Procedures Act that mandated "decisional independence" of trial examiners whose hearings created a record. It was understood by the Republican Congress that passed the act that steps would be taken to change the political views of the cadre of trial examiners. "[M]en of bias," Senator Alexander Wiley of Wisconsin wrote bitterly, describing them, "of ideological preconceptions, of subservience to pressure groups, of habits of unfairness, of disregard of the true values and weight of evidence."[4] In 1972, to skip ahead but explain the nomenclature of the rest of the chapter, the Civil Service Commission decreed that the "trial examiners" and "hearing examiners" of the agencies should be called "administrative law judges."

By then, the best that opponents of administrative agencies could do was to separate the judicial from their other functions. There was no escaping the agency device. It had become obvious that judging in the commercial context would have to move for most purposes onto an administrative chassis. Karl Llewellyn noted in his book on "the common law tradition" that America and England had taken an immense leap of faith in permitting the laws for a modern society to be made by judges "who are specialists only in being unspecialized."[5] Much of the modern flap about "expert testimony" ("opinion testimony," D.C. district judge Charles Ritchey called it, with reason) merely reveals the inadequacy of court proceedings before inexpert judges as a way to get at the truth or even the real disagreements of technical disputes. As late as 1990, when George H. W. Bush was president and deregulation was a matter of faith and morals at both ends of Pennsylvania Avenue, Congress passed and the president signed an "Administrative Dispute Resolution Act" to encourage the use of expert judges.

Much of the decision making in the interface of government and the private sector is now done in administrative agencies, where ALJs decide whether poor devils qualify for disability payments under the social security laws, whether power-and-light companies are exploiting their inevitable monopoly position to defraud their customers, whether labor unions (or employers) are entitled to a new election to choose representation of the workers in some company or factory, whether a property developer is endangering a fish that swims in a creek that bisects his property or a bird that nests in a bush, whether a stockbroker or commodities broker cheated his customers, whether an applicant for a license to broadcast on a certain frequency at a certain power should get the license, whether a contribution to a political party is "hard" money or "soft" money, and so on ad infinitum. "Hard-charging administrators don't like us," says one of the ALJs. "They lose control when the case goes to the ALJ. But really we're their best friend, because they need a clean record, and we give that to them." Patricia Wald, when chief judge of the Court of Appeals for the D.C. Circuit, noted in a speech to the federal bar association that in the age of deregulation there has been "an ossification of the federal rulemaking process, to the point that some agencies now prefer to make their legal interpretations and policy choices through the adjudication rather than the rulemaking process."[6]

The offices and hearing rooms for ALJs are often if not always in buildings not otherwise occupied by the agency. ("I don't see anybody but the accountants," says chief administrative law judge of the FCC, Richard Sippel, whose office is in the same building but in the basement.) Far from Washington, ALJs usually work in office buildings rather than courthouses. The hearing rooms are very much like courtrooms, with raised platforms for the judge's bench, a well for the lawyers and the various clerks, and (normally empty) wooden benches for forty to seventy-five members of the public. The well includes a desk for recording machinery or a court reporter, for these proceedings are all on the record.

Like Article III federal judges, ALJs serve unlimited terms. Their decisions and opinions are published. Even before 2005, when the Department of Health and Human Services added or was supposed to add five hundred ALJs to handle Medicare disputes, there were more than twice as many administrative law judges as there were federal district judges. The caseload of the ALJs "dwarfs that of the federal court system," to quote a 1992 report of the Administrative Conference of the United States.[7] Noting 500,000 social security cases adjudicated by ALJs every year, Ronnie A. Yoder, chief administrative law judge of the Department of Transportation (and a tenor who has sung professionally in his time away from the office), writes that "in terms of the impact on individual Americans, the role of the ALJ is far closer to more people than the constitutional judiciary."[8]

In *Butz v. Economou* in 1978, the Supreme Court declared that "the role of the modern federal hearing examiner or administrative law judge . . . is functionally comparable to that of a judge. . . . He may issue subpoenas, rule on proffers of evidence, regulate the course of the hearing, and make or recommend decisions. More importantly, the process of agency adjudication is currently structured so as to assure that the hearing examiner exercises his independent judgment on the evidence before him, free from pressures by the parties or other officials within the agency."[9] Most ALJs feel that their findings of fact are final, and that the agency is not empowered to change them. Indeed, in her speech to the ALJs, Judge Ward quoted from an opinion in her court that "this case turns not on the construction of regulations or on statutory interpretation but on the weighing of evidence and reasonable inferences made therefrom. Thus our deference runs not to the policymaking body . . . but to the ALJ, the factfinder who oversees the adjudicatory proceedings." The ALJ is supposed to be on particularly high ground where the decision is on "demeanor testimony"—i.e., should you trust this witness or that. "Our function," says NLRB chief ALJ Robert Giannasi, "is to decide who is telling the truth."

The authors of the 1992 Administrative Conference *Recommendations and Reports* disagree, announcing flatly that "if an agency and an ALJ disagree with respect to a finding of fact, it is the agency's finding that is entitled to deference on judicial review."[10] Yoder says there is no question the agency can change the ALJ's findings of fact. In both cases, of course, the court reviewing the administrative decision (a district court if it's a social security benefits case, an appeals court if it's a large matter from an agency with regulatory powers over industry) will insist that any finding of fact be supported by "substantial evidence." Congress can specifically structure the situation, by design or carelessly, so that the ALJ outranks the agency in appellate situations. Under the Black Lung Benefits Act appeals go from the Department of Labor to a Benefits Review Board, which is enjoined to take its findings of fact from the ALJ. If there is a further appeal from the review board to the federal district court, the judge is under orders to take the facts from the ALJ.

In any event, the ALJ is an employee of the agency, and his decisions will not take effect if the commission or board that runs the agency blocks them. (Normal procedure is that ALJ decisions are published, to take effect after a waiting period during which a litigant can appeal to the agency itself. In the absence of such an appeal, the decision is final.) Some judges worry that this makes the ALJs the servants of political masters. Others, more subtle, feel that the corps of ALJs become the heart of the bureaucracy, interpreting the commissioners' decisions to mean what the agency's veterans want them to mean.

George Painter thought that accusation a libel. Wispy-haired, over seventy, cherishing a reputation as cantankerous, the original hearing officer for the agency when it was created in 1975, he was in 2005 one of two ALJs at the Commodity Futures Trading Commission. He had lived through the terms of two CFTC chairmen who were antagonistic to their own agency's work—Susan Philips, whose Ph.D. dissertation at the University of Iowa had said that the Securities Act of 1933 was a waste of time and companies should not be compelled to issue registration statements before selling stock to the public; and Wendy Gramm, wife of Senator Phil Gramm, whose rulings permitted Enron to hide what it was doing in the energy exchange, where it ran the show and was counter-party to every trade. (She later went on the Enron board and, if her husband is to be believed, suffered just desserts because she took her director's fees in Enron stock that became worth-less.) Under their leadership, Painter's work was often made meaningless, but he was a good sport about it.

"Recently," he wrote in a letter to *Judicature*, "the regulated industry persuaded the agency I work for to give a new 'interpretation' to a regulation, 17 CFR 1.35 (a-1)(i), that has been of vital importance in detecting schemes to launder money, bucket orders, or cheat on taxes. The interpretation is, in my opinion, equivalent to a ruling that pigs fly. But I am bound by that interpretation. Once in place, it isn't smoke and mirrors. It is the law to every employee of the agency. And it is most unlikely that Justice Scalia, the literalist, will ever have an opportunity to review these flying pigs."

Judicature did not print the letter, so George Painter sent it to me.

2

"We are appointed on merit," says Brenda Murray, chief ALJ for the Securities and Exchange Commission, a gray-haired lady who strides about her conference room. "As opposed to Article III judges. You don't get here because you know a politician."

Actually, the tale of appointments to ALJ positions is long and peculiar and confusing. The Administrative Procedures Act of 1946, as noted, was written to a large extent by enemies of the administrative agencies, and their decision to insulate the "examiners" from pressures in their agency was in their own minds conditioned on sweeping a new broom through the rosters. All incumbent examiners were required to reapply for their jobs. The law gave the Civil Service Commission power to dismiss any of the 196 existing examiners who were found "unqualified." The CSC appointed a six-member "board of examiners," several of whom were well-publicized critics of the existing staff. And this board promptly disqualified or demoted more than a quarter of the incumbents, including twenty-seven of forty-one examiners at the NLRB.

Meanwhile, the commission set about designing a civil service exam that could be taken by applicants for ALJ positions—including credit for relevant experience, an essay on administrative law, and interviews—to be graded on a scale of 0 to 100. Agencies that wished to hire ALJs would be required to take one of the top three candidates as ranked by the exam, in best Civil Service procedure. Veterans were to get a five-point bonus on their score; disabled veterans, a ten-point bonus. But by the time the CSC was ready to publish the results of its exam, there were very few jobs. The incumbents had mobilized, put pressures on Congress, sued, publicized their plight, and in the process procured the resignation of five of the six members of the CSC's special "board." Virtually all the incumbents were thereupon declared qualified, and the list to take the exam was closed until 1954.

With the passage of time, ALJs became the responsibility of the government's Office of Personnel Management, and the Civil Service Commission was replaced by the Merit Selection Protection Board. The exam matured, grew more complicated, including a description of the two most important cases in the applicant's experience and the names and addresses ("vouchers") of at least twenty-six people who could give personal reference letters. Candidates had to show seven years of experience as a lawyer or a judge, had to write a "model decision" in an administrative law case, and had to perform well in a one-hour interview with a panel of three interviewers from OPM. Grading standards bounced about, with the weight given to experience ranging from 50 percent to 70 percent, the weight given to personal references from

40 percent to 10 percent. Letters were also sent to judges before whom the candidate had appeared and lawyers who had represented the other side of his (or her) cases. The panel interview was structured by professionals in such matters, and a full five hours were allocated to the creation of the "model decision," which was then graded by a law professor.

A minimum grade of 80 was required to qualify as a potential ALJ, and the veterans' bonuses were not applied until all the other factors had been tabulated. In the 1960s and 1970s, agencies were allowed to specify the experience they thought was needed to be an ALJ in their shop ("selective certification"), and applicants with such experience could be hired by an agency that said it needed such experience even though they were not among the top three on the merit list. Then in the late 1990s a federal appeals court threw out the grading procedures as too subjective (roughly 80 percent of candidates were failing), and the Office of Personnel Management closed what was already a long list of qualified applicants: No further exams were given, except for disabled veterans. It also stopped giving selective certification, demanding that an agency with an unoccupied budget slot for an ALJ take one of the three top people on the current list, whether they have shown any interest in the work of this agency or not.

The safety valve is an unlimited right of lateral motion. Once an ALJ, always an ALJ. The agency with by far the largest number of ALJs is the Social Security Administration, now with more than 1,100 of them. It may order new ALJs from OPM in batches of a hundred. OPM has ruled that instead of being held to one of the top three, Social Security can choose a hundred from the top three hundred. This provides considerable variety of background among the entrants. The work of a social security ALJ is pressured and repetitive, what the ALJs call the "rocket-docket system," under which nobody knows anything about the cases to be heard today before the actual hearing begins, and the judge is handed a list of some dozens of cases to be finished up today.

The system is insane. Applications for disability payments go to a federal social security office, where a clerk asks a few questions (if you are actually working, you can't get disability payments) and sends the applicant to a doctor. If after receiving the doctor's report he denies "the grant," the applicant appeals to a state office. If the state disallows, he can appeal to a board of state officials, and if they turn him down he can appeal back to the Social Security Administration, which sends in an ALJ. This happens about 500,000 times a year in the United States, lumping together disability income and supplemental security income cases. The ALJ holds a hearing with testimony on the record, and if the ALJ also turns down the applicant (and he still has enough money to pay a lawyer), the case moves on to a federal district court. The Social Security Administration is not represented at the hearing, which is not supposed to be an adversary affair.[11] During the Reagan years, when government was especially concerned that poor people might be cheating it (Ronald Reagan's favorite piece of country music was something about a "welfare Cadillac"), SSA did employ lawyers to oppose grants, and sought to set a benchmark of decisions for the claimant, disciplining ALJs who gave more grants than the average. Courts questioned this practice, and it was dropped, though not until after the

ALJs at the Social Security Administration had formed a union, which survives.

Many SSA judges are quite prepared to continue their career elsewhere. If the SEC needs an ALJ with some securities expertise, or the NLRB needs someone who has worked in labor relations, they can go to the Social Security roster, ask SSA for permission to poach, and approach the judge they want. There is another side to the subject, too. Susan Biro, chief ALJ at the Environmental Protection Administration in 2004, is a cheerful young woman whose private sector experience was with small firms in Washington. She had been hearing social security disability cases in the Bronx two years before she became the first and most important arbiter of whether or not a proposed shopping center encroaches on wetlands. She is quite content to employ judges who are without training in environmental matters: "Our credibility is at stake. Environmental law is an area where people don't revolve. They're either on one side of the equation or the other, part of the regulatory community or the regulated. So we want people with no background." EPA administrative law judges, of course, hear only cases brought by the agency's general counsel. If people wish to make a complaint that someone is violating environment rules, they go to the agency's investigative arm, which decides whether the agency should bring charges and propose remedies.

Even more than trial judges, ALJs have become expert at settling cases. "Outreach," says Biro, "is a big part of our agency. Our effort is to bring people into compliance." (Some kinds of case can't be settled: the Labor Department's John M. Vittone points out that someone claiming benefits under the Black Lung law either has black lung or he doesn't. If he does, he gets a fixed benefit, so there is no bargain to be struck. Marshall J. Breger, writing a review in the *George Washington Law Review* of a 1989 book on "Defining Administrative Law," pointed out a number of ways that administrative law judges had moved toward processes better suited to the disputes their agencies had to solve. The Federal Energy Regulatory Commission, for example, employs "settlement judges" who serve as "neutral evaluators" to examine disputes between energy producers and energy consumers. The Environmental Protection Administration has established an "alternate dispute resolution" process.

"The use of decision makers with technical expertise," Breger wrote, "means less power for the lawyers. . . . The Administrative Conference recently . . . recommended that medical experts become more centrally involved in disability decisions instead of relying on legally trained decisionmakers." Because administrative agencies have explicit rulemaking authority, the judges who work for them may have an expanded view of their function. Breger points out that the various "sunshine acts" requiring public information about rulemaking processes have driven some agencies to a common-law approach to rule changes, letting the judges create precedents from actual cases. The National Highway Transport Safety Agency was rebuked by the courts when it tried to write rules governing automobile design, and moved instead to recall orders.

The origin of the "settlement judges" at FERC is especially interesting. In 1976, Southern Natural Gas, a Georgia company operating across state lines, cut back on its allocation of product to a General Motors automobile factory, in favor of a fertilizer manufacturer, both of which came to FERC to compel delivery. During the proceeding, ALJ Curtis L. Wagner Jr. got a phone call from the governor of the state, asking if he could be heard as a witness, not just as governor but as a peanut farmer who knew how important this fertilizer company was to his crop. All parties consenting, Jimmy Carter was called as a witness, and asked as a further favor that he get an extended luncheon recess on the day of his testimony, so he could declare his candidacy for the presidency at a National Press Club lunch. Judge Wagner ruled for the car company ("which is why I am not on the Supreme Court," he says cheerfully in his twenty-eighth year as chief ALJ for the agency), but before the commission could decide whether to accept his ruling the new governor of Georgia called and asked whether maybe this thing could be settled. The commission referred the case back to Judge Wagner, who did indeed settle it. By then he was the agency's *chief* ALJ, and the commission asked him if he could codify what he had done in the Southern case.

More than 90 percent of the cases heard by the FERC are settled in conferences with one of the agency's now fifteen ALJs sitting as "settlement judges." All ALJs of this agency receive formal training in mediation techniques. The system is unlike that used in the courts, where the judge who will hear the case usually supervises the settlement conferences. At the FERC, all complaints are first referred to an ALJ acting as a settlement judge, and all proceedings before him are under seal. The settlement judge may have no contact with the litigants or their lawyers except in the course of the settlement procedure, and is forbidden to discuss the case with anyone at the agency. If the case fails to settle, the settlement judge may not discuss it with the ALJ to whom it is then assigned. When the commission reviews the findings of the ALJ, it may not solicit the views of the settlement judge. Similarly, the "alternate dispute resolution" process at the Environmental Protection Agency is completely confidential, and if the process fails (about four-fifths of the time it succeeds), all the files on the case are destroyed before it goes to another ALJ.

We are talking here about what may be very substantial matters. In the El Paso case that grew out of the Enron-manipulated price spike in the supply of natural gas to California, Judge Wagner found that El Paso had indeed abused its market power. "The decision was the lead story in *The New York Times*," he notes reminiscently, "ahead of Iraq. El Paso took out full-page ads in the *Times, The Washington Post*, and *The Wall Street Journal* to say I was crazy." El Paso finally settled the case by paying the California parties *six billion* dollars. The cases can also be very complicated. "Our hearings," FERC chief judge Wagner told a training session for the federal energy bar, "are almost all multiparty hearings (unlike court trials, which commonly involve just a plaintiff and a defendant)—and it takes considerable skill for the administrative law judge to maintain control over the hearing and to move it along expeditiously."

The FERC case with the longest opinion (971 pages, following 411 days of hearings before two judges) was one involving the Alaska Pipeline and the responsibilities of the seven partners who owned it to provide high-quality oil to run through it. Producers who send lower-grade petroleum through the pipeline must pay into an "Alaska Pipeline Quality Bank." The disagreement was among the producers, not involving the government, but the law directs such complaints to FERC, not the courts. FERC has been here before; district judges have not. The decision to award the quality bank more than $9 billion was still before the commission for approval in fall 2004, and Senator Ted Stevens (R-Alaska) in his capacity as chairman of the appropriations committee put an amendment into FERC's appropriation forbidding the agency to spend money to increase the penalties imposed by the ALJ on companies that had in effect watered the oil they put in the pipeline. "Decisional independence" is something Congress imposes on the relationship of the judges with their agency, not on the relationship of the judges and Congress.

In 1978, a team of investigators headed by Yale law professor Jerry L. Mashaw studied decisions on disability claims by the ALJs of the Social Security Administration. They found that letters from congressmen energized the process of "allowing" the claims, though "we are unable to advance a legitimate reason why a congressional inquiry should influence the amount of delay to which a claimant is subjected." And they noted admiringly one ALJ who "has completely insulated himself from congressional influence. Inquiries are answered by members of his staff, who are instructed not to mention the matter to the ALJ and to keep congressional inquiries out of the files that he reviews." The Mashaw team also wrote chillingly that "the outcome of cases depends more on who decides the case than on what the facts are," and that appeals to the court system were meaningless: "We can find little, if any, contribution to accuracy or consistency resulting from judicial review."[12]

One notes in passing that by the rules of the game an ALJ engaged for the past four years in deciding whether claimants should be allowed $5,500 a year to help them survive a disability may be transferred tomorrow, with no training or education whatever, to the energy agency or the EPA or the Defense Department's contract office to make decisions determining the fate of immense enterprises. And he gets the same pay, too. It's the American way. We are out of our minds.

13 THE POLITICS OF SUPREMACY

The reason the public thinks so much of the Justices of the Supreme Court is that they are almost the only people in Washington who do their own work.

—Louis D. Brandeis (1934)[1]

PERHAPS THE STRANGEST THING ABOUT the Supreme Court is the amount of time its members spend with each other, all alone—no staffs, no clerks, no marshals or messengers—around the big mahogany table in the conference room beside the office of the chief justice in the marble mausoleum beside the Library of Congress on Capitol Hill. It is a separate self-governing social system. Though the salaries of the justices are set by the Congress, the budget for the courts goes directly from the chief justice to the Office of Management and Budget and the president, who must communicate it as written to the Congress. The Court hires its own clerks and marshals and information specialists and cleaning help, and runs its own cafeteria for its employees and visitors (Justice Stephen Breyer, who is something of a gourmet, has been for some years the chair of the committee that supervises the food). Apart from a handful of cases that the Constitution or a judiciary act requires the Court to hear (the "original jurisdiction" cases involving disputes between the states, and the cases like the challenge to the campaign finance reform laws where Congress writes into the statute itself that the Court must hear the appeal from the three-judge district court to which the statute directs litigants to take their challenges), the Court controls its own workload.

Each "term" of the court runs from early October to June. The court sits in Washington until April of that term for seven two-week sessions in which cases will be heard and occasionally decided, and then from April through June for the private preparation and public presentation of opinions. Opinions are printed in the Court's own print shop and handed out (also placed on the Web site) as they are delivered from the bench. On Monday, Tuesday, and Wednesday of each session week, from ten to noon and then again from one to three in the afternoon, cases are argued in public by counsel (with interjections from the bench—except for Justice Clarence Thomas, who almost never speaks, today's Supreme Court is what judges call a "hot court" that peppers counsel with questions and comments—and the substitution of Roberts for Rehnquist has made it hotter).

On Wednesday afternoon following the open session, the Conference (a capitalized noun, meaning the nine justices) meets to discuss and conduct a preliminary vote on the cases argued on Monday, usually three or four of them. Thursday the court does not sit, and there is no Conference. Everybody has a chance to read, talk with "brethren," and discuss with the law clerks in his or her office. Each justice is entitled to hire four law clerks, nearly all of them very recent graduates of high-prestige law schools, seasoned by a year of clerkship for an appellate judge. They have cut their eyeteeth editing and writing law review articles that mimic appellate court opinions. (Or vice versa: There is some feeling among legal academics that the Court's opinions mimic law review articles, which is not necessarily good for the country.) Justice John Harlan, who spent most of his career in private practice, liked to say that staffing arrangements, the independence of each justice's chambers, made the Court into nine small law firms.

Many in Washington would now dispute Brandeis's assertion that the justices do their own work, the argument being that the clerks prepare drafts of opinions. In Brandeis's time, Learned Hand on the Second Circuit Court of Appeals told his clerk, Charles Wyzanski, that the only drafting he should do was preparation for himself to be the wall against which Learned Hand could bounce the ball. Given their role in disposing of the requests for certiorari, there can be no question that today's clerks do make direct contributions to the output of the Court, but lawyers do not need too much practice reading the opinions of the Court to feel fairly confident that one can match the words with their author, and the clerks are there only a year or two.

Friday is Conference day: The justices assemble and shake hands (an invariable ritual) at 9:30 in the morning, and go at it, just the nine of them, arguing the cases, with forty-five minutes off for lunch, usually until the late afternoon. If a message to a justice is considered important enough (anything much less than a death in the family will not qualify), a messenger may knock on the door, which will be opened by the most junior justice, who will deliver it to its designated recipient. The chief justice, of course, is never the most junior. Justice Breyer, who had been looking forward to freedom from this role after ten years of juniority, found himself still on duty when the first replacement on the Court was a new chief justice. Then Justice Alito took over.

In considering how to rule on cases, the Chief speaks first, summarizing the case as he sees it. Next to speak is the associate justice with the greatest seniority, and the discussion moves down to the newest arrival. Lawyers arguing cases before the Court are strictly controlled in the time they can have—half an hour is almost always the top; Chief Justice Charles Evans Hughes reputedly could cut off counsel in the middle of an "if." But in Conference there is no limit on how long each justice can speak other than his own sense of what strengthens his argument. Among the demands on the Chief is subtly to influence that sense in a way that will not be resented. (Felix Frankfurter once said that watching Hughes preside was like watching Toscanini conduct.) Both the Chief and the most junior of the justices keep a record of the vote, and most justices keep their own notes on what was said by whom. On Monday morning the chief justice parcels out to himself or others on his side the task of writing an opinion in each case where he was in the majority, and if the Chief is in the minority, the job of assigning the opinion falls to the most senior of the justices in this majority.

Discussions in the Conference never become a matter of public record. Indeed, it is one of the accomplishments of the Court that there have been very few leaks from what are often highly contentious discussions. Not infrequently, having no public stake or pride in their first impression, justices change their minds between the start of discussion and the preparation of written opinions. What is *said* does not matter at the Supreme Court. Only what is written counts, and then only after each justice has decided each case for himself or herself, and has signed on to a brother's opinion or prepared a concurrence or dissent. Most justices destroy any notes, and early drafts of opinions, once the decision is published. Justice Brandeis put his drafts through the print shop because he liked to edit on printed pages rather than on typescript. This produced a lot of work for the print shop, for Brandeis was a perfectionist; he put one opinion through fifty-three different printings. Today, of course, most editing is done on computers.

In addition to preliminary decisions on the cases argued Tuesday and Wednesday, the Friday conference considers petitions for certiorari (writs commanding that lower courts forward certified copies of the record in cases the loser wishes to appeal to the Supreme Court). About seven thousand such petitions are filed each year. The filing fee is $300, which can be waived if individuals file *in forma pauperis*. These pro se documents, the petitioner trying to make his case for himself, constitute about four-fifths of the petitions. The others are filed by lawyers, and accompanied by printed briefs, often long printed briefs. Copies of petitions for certiorari and the associated briefs are distributed by the clerk of the Court to the chambers of the justices as they arrive. Something less than a hundred of these petitions, including no more than a handful *in forma pauperis*, will be heard by the Court. The 1925 Judiciary Act began an irreversible process of expanding the Court's control over its docket, which is now virtually complete. Only a state or a federal agency appealing against a lower court decision that its law violates the U.S. Constitution can claim a *right* to a hearing at the Supreme Court.

The Court's rule on granting "cert" has been—the memory of man runneth not to the contrary (even in 1925 its origin was lost in the mists of history)—that a petition receiving four votes triggers cert and the case will be heard. Less than four votes, cert is denied. Every once in a while trouble arises from the difference between the five votes needed for action and the four needed for cert. Linda Greenhouse, in *Becoming Justice Blackmun*, tells the story of a death-row inmate who got the four votes needed for his case to be reviewed but not the five votes needed to order a stay of execution. The Court was confronted with the embarrassing possibility that it could invite arguments about the fate of a man already executed. Various ways to amend the rules were pondered—Rehnquist as a good conservative stood out against changes—until Justice Lewis Powell, who always thought the rule of four was nonsense (so did Justice John Paul Stevens, who complained about it publicly in a lecture at New York University in 1982[2]) grumpily provided a fifth vote to stay the execution. Testifying before the Senate Judiciary Committee in his confirmation hearings, John Roberts said that, in similar circumstances, he would gladly provide the fifth vote himself.

In the Rehnquist Court, one of the law clerks of one of the justices (all but two of them had four clerks each) prepared a memo on each petition for cert, and the memo was circulated to all the chambers. Justice John Paul Stevens did not participate in this division of labor. He asked his clerks (until 2000, he kept only three) to prepare memos on each petition for his consideration. These petitions for cert make up much of the workload by the small law firms in the chambers and by the justices at the Friday Conference. In the 1920s, when there were no more than twenty or thirty petitions per Conference day (which was then Saturday, not Friday), all were listed on the docket and brought up for discussion. In the 1940s, the chief justice would circulate a "dead list" of cases that struck him as unworthy of discussion, and unless a justice asked to take up one of them, these cases were simply dismissed without mention at the Conference. By the time Rehnquist took over, there were more than a hundred petitions per Conference day, and he circulated a "discuss list" of petitions that should be brought to the Conference.[3] All the justices had of course been given copies of the pool memos from the clerks and many had probably at least glanced at the petitions in question. Any justice could add a name to the Chief's "discuss list" if he or she thought there might be three others who also thought the case should not simply be thrown out. Justices can and do dissent from the Court's denial of cert, presenting their reasons why they think the appeal should be heard. Justice Byron White did so often in the 1980s, on the grounds that the Court was permitting the continuance of too many disagreements between the courts of appeal.

Among the major tasks of the chief justice is summarizing for the Conference each case that remains among the living. By common consent, Rehnquist was outstanding in his capacity to do that fairly, quickly, and with a sense of humor. Sometimes, the Court gives its reasons for granting cert, asking the attorneys who will argue the case to answer certain questions. But the Court does not give reasons for refusing to hear an appeal, which is what usually happens. The Court these days rarely hears more than ninety cases a year.

2

Of the making of books about the Supreme Court of the United States there is no end. Still, the institution is grievously misunderstood, in part because the founding document is so short and open-ended, and in part because the governing rules—the words of that document—are subject to reinterpretation and open doors to legislative change. The Court's appellate jurisdiction is laid out in seven quick phrases separated by dashes and semicolons. Essentially, it consists of cases involving federal law or the Constitution, or matters overseas, or disputes involving citizens of different states or a choice between different state laws. It can be exercised only "with such exceptions, and under such regulations as the Congress shall make."

The Constitution was explicit about what the Congress could do to the Court and could not do (judges could not be fired, and their pay could not be reduced), but it said nothing about what the Court could do to Congress. The Court, Alexander Hamilton assured the state legislatures in *The Federalist*, would be "the least dangerous branch, having neither force nor will." But there is a degree of dissembling in all this, for the sociopolitical purpose of the Supreme Court is to establish the uniformity of the law across a continental empire, and for that purpose its decisions must be final.

Chief Justice John Marshall, a plain, blunt Federalist Virginian in broadcloth, a relative of Thomas Jefferson, but no friend of his, leaped into the void in 1803 to claim that in the absence of a law limiting its jurisdiction the Court had the power—indeed, the duty—to declare an act of Congress unconstitutional and thus nonexistent. [See page 77.] Jefferson and James Madison thought this "judicial review" was a step too far. So did Learned Hand, greatest of the appellate judges of the middle of the twentieth century, who wrote that "I have never been able to understand on what basis it does or can rest except as a *coup de main*."[4] Highly competent testimony exists to argue that this power or duty is not even necessary. "I do not think the United States would come to an end," Justice Holmes said in a speech to a Harvard Law School alumni dinner in 1913, "if we lost our power to declare an Act of Congress void." Then Holmes added, "I do think the Union would be imperiled if we could not make that declaration as to the laws of the several States."[5] This power is not in the Constitution at all, but it is the True North of the Court's jurisdiction. The concession the Court makes is that when lower courts throw out state legislation as contrary to the Constitution, the Court *must* hear the appeal.

And no decision is ever *really* final, because political apparatus can amend the Constitution, and because today's Court can overrule yesterday's. Writing in 1944, when the Court's reversal on New Deal legislation was a recent memory, Charles Wyzanski argued that "the Supreme Court has, I believe, never, unless the Child Labor Tax case be taken as an exception, refused to uphold the constitutionality of a measure which in substantially the same form has twice secured the adherence of a majority of Congress. . . . From American history it can be persuasively argued that judicial review is a mere device to appeal from Philip drunk to Philip sober."[6] History still gives more support to that idea than one could gather from the current political scene, where the abortion question keeps getting regurgitated and swallowed and regurgitated again. Especially when dealing with the powers of the other, coequal branches of government, the Court must persuade as well as give orders. If the opinion fails to persuade, the Court will not in fact achieve the finality it asserts.

The supreme courts of the several states exist essentially as courts of error and appeal, correcting the record and results of private lawsuits, state regulations, and state criminal convictions. The Supreme Court of the United States has a *nationalizing* function. The "judicial power of the United States," after all, is what Article III vests in the Court. Its purpose is to establish in the areas of its competence a commonality of law for the country. Legislation passed by the Congress and signed by the president must mean the same thing everywhere in the country.

Even where there is no legislation, there may be a need for law. Justice Joseph Story was wrong when he posited a "federal common law" that would be written and enforced by the federal courts whether state courts agreed or not, but there were reasons why the error persisted for a century. In many matters, including the commercial, it was necessary for the government of a continent to offer the same rules to all participants in its jurisdiction. Appointed for life by the president "with the advice and consent of the Senate" (which in the nineteenth century rejected almost one out of three of the presidents' choices), the nine justices of the Supreme Court (the number doesn't have to be nine: George Washington's Court had six, Lincoln's at one point had ten) speak for the law itself, the nation's law—or, as Marshall insisted, for the "we, the people" who adopted the Constitution, though we were not in fact consulted. Meanwhile, at some level we do live in a federal system, a union of states, and failing anyone else who can do it, the Supreme Court is responsible for allocating functions between the national power and the states. It is all at least a little strange.

In the next chapter, we shall note the historian Gordon Wood's concern about the "demystification" of law. He speaks exactly to the strengths of the historic Court and the problems of the modern Court. The illustration in detail can be found in Linda Greenhouse's admirable book about Justice Harry A. Blackmun, built on the papers this packrat kept through a long life in law and justice. Justice Blackmun must have had an interesting mind when young—no less than Charles Wyzanski, a Harvard Law School classmate, invited him to Washington to work in Franklin Roosevelt's Labor Department in 1934—but there is a cloak of banality over most of the papers he and his colleague exchanged in the process of deciding the cases Greenhouse describes. In large part, this was because the disagreements of the justices were not over the facts of the case and not over the law to be applied, but over the policy aspects, the future activities within the society that the Court's decisions would promote or frustrate.

Historically, the common-law judges of the British tradition have made law by way of deciding real cases affecting real litigants. Let justice be done in the individual case, said Lord

Mansfield in Latin, though the heavens fall. The constitutional law judges of the American tradition echoed the British
judges' concern that the cases they hear involve real disputes,
not arguments about what the law ought to be. Except in
Massachusetts, no American trial or appeals court will give
advisory opinions to state or federal authorities, and the
Supreme Court for generations has had a rule that wherever
possible cases will be resolved without recourse to exegesis of
the Constitution. Thus, the law, inescapably abstract, will remain tied to the life of the community. But increasingly in the
second half of the twentieth century, the Supreme Court of
the United States has decided cases by making law.

This discovery of new potential in the Constitution was
especially characteristic of the Warren Court. One remembers the chief justice, shaking his large head, reading from
the center of the great bench decisions detailing the injus-
tices an appellant had suffered at the hands of the police or
his employer or some bigot or the manufacturer of some defective product. Starting from the premise that there ought
to be a law against such outrage, Warren would eventually
find a law somewhere that compensated victims and controlled the future performance of victimizers. One of today's
justices, who clerked in the Warren days, notes that the violations of civil rights were then so egregious that they dominated the decision making on whether to hear a case and thus
by extension the decision in the case, whereas now the law itself is in good shape and individual cases won't change it.
And this may be so. (Rehnquist as a clerk to Robert Jackson
in the first year of the Warren Court wrote memos opposing
the sentimentality of accepting cases because the petitioner

had been wronged, and remained consistent in this attitude for more than fifty years; in this area, Roberts will almost certainly be a Rehnquist clone.) Justice Hugo Black, former senator from Alabama and former member of the Ku Klux Klan, told a television interviewer shortly after the decision in *Brown v. Board of Education* that he didn't rely on any high-falutin arguments about distinguishing schools from railroad dining cars to decide that case: "I lived in the South, practically until I came up here. . . . I didn't need any philosophy about changing times to convince me that there was a denial of equal protection of the laws."[7]

The functions of the Supreme Court in the narrative of our history have changed from time to time. John Marshall was chief justice for thirty-four years, and nationalized the enterprise of self-government, mostly through his personal command of jujitsu, turning each enemy's practical strength against him. We have noted that Marshall in *Marbury v. Madison* gave Madison the victory in the dispute by refusing to order that Marbury's commission be delivered to him—but only because the Judiciary Act of 1789, which purported to give the Court authority to issue such an order, was unconstitutional. When Congress exceeded its authority under Article I, Marshall ruled, the Court was empowered, nay, commanded, to disfranchise the legislature. In *Cohens v. Virginia*, Marshall let stand a state ban on the sale of the lottery tickets the federal government had authorized to help build the District of Columbia—but only because the Congress had not specifically included sales in Virginia as part of the legislation that established the lottery. If Congress had declared that the tickets could be sold across the river, then Virginia would not have had the legal authority to prohibit the sale. Again, the power of the federal government is asserted in principle, but in the specific matter the government's antagonist wins.

Marshall's great tool was the opinion of the Court. In the Court's first dozen years, pre-Marshall, its judges like British judges read their separate opinions from the bench. Marshall from his arrival in 1801 persuaded his colleagues that there should be one opinion "for the court," and that the chief justice if part of the majority should assign the task of writing it, usually to himself. Another trick that goes back to Marshall (Warren Burger tried it a couple of times in the 1970s) was the chief justice shifting his vote on a case so that he could write the majority opinion and control the message that would be sent by a Court that in reality disagreed with him.

Roger Taney, who succeeded Marshall, served almost twenty-eight years, and like Marshall died in office. President John Adams swore in Marshall, and President Abraham Lincoln was running for reelection when Taney died; between them, these two men served with fifteen presidents. Taney's first nomination by Andrew Jackson to be an associate justice was turned down by the Senate (which had previously rejected his nomination to be secretary of the treasury), and the seat he had been unable to take was still unoccupied when Marshall died. Jackson boldly nominated Taney to replace Marshall, and the aggressive states'-rightser Philip Barbour, a Virginia congressman, for the vacant seat. (Barbour, who died young after serving only five years, thought that except where the Constitution specifically authorized federal interference, the separate states of the union had all the sovereignty of a foreign nation. In fairness, he did not push these views too hard on the bench, and Justice Joseph Story, who was a Harvard law professor on the side and had no truck with such ideas, greatly respected his mind.[8]) The Senate confirmed both of Jackson's nominees in a session of which no records were kept.

But just as it became the function of the Burger Court in the 1970s to confirm most of the Warren Court's innovations (it was Burger who wrote the unanimous opinion in that forced the Charlotte, North Carolina, school district to bus pupils across municipal boundaries for racial balance), it had been the function of Taney's Court in the 1840s to enforce against attack most of the national powers Marshall had asserted for the federal government. As Gerald Dunne wrote in his biography of Justice Story, Marshall had achieved "the transformation of the Supreme Court from tribunal of justice to an organ of government."[9] Taney had grown up as a Federalist in his native Maryland, but had become Andrew Jackson's most faithful servant. Somewhat to his own surprise, he had also become a master of compromise: a Roman Catholic himself (the first such to sit on that bench), he was married to an Episcopalian; he and his wife agreed to bring up boys as Catholics and girls as Protestants. They then had six girls. It was Taney who found the way to assure that states would not try to restrict the activities of out-of-state corporations to favor their own, establishing the rule that absent specific legislated prohibitions a corporation chartered in one state could assume that it was authorized to do business in the others.

The one big exception to Taney's record of grumpily accepting the national power, an exception that has left Taney's name an abomination in American history, was the law of slavery. Taney insisted that state powers to classify Negroes as chattel possessions—and to maintain the private property rights of the individuals who owned these possessions—could not be abrogated by the national government. In the Dred Scott decision of 1857 he declared that the Missouri Compromise of a generation before had been an unconstitutional usurpation of power by the national government. It was the first time since *Marbury*, fifty-four years before, and only the second time overall, that the Court had invalidated an act of Congress. The decision was especially pernicious because it extended the power of the slave states to send police into other states to seize "fugitive slaves." (This power rested primarily on Article IV, Section 2, of the Constitution, which required that any "person held to service or labor" in one state who had escaped to another "shall be delivered up on claim of the party to whom such service or labor shall be due." But judges in the Free States were refusing to do it.) Less noticed in the uproar was Taney's insistence on the sacred nature of private property, which formed the foundation for the next generation's insistence on "equal protection of the law" and "substantive due process" before either Congress or the states could trespass on "liberty of contract," which included, for example, the freedom of a ten-year-old child to bargain wages and working conditions with the owner of a factory. "There is no greater inequality," Felix Frankfurter noted bitterly in 1912, "than the equality of unequals."[10]

The later years of the nineteenth century saw what some historians consider intellectually the strongest bench the Supreme Court has ever known—Miller, Field, Harlan, Gray, Fuller. (Several of them were also physical giants: Harlan was six foot three, Gray was six foot six. Fuller perhaps does not merit inclusion in the list. He had married money, and was most ingenious at finding ways the Constitution could be construed to defend the interests of the rich. In 1895 he wrote opinions invalidating the income tax and declaring that manufacturing activity is not commerce and thus not subject to federal control, something that Justice Clarence Thomas alone in the world believes today. But Holmes thought "he was extraordinary. He had the business of the Court at his fingers' ends, he was perfectly courageous, prompt, decided . . . with a humor that relieved any tension with a laugh."[11]) Felix Frankfurter wrote that the reactionary Justice Joseph Bradley (on the Court from 1870 to 1892, eviscerator of the Civil Rights Act of 1875, precursor of Justice Thomas in his affection for the Eleventh Amendment) was "one of the keenest, profoundest intellects that ever sat on that bench."[12] To some degree our notions of what Supreme Court opinions ought to be—certain, pompous, based on eternal verities—are still inherited from that period.

Every once in a while, one of these highly formal opinions would support government efforts to remedy the most enormous inequalities of bargaining power. The state of Illinois was permitted to set storage fees at wheat silos owned by railroads in Chicago, the Interstate Commerce Commission was created to regulate railroad rates, the Constitution was found to tolerate the Sherman Antitrust law (Fuller found a way to use it against labor unions), the state of Oregon was permitted to set maximum hours of work for women. Most of this happened in Theodore Roosevelt's second term, when he was on the rampage about judicial interference with his programs.

("I may not know much about law," he said in 1912, "but I do know one can put the fear of God into judges."[13]) But most social legislation attempted by the states in the early twentieth century ran afoul of these legal philosophers, who thought the life of the law was logic, and saw the common law, in Holmes's contemptuous phrase, as "a brooding omnipresence in the sky."

In his book about the Supreme Court, Chief Justice Rehnquist runs through a list of the rejections by the Court of social legislation, state and federal, in the first thirty-five years of the twentieth century. "[T]he laws the Court was thus setting aside," he writes, "were the response of legislators in countless states to keenly perceived and prominently publicized problems of the day. The Court was in the process of sowing a wind, with the whirlwind to be reaped years later."[14] The whirlwind from Justice Rehnquist's point of view was of course the Warren Court, where for several brief shining moments it seemed possible that the judiciary could take the leading role in the reformation of an unjust America. Even the conservatives were Democrats—Jackson, Frankfurter, Tom Clark, Byron White.

Among the taped conversations of President Lyndon Johnson in the White House is one where he discusses nominating Thurgood Marshall to the Supreme Court: "And my judgment is with Hugo Black, Bill Douglas, the Chief [Warren], Abe Fortas . . . they'll just have a field day."[15] Right-wing groups have looked foolish in the early 2000s, seeking to hobble a Supreme Court on which seven of the nine justices are Republicans appointed by Republican presidents, but forty years earlier there was a thirst for activism. Justice Brennan could look at the court calendar for the year ahead and find opportunities to advance freedom, as he did once, famously, before a *Harvard Law Review* dinner. Charles Reich, a Yale law professor who had been a law clerk to Justice Hugo Black, wrote a best-seller called *The Greening of America*, which called on the Court to expand the Bill of Rights, establish a long list of entitlements for every American, and order elected officials both state and federal to care for the environment, equalize the chances of minorities, help suspects defend themselves against police and prosecutors, and so on.

I myself was then chairman of a New York City local school board and a member of the president's Panel on Educational Research and Development in Washington, and I vividly remember a professor at the Harvard Graduate School of Education proclaiming that the Court was about to demand that school integration be achieved by busing children back and forth across the municipal boundary lines separating cities from suburbs. The resulting pressure on school budgets, he said, would require the politicians to raise school taxes enough to dramatically improve the education offered to blacks and to solve the American dilemma. I brought word to him from the field that he was crazy, but he didn't believe me. Progress by lawsuit was the wave of the future. "Although the relevant boundary line cannot be drawn precisely," the University of Chicago political scientist Gerald N. Rosenberg writes in *The Hollow Hope*, a deeply researched book about the gap between what "public interest" lawyers thought they had achieved and what in fact they did achieve, "there is no doubt that the aim of modern litigation in the areas of civil rights, women's rights and the like, is to produce significant social reform."[16]

As late as 1983, so sophisticated an observer as political scientist Sheldon Goldman could write that "one contribution
that the courts, and especially the Supreme Court, uniquely
make for conflict resolution in American society is to offer
oppressed groups a forum for treating demands that otherwise are untreatable because of the control exercised by entrenched majorities whether they be in a national or local
electorate, a legislative body or a local government area such
as a school district."[17]

3

And this, as Learned Hand had warned in the early years of
the Warren Court, spawned the other whirlwind, the politi-
cization of appointment to the federal bench, and the intrusion of ideology in elections to the state supreme courts, the
insistence that courts be "accountable." In the next chapter
we shall note that there is a great difference, hidden from
contemporaries but obvious in the eye of history, between the
detailed Brandeis brief that supported action by a legislature
and the detailed Brandeis opinion that informs the action of a
court that must find a rule to justify its orders to the litigants.

When Franklin Roosevelt railed against the nine old men
who were declaring the New Deal legislation unconstitutional, he was not asking for a bench that would impose the
New Deal on an unwilling Congress and executive branch.
President Dwight Eisenhower did not like the Warren Court
because it was in effect ordering him and other officials, federal and local, to do things they did not wish to do. Eisen-

hower did not make a public statement praising the decision in *Brown* until he had been out of office for three years. When Governor James F. Byrnes of South Carolina (formerly a Supreme Court justice and secretary of state under Harry Truman) complained that someone had overheard Assistant Attorney General Warren Burger (yet) say that Eisenhower would not appoint anyone to a federal bench who advocated segregation, Eisenhower hastened to reassure him that he had been misinformed.[18] Official resistance to school desegregation in the South was all but universal among Southern politicians. In 1956, all but two senators from the South (the exceptions were Lyndon Johnson of Texas and Albert Gore Sr. of Tennessee) signed a "Declaration of Constitutional Principles" declaring that the unanimous opinion in *Brown* had "no legal basis."[19]

The Warren Court single-handedly prohibited segregation here, there, and elsewhere, at a time when the Southern senators, commanding the committee chairs through seniority and empowered through the filibuster to prevent the scheduling of legislation they did not want, could and did see to it that no substantial civil rights bill was even considered in the Congress. (In 2005, in one of the great illustrations of the meaning of the word "chutzpah," a United States Senate controlled by Southern Republicans apologized for the failure of the United States Senate controlled by Southern Democrats to pass antilynching legislation in the twentieth century.) The Court rewrote obscenity laws, gave specific meaning to the generalities of the Bill of Rights in protecting people accused of crime and providing remedies for victims of discrimination, and cheerfully accepted private lawsuits brought to enforce environmental protection goals that Congress had not intended to be taken seriously.

A court that tells you to bus your child to a school miles away or throws out laws prohibiting the sale of pornography in your neighborhood or forbids your town to license developers to build nice housing on wetlands affects public attitudes toward government and elected officials' attitudes toward courts. Political leaders find it profitable to second-guess the judiciary. As early as 1970—or as late as 1970, *Brown v. Board of Education* having been decided in 1954—Vice President Spiro Agnew campaigning in congressional districts in the South was promising Southern voters that if they gave President Nixon a Republican Senate his next appointment to the Supreme Court would be a Southern conservative. Chances to appoint to the Supreme Court are few, but between the creation of new seats and the resignation or retirement or graduation to senior status of existing judges, presidents every year get several score of appointments to district and circuit courts.

Examining these appointments historically, Sheldon Goldman finds it "useful to make a distinction between a president's policy agenda, partisan agenda and personal agenda."[20] Obviously, the three may come together. A potential nominee may be a personal friend, share the president's substantive goals, and inspire senators or congressmen or the worker bees of the president's party. And everything necessarily runs through the Justice Department, which has daily contact with government attorneys and others in every district in the country—and supervises the Federal Bureau of Investigation, which formally reports on every candidate the White House is considering. Officially, it is always the Justice Department that recommends the candidate to the White House, though often enough (always when the nomination is for a Supreme Court seat) the White House sends over at least some of the names.

The more calm the relationship between the courts and the politicians, the more likely a president will regard judicial appointments as the most dignified form of patronage. It is, after all, a lifetime appointment, and rewards friends and the friends of friends, as Harry Truman did. (Truman's first appointment to the Supreme Court was a Republican senator who had served on the wartime committee that made Truman's reputation.) District court judgeships are to a significant degree in the gift of the senators from that state who are members of the president's party, and who by the rules of senatorial courtesy can usually prevent the Judiciary Committee from considering any nomination they dislike. Lyndon Johnson when majority leader put a stop on *all* judicial nominations until Eisenhower picked a friend of his for a district court in Texas. (Thirteen nominations were sitting under the dust in the Judiciary Committee's in-box before the president gave up and proposed Johnson's friend for the vacant seat.) Goldman's book is replete with situations where a complicated negotiation promotes a district judge to the circuit court, leaving a vacancy on the district bench for a senator's choice. New York senators Daniel Patrick Moynihan (a Democrat) and Alphonse D'Amato (a Republican) worked out a deal whereby when the president was a Democrat D'Amato got one choice in four and when the president was a Republican Moynihan got one chance in four. D'Amato, who was known as Senator Pothole because of his assiduous attention to the pork-barrel demands of his constituents, took his function seriously in the judicial area, and the federal district courts in both the Southern (Manhattan) and Eastern (Brooklyn) districts in that state are still unusually distinguished.

During the Truman administration, the American Bar Association established a Standing Committee on Federal Judiciary to give ratings to candidates for judgeships. There were at first four possible ratings—exceptionally well qualified, well qualified, qualified, and unqualified. Truman liked to say in public that the appointment of federal judges was the most important thing he did, and in theory he welcomed the ABA's original modus operandi, which was the submission of a list of four to six candidates the lawyers would like the president to consider. After the committee had successfully lobbied against two of his nominees, he became somewhat less enthusiastic, but a scandal in the Justice Department forced a reorganization that brought in Ross Malone, a New Mexican lawyer who was on the ABA Board of Governors, to be deputy attorney general. Malone negotiated a treaty with the ABA by which the Justice Department would submit to the ABA committee the names under consideration to fill judicial vacancies before anyone was announced to the public. The Judiciary Committee would learn and could publicize the rating the ABA assigned.

The Truman administration was winding down, and in fact Truman made no nominations under the new system, but Dwight Eisenhower and his attorney general, Herbert Brownell, found it in place in 1953 and kept it as part of the formal procedure. In his memoirs, Eisenhower wrote that he told Brownell "that I would appoint no one who did not have the approval of the American Bar Association." (Before names went to the ABA, however, they were run through the Republican National Committee.) After 1956, the nominee's ABA rating was included with the Justice Department recommendation that went to the Senate. Brownell, a Wall Street lawyer from Nebraska, was a sophisticated attorney general with a strong belief that appointing judges widely admired in the legal community would be good politics. Still, there are limits, and Goldman reports that 6 percent of Eisenhower's appointees were rated "not qualified" by the ABA.

In fairness, it should also be noted that the ABA ratings were not always authoritative. The standing committee had a standing rule against anyone older than sixty, its members didn't think much of women or blacks, and its domination by the establishment meant that lawyers from the civil rights or environmental movements were rarely praised. James R. Browning, later chief judge of the Ninth Circuit, who had been secretary of the Supreme Court for three years and was highly admired by its justices, was rated "not qualified" for the circuit by the ABA in the Kennedy years, partly no doubt because of his "liberal" political views, but also because he had been working in Washington, and the lawyers the ABA committee consulted on a Ninth Circuit appointment were living on the West Coast. Left-wing law professor Anthony Amsterdam suggested that "screening for the lower courts is a matter of asking round over the lunch table at whatever restaurant gets the carriage trade for the local commercial lawyers."[21]

The more the courts are perceived as making policy, the greater the emphasis a president will put on placing on the bench, and especially on the Supreme Court, judges who he believes share his views. In the Nixon administration, a young White House staffer named Tom Charles Huston wrote a paper urging the thought that "through his judicial appointments, a President has the opportunity to influence the course of national affairs for a quarter of a century after he leaves office. . . ." The Warren Court, Huston noted shrewdly, had "opted for active combat in the political arena, and judges have thereby forfeited their claim to impartiality and detachment. . . . *In approaching the bench, it is necessary to remember that the decision as to who will make the decisions affects what decisions will be made.*" (Italics in the original.)[22] The memo went to H. R. Haldeman, the president's chief of staff, who showed it to Nixon, who liked it a lot and passed it to Deputy Attorney General Richard Kleindienst with the notation "RN *agrees.*" Meanwhile, Nixon's attorney general, John Mitchell, had announced that the new administration would no longer consult the ABA. He showed that he meant it by keeping the ABA in the dark while he and Nixon decided that Warren Burger, author of numerous opinions and speeches about how the Warren Court had crippled law enforcement, should succeed Earl Warren as chief justice.

This was not the only vacancy on the Court in the spring of 1969. While sitting on the bench, President Johnson's buddy Abe Fortas, who had never much wanted to be a Supreme Court justice, had quietly accepted speaking fees and consultancies from educational institutions and foundations controlled by friends. The press machine at the Nixon White House took the opportunities Fortas had offered to create the appearance of great scandal and Fortas returned to the private practice of law. Nixon, who had promised in his campaign that he would appoint a Southern conservative to the Supreme Court, nominated Clement Haynsworth, a plausible judge on the Fourth Circuit Court of Appeals, for the vacancy. Haynsworth when young had been involved in various anti-union activities, had voted in cases where arguably he had a pecuniary interest (an especially damaging charge given the reasons Fortas had been forced out), and had given no support to the Warren Court's civil rights decisions. His enemies beat him in the Senate. Attorney General Mitchell then found a much less plausible appeals court judge, G. Harrold Carswell, who was an undistinguished judge and whose private life was a mess beyond the imaginings of the earnest conservatives who supported him. After Carswell, too, was beaten on the Senate floor, Nixon gave up on the South and nominated Burger's childhood friend Harry Blackmun. This experience left Nixon sour on Tom Charles Huston's suggestion, but it was front and center in the White House when Ronald Reagan took office ten years later.

Reagan really and truly disliked what he knew of the decisions of the Warren Court, including those affirmed by the Burger Court, and unlike his predecessors Reagan had no friends or former colleagues who were candidates to be a justice. His administration, writes the political scientist David Alistair Yalof, aimed "at influencing judicial action directly by fundamentally changing the political makeup of the courts. Early in Reagan's first term the selection of conservative judges at all levels of the federal judiciary assumed its place as a central element in his administration's overall political strategy."[23] Campaigning, Reagan had promised to nominate the first female Supreme Court justice, and his attorney general,

William French Smith, told him that Sandra Day O'Connor on the Arizona Court of Appeals was a good one, which meant that he started with someone who was not conservative on all issues. His most doctrinaire nominee, Antonin Scalia, refused (not unreasonably) to testify about his beliefs to the Senate Judiciary Committee—he wouldn't even answer a question about whether he thought Marshall had been right in *Marbury v. Madison*. He sneaked under the radar while senators who might have fought him concentrated their fire on the simultaneous elevation of Rehnquist from associate to chief. It is significant that every one of Reagan's five nominations to the Court (two of the five didn't make it) was already an appeals court judge.

It is also true that justices frequently let down the presidents who appointed them for political reasons. Theodore Roosevelt never forgave Justice Holmes for voting against him in the *Northern Securities* case, and Truman was furious at Justice Clark for being part of the six-vote majority that forbade the president's seizure of the steel mills in the Korean War. People's views can change with time on the bench. Harry Blackmun when new to the bench voted so often with Chief Justice Warren Burger that the press spoke of the two as "the Minnesota Twins," but by the second five years of his time on the Court he was voting more often with the liberal William Brennan than with his conservative Chief.[24] The Reagan administration crusaded for the reversal of *Roe v. Wade*, but two of Reagan's three appointees, Justice O'Connor and Justice Kennedy, helped form the majority in *Planned Parenthood v. Casey* to reaffirm Blackmun's central finding in *Roe v.*

Wade. The Oxford Companion to the Supreme Court of the United States, published in 1992, argued that Justice David Souter, appointed to the Supreme Court in 1990 by George H. W. Bush, was likely to be part of a new conservative majority; in 1991, "he voted with Chief Justice William H. Rehnquist in 86 percent of cases."[25] But he voted with O'Connor and Kennedy in *Casey*, and by the end of the decade, Justice Souter was probably the least conservative member of that bench. When Justice Blackmun, who had made a similar journey, retired from the Court in 1994, Souter sent him a letter that illustrates the desired relations within the Court: "[f]or four terms you have been to me the wisest and kindest elder brother that a junior justice could ever dream of having."[26]

4

The Constitution mentions a chief justice exactly once, as the person who will preside when the Senate constitutes itself as a court to hear articles of impeachment against a president. From Washington to Grover Cleveland, presidents appointed a "chief justice of the Supreme Court of the United States." When Cleveland appointed Melville Fuller, however, for reasons nobody has ever explained, the new justice was sworn in as simply the chief justice of the United States, and that form has persisted. In recent years the job of chief justice has indeed become much larger and more difficult than the job of associate justice, involving administrative responsibility for more than 20,000 employees.

It is the Chief (with the consent of the Judicial Conference, which he chairs), who appoints the director and deputy director of the Administrative Office of the U.S. Federal Courts. He chairs the board of the Federal Judicial Center, where the system's research and training programs are developed. Twice a year there are meetings of the Judicial Conference of the United States, which consists of the chief judges of the twelve geographic and one subject-matter circuits plus one district judge from each circuit; the chief justice presides at the meetings, the associates do not attend. The Judicial Conference deals with rule changes and budgets, and works mostly through committees of federal judges; the chief justice appoints all the members of the committees. (The Chief also appoints all the judges on the FISA court, which is authorized under the Foreign Intelligence Surveillance Act to give the FBI and the National Security Agency extraordinary powers to tap phones and seize information when the government alleges terrorist skullduggery. This is the court George W. Bush decided a president could ignore when he wanted to tap telephones.) The Supreme Court as a whole approves any rule changes before they are submitted to Congress; otherwise the justices have no role in administration. By a tradition dating back to the time when justices rode circuit, each associate justice is responsible for hearing emergency appeals from one or two circuits, and that justice will participate in the ceremonies around the annual meeting of his *circuit's* judicial conference. But that's a social occasion.

Political scientists distinguish between "social leadership" and "task leadership" in small-group decision making. The chief justice, ideally, should do both. William Howard Taft, a genial fellow who had been a successful colonial administrator in the Philippines before he became a not very successful president, handled the social part of the job with easy aplomb. Among other things, he got Justice McReynolds to shake hands with Justice Brandeis. "Things go happily in the conference room," Brandeis wrote to Felix Frankfurter, describing the change when Taft took over from Chief Justice Edward White. "The judges go home less tired emotionally and less weary physically."[27] Because the justices spend so much time with each other, all alone in the conference room, the social leadership question is profoundly important. Task leadership can be delegated—behind the scenes, Taft relied on Justice Willis Van Devanter to make assignments and get the work out—but social leadership is a necessity. Charles Evans Hughes was an immensely imposing figure who had been governor of New York and secretary of state and had gone to bed on election night in 1916 convinced that he was the next president. He then became by far the most successful corporate lawyer of his time. Returning to the Court, he ran a tight but happy ship; when the argumentative Harlan Fiske Stone succeeded him, "It took the Court twice the amount of conference time to decide the same number of cases decided by the Hughes Court."[28]

No doubt chief justices can have agendas, but in the end they are controlled or at least limited by the documents, the precedents, the political tone, the *function* of the institution. Marshall was a nationalist, but had to admit in *Barron v. Baltimore* that the Court was not empowered to apply the Bill of Rights to state actions. (This attitude interestingly survived the post–Civil War Fourteenth Amendment that arguably was intended to extend the scope of the Bill of Rights; not until 1925 in the *Gitlow* case did the Court insist that states could not legislate against free speech.) Warren Burger became chief justice because Nixon liked some tough-on-crime speeches he had made while on the D.C. Circuit, but Burger found that the idea of limits on search and interrogation by the nation's police forces had been built into the culture, including the culture of law enforcement.

In his book about the Supreme Court, Chief Justice Rehnquist sought to clothe himself in the robes of Justice Holmes. His philosophy, he argued, like Holmes's, allowed maximum freedom to the legislatures, especially the state legislatures, where experiment can thrive. His guiding belief, at least in his book, was that policy is made by legislatures. Courts convert that policy into judgments in specific cases, giving states immunity from federal law as the Supreme Court sees fit. Starting in 1990, Justice Rehnquist's crusade to enhance the powers and especially the immunities of the states allowed state universities to violate copyright, patent, and trademark laws, denied a student raped at college the right to sue the college for failure to protect her, and permitted a state marine facility to discriminate among users in ways prohibited by federal law. As Senior Judge John T. Noonan Jr. of the Ninth Circuit—Jesuit trained, Republican noted earlier, and my Harvard classmate (appointed to the bench by Ronald Reagan)—blew his stack book-length, and the argument is worth noting:

"The Court has conceived itself as a neutral umpire above the fray. It does not think of itself as a player. It does not look at itself as an entity wielding the nation's power. It identifies with the Constitution itself. Identification of this sort confers upon it invisibility to itself.

"Abstractness accompanies this invisibility. The court's decisions here are driven by abstractions. A mind-set, not uncommon in judges, rejoices in rules because the rules appear to provide certainties. Recitation of the rules boxes the facts into established categories. The expenditure of energy in thought is reduced.

". . . Facts should drive cases. . . . Forget the facts, and you forget the persons helped or hurt by the decisions.

"For the Supreme Court, proceeding as it appears to proceed in these cases with an agenda, the facts are of minor importance and the persons affected are worthy of almost no attention. The court is focused on the large questions of constitutional law and on grand conceptions, such as sovereignty. The people and their problems that have been grists for the constitutional mill are incidental."[29]

In 2005, perhaps because illness had reduced his influence, history seemed to catch up with Justice Rehnquist. The Supreme Court by its nature is a nationalizing body. Its function in governance is to make sure important laws are the same everywhere in the country. Rehnquist and Thomas had held the fort against the logic of their job and the history of their Court. Thomas went so far as to renounce the claim that the states'-rightsers were merely giving texts their literal meaning. ("The preeminent purpose of state sovereign immunity," Thomas wrote grandly in ruling that the Federal Maritime Commission might order a privately owned but not a state-owned marina to find a berth for a cruise ship, "is to accord States the dignity that is consistent with their status as sovereign entities. . . . We have understood the Eleventh Amendment to stand not so much for what it says, but for the presupposition of our constitutional structure which it confirms."[30]) The historian Bernard Bailyn notes an oddity in Justice Thomas's opinions from the 1990s: In the period 1995–99, he cited *The Federalist* (presumably authoritative on the Founders' intent) less often than any of his brethren—but he led the bench in the number of times he cited *The Anti-Federalist*, the arguments of those who wished to see the draft Constitution defeated.[31]

The Rehnquist Court in his last days on it ruled over his dissent that the state of California could not legitimize the medical use of marijuana when federal law prohibited possession of the weed. And later that week the Court, with Rehnquist and Scalia and Thomas in the minority, okayed as constitutional a municipal condemnation and acquisition of people's homes for the purpose of building a hotel and convention center in a bad area of New London, Connecticut. The previous year, the Court had approved the enforcement of wetland restrictions on property owners' right to build, delivering a body blow to a doctrine Rehnquist had pushed forward, that the Constitution prohibited governments from "taking" property without compensation, and that regulations that reduced the value of property constituted a "taking."

Rehnquist's triumph as an administrator was a deep cut in the number of cases his Court heard during the course of a term. In the last days of Warren Burger, the Court accepted and decided almost two hundred cases a year; the Rehnquist

Court heard fewer than one hundred. Noonan's charge of abstraction holds: Rehnquist had less interest in the plight of the unlucky, or the Court's function in redressing balances, than any chief justice since Taft. His court put cases on the docket because the circuit courts or the state supreme courts disagreed in their interpretations of federal law or the federal Constitution—or sloppy work in the Congress demanded judicial pronouncement on what the law means—or new technologies demanded redefinition of old principles—or the government was doing something arguably beyond its legislated or constitutional authority. In fairness, it should be noted that on occasion even this very conservative court took time to vindicate the rights of very unimportant people, like the Haitian immigrant who was deported from his wife and kids because he had been involved in an automobile accident while DUI. Also that one does not hear from this part of the firing line the twaddle about "finding" law rather than "making" law that afflicts the political arguments about the selection of judges. Justice Rehnquist knew perfectly well that courts cannot avoid legislating interstitially—in molecular, as Holmes put it, rather than molar motion.

5

There remains the question of whether the U.S. Supreme Court is a court at all. Charles Curtis more than fifty years ago said it was not, and that anyone who believed it was had simply not been paying attention. Certainly, as Judge Noonan complained, the modern Supreme Court lacks what we have

earlier considered the first attributes of a court—the requirement to hear what comes before you, and concentration on
the litigants and the resolution of the specific dispute that
brought the matter before the bench. Even the case of the
Haitian immigrant fighting deportation as an immoral person
because he had driven a car under the influence was heard in
the Supreme Court not because an injustice had been done to
him but because the Immigration and Naturalization Service
had become cavalier in its definitions of the "crimes" that disqualified immigrants from becoming citizens. Once upon a
time, the first rule of decision in the Supreme Court was that
if a decision could be made without getting to the larger constitutional or philosophical issue in a case, the decision would
be anchored in the specifics, not the general principles. But if
the Court is to take only eighty-odd cases a year, the criteria
for selection must be the importance of the larger questions
embedded in the dispute.

It is a significant fact that most of the great figures in the
history of the Court had never been judges in any court be-
fore they were appointed to the Supreme Court. The list in-
cludes Marshall, Story, Taney, Miller, Hughes, Brandeis, Black,
Frankfurter, Jackson, Powell, Warren, and Rehnquist. The
Court at the end of the Roosevelt administration included
Hugo Black from the Senate, Robert Jackson from the attor-
ney general's office, Felix Frankfurter from the Harvard Law
School, and Harlan Fiske Stone from the Columbia Law
School, Frank Murphy from a governor's chair, and William
Douglas from the Securities and Exchange Commission. To
the extent that they were supposed to predict the results of

their decisions, they had experience outside the courts and the law schools to help their understanding.

One comes back to the unique relationship. In public and in private, the justices say that social relations among the nine are warm. They spend more time with one another than most husbands and wives, go to one another's grandsons' christenings. It is a work environment unlike any other. Somebody once suggested to Justice Robert Jackson that it took a justice three years to become comfortable at the Supreme Court. Jackson said, "More like five." There have been some famous feuds—the anti-Semite McReynolds would not speak to Brandeis; Black and Jackson and then Black and Douglas were at daggers drawn after a decade of partnership; Blackmun, who had been best man at Burger's wedding, did not attend Mrs. Burger's funeral. Still, there remains the requirement of the *system*. "When you are going to serve on a court of that kind for the rest of your productive days," Earl Warren told public television shortly after his retirement, "you accustom yourself to the institution like you do to the institution of marriage, and you realize that you can't be in a brawl every day and still get any satisfaction out of life."[32] Rehnquist no doubt deserves the credit for the good cheer universally reported in recent years. In cementing personal relationships, efficiency itself improves tempers and promotes good manners. And behind Rehnquist's sourpuss visage and the sourpuss politics there was apparently a very amusing man—and a very fair Chief, who distributed the opinion-writing chores in his gift to make sure everyone had interesting work. (Roberts by all reports has sustained the atmosphere. He even plays in the poker game.)

In 2001, there were tales that personal relations on the Court had been disrupted by the disputes over *Bush v. Gore*, when the Supreme Court in effect chose the president of the United States following an indecisive election. Justices on both sides denied the stories, but they may have been true for a time. From the outside, the question was why a court that has historically fought to control its docket, make its own decisions about which cases it will hear, took jurisdiction in this case.

Books have been written, men have died, and worms have eaten 'em, but they are all, I suspect, too rational. The position here, essentially Judge Posner's position, is that the Court had to take the case because there was no other authoritative body. The Florida Supreme Court, all Democrats, were guaranteed to be in conflict with the Republican-controlled Florida state legislature and the egregious Florida secretary of state, a Republican woman with greater ambitions. If the decision about which slate of electors to accept were left, as the Constitution left it, in the hands of the House of Representatives, months of nastiness would end with a less-than-authoritative vote, one per state, each state giving their single vote where the majority of its House delegation wished to put it.

The villainy in this matter was the decision by the television networks and the wire services to declare George W. Bush the winner of the election when in fact there was no winner. Confirming what everybody had been told by the most public authority figures in the country might be unfair, for there could be little doubt that many more votes intended for Gore had not been counted—because of a confusing ballot in Palm Beach County and organized disenfranchisement in the black neighborhoods of the geographically huge municipality of Jacksonville. Still, telling the Bush supporters that the election the media said they had won was to be reversed in the courts would have inspired strong, even violent resistance by elements in this society—many of them established, tightly organized, and rich—who were not used to losing. On the other side, the people who had been told by the networks that their candidate had lost were mostly people who were used to losing, and would accept the result. In retrospect, it is not obvious what the Court could have done to validate a Gore victory, especially given the nature and habits of the leadership of the House. It was much easier, and arguably better for the country for the Court simply to tell the public that the network anchors got it right.

This was the second time the Supreme Court had in effect decided an election. In 1876 Democrat Samuel J. Tilden of New York had won the popular vote, and had received more votes than Rutherford B. Hayes in four Southern states, all of which Hayes needed to win in the electoral college. The Republican-dominated governments of these former Confederate states, which had not yet regained full self-government and were occupied by Union troops, manipulated the ballot count. Presidents were not inaugurated in those days until March, so there was some time to sort it out. Congress appointed a commission of five representatives (three Democrats), five senators (three Republicans) and five Supreme Court justices, one of whom was supposed to be neutral, to determine which electors would be permitted to vote in the electoral college. The individual neutral, unfortunately, had left the Court to take a seat in the Senate, and the substitute for him, Justice Joseph Bradley, was a dedicated Republican. At first, apparently, Bradley was inclined to elect Tilden, but his friends prevailed. Hayes took office with a quid pro quo to the Democrats that federal troops would be withdrawn from the South.

Though there is no point in saying that the Supreme Court is "wrong" in its interpretation of the Constitution—remember Justice Jackson's comment that "we are not final because we are infallible, we are infallible because we are final." There was more farce than logic in Justice Kennedy's solemn opinion, unsigned, per curiam for the Court, that recounts in selected districts with arbitrary counting rules would deprive voters in other districts of due process and the equal protection of the laws. Kennedy also suggested that the Court never ever wanted to see a case like this again. Invited by the opinions of the Court to establish some other system to deal with disputed elections, Congress ignored the problem, as it usually does. It is the prerogative of legislatures, and the reason we have "activist courts."

6

After half of a term, no one—certainly not this occasional visitor—can confidently predict where the new chief justice will take the Court. The great question before the Court in the closing years of the Bush Administration is obviously the power of the president. Not to put too fine a point on the matter, the White House since late 2001 has declared that a "unitary executive" has the power to arrest anyone as a danger to the state and keep that individual in prison without charges (let alone the opportunity to respond to charges in open court) for so long as is convenient for the government. In addition, the executive branch has arrogated to itself the power to declare any information "secret," as the Russians and the Chinese do, not to be revealed to or by the press. One notes again with horror the complicity of the press in seeking punishment for those in the White House who leaked the name of a CIA agent to selected reporters. To the extent that the court runs for cover—as it did in the various Red Scares of the 1910s, 1920s, 1940s, and 1950s, Americans could lose much of what their parents considered their birthright.

There can be little doubt that Learned Hand was right— that a constitution only a court can save cannot be saved. But the court has brakes that it can apply to make time for the public and the Congress to do a more sensitive cost-benefit analysis between the guarantees of the First Amendment and repressive actions taken allegedly and sometimes truly as defenses against terrorism. The decision invalidating the creation of military commissions to try the denizens of Guantánamo is less encouraging than its reception indicated, for Chief Justice Roberts had okayed these courts as an appeals court judge before his elevation, and the opinion that stressed the nation's treaty obligations was by an eighty-six-year-old justice. Perhaps the outstanding statement of the true obligations of the people who work in government was given by the future Justice Brandeis when he was counsel for Louis Glavis, who had leaked the fact that Taft's secretary of the interior was conspiring with private interests to loot the national forests.

"The danger in America," Brandeis told a congressional

committee, "is not of insubordination, but it is of too compla-
cent obedience to the will of superiors. With this great government building up . . . we need men in subordinate places
who will think for themselves and will think and act in full
recognitation of their obligations. . . . They cannot be worthy
of the respect and admiration of the people unless they add to
the virtue of obedience some other virtues—the virtue of
manliness, of truth, of courage, of willingness to risk positions, of the willingness to risk criticisms, of the willingness to
risk the misunderstandings that so often come when people
do the heroic thing."[33]

14 THE LOSS OF AUTHORITY

*Our judicial system . . . is intellectually the weakest part of our govern-
ment. It has the least opportunity to get adequate information on the issues
which it has to decide. Which of us who wants to inform himself on one of
the principal current issues will be satisfied with listening for a few hours to
a couple of lawyers and reading their briefs?*

—Morris Raphael Cohen[1]

*[C]hanged conditions often deprive precedents of reliability and cast us more
than we would choose upon our own judgment. But we act in these matters,
not by authority of our competence, but by force of our commission.*

—Justice Robert H. Jackson[2]

*When the Realists exploded the Langdellian myth of a science of law, they
replaced it with the idea of law as a purposive activity. The exercise of legal
power now must be premised on its undocumented connection to the realization of accepted public values. A logical methodology whose functional
underpinnings cannot be analyzed in legal argument seems unlikely to survive in the modern administrative state.*

—Jerry L. Mashaw[3]

———————————

WE CONTRAST TWO SUPREME COURT
opinions, twelve years apart, both asserting that
the Constitution protects a right of privacy:
"Today," Justice Tom Clark wrote firmly in *Mapp v. Ohio* in

1961, "we hold that all evidence obtained by searches and seizures in violation of the Constitution is . . . inadmissible in a state court. . . . Having once recognized that the right to privacy embodied in the Fourth Amendment is enforceable against the States, and that the right to be secure against rude invasions of privacy by state officers is, therefore, constitutional in origin, we can no longer permit that right to remain an empty promise. . . ."

In 1973, Justice Harry Blackmun, who had been counsel to the Mayo Clinic before he became a Supreme Court justice, struck down state laws prohibiting abortion. "We forthwith acknowledge," he wrote, "our awareness of the sensitive and emotional nature of the abortion controversy, of the vigorous opposing views, even among physicians, and of the deep and seemingly absolute convictions that the subject inspires. One's philosophy, one's experiences, one's exposure to the raw edges of human existence, one's religious training, one's attitudes toward life and family and their values, and the moral standards one establishes and seeks to observe, are all likely to influence and to color one's thinking and conclusions about abortion. In addition, population growth, pollution, poverty, and racial overtones tend to complicate and not to simplify the problem."

Clark closes the question, in the established manner of the court of last resort. You may agree, you may disagree, but the law is the law. Blackmun opens the door to all sorts of discussions and objections. And he got them.

2

The returning visitor cannot ignore the loss of intellectual distinction that characterizes American law at the beginning of the twenty-first century. I do not say this gladly. Law was once a magisterial study, a subject that could entrance great minds for all of their lives. "When I think thus of the Law," Justice Oliver Wendell Holmes Jr. told a meeting of the Suffolk Bar Association in 1885, "I see a princess mightier than she who once wrought at Bayeux, eternally weaving into her web dim figures of the ever-lengthening past—figures too dim to be noticed by the idle, too symbolic to be interpreted except by her pupils, but to the discerning eye disclosing every painful step and every world-shaking contest by which mankind has worked and fought its way from savage isolation to organic social life."[4]

Lord Mansfield had trumpeted to England, *"Fiat justitia ruat coelum"*—Let justice be done though the heavens fall.

For Roscoe Pound, the distinction was between what were "merely laws, expressions of the popular will for the time being, [and] law, an expression of reason applied to the relations of man with man and of man with the state."[5]

Law was reason; the extension of reason to a society, the movement from status to contract, was the noblest work of man. Judges served and executed not merely the laws, but law itself.

In truth, this romanticism, this separation of law from life, did not serve the nation or the judges well in the late nineteenth and early twentieth century, when the Supreme Court in the United States insisted that a corporation was a person, and entitled to the same protections against the state that were enjoyed by human beings and guaranteed for them by the Constitution. And here appellate decisions could be imposed on the lower courts, because the corporations had lawyers. Breaking that fallacy, forcing upon the courts a realization that law had *obligations* to society, was the work of two, perhaps three generations of "realists." We have, philosopher John Dewey noted sourly, a government of lawyers, not of men. The world of fact had to intrude on the idealizations of law. It was not understood by the realists, brilliant men but like all men and women prisoners of their time, that the majesty of the law, the ideal of judges enforcing a rule of law, grew from its retrospective nature. The judge finds the facts from the evidence, and, with the help of the advocates in his courtroom, the law that applies to these facts. If the result is distasteful, there may be something wrong with the law, and we ask the legislature to fix the law. But we judges know what the law *is*: Indeed, Chief Justice John Marshall in 1803 made it the backbone of Article III of the Constitution that the judges are *compelled* to tell the world what the law is.

The founder of the school of legal realism, of course, was Justice Oliver Wendell Holmes Jr., born when William Henry Harrison was president and still alive for the inauguration of Franklin D. Roosevelt. He enlisted in the army at the start of the Civil War and fought for three years, at Antietam and Vicksburg, in the Peninsula and Wilderness campaigns. He served on the Supreme Court from 1904 to 1931, following a distinguished career as associate justice and then chief justice of the Massachusetts Supreme Judicial Court. He was already sixty when he came to Washington, with a great reputation as a scholar and teacher. But he thought it important to consider not just legal history but the practical results of legislation and judicial opinion. Law, he once wrote, quoting the nineteenth-century British social philosopher Herbert Spencer, was the governance of the living by the dead. General propositions, he wrote, do not decide concrete cases. And continuity with the past, he wrote, is never a duty, merely a necessity. His father had been a leading poet and essayist of the great days of Boston, a contemporary of Emerson and Thoreau. Holmes was a phrasemaker in the nation's highest tradition.

Though Holmes and his contemporary and friend William James quarreled about almost everything else, Holmes looking at the function of the judge had no quarrel with James, who wrote as though stating something obvious that "given previous laws and a novel case, the judge will twist them into fresh law."[6] A changed world could not be governed by the letter of a law written before the changes had occurred. Law professor and philosopher John Chipman Gray, another Holmes friend and contemporary, once asked, "What was the law in the time of Richard Coeur de Lion on the liability of a telegraph company to the persons to whom a message was sent."[7] And that sort of problem never goes away. Asked to rule in 1968 on whether one of the newfangled cable television companies had to pay broadcasters for the signal it was carrying over the hills and selling to hotels that otherwise could not offer their customers the programs, Justice Potter Stewart (whose majority opinion said it didn't) commented bitterly, "We take the Copyright Act of 1909 as we find it."[8] It is simply childish to demand that judges "find" preexisting law to decide cases arising under a technology or in social and economic circumstances quite different from that in use when the "preexisting law" was written. But this does not, as Holmes often wrote, give judges authority to write new law. "I should always be sorry," he wrote in a letter, "if I could not get any reason more definite than [that the decision is] in consonance with our sense of justice."[9]

"I always say the chief end of man is to form general propositions," he wrote to the English judge Frederick Pollock, "—adding that no general proposition is worth a damn."[10]

Someone who lived as long as Holmes did was likely to come down at different times on different sides of complex issues, and he did. In a letter to John C. H. Wu, a Chinese legal philosopher and judge, a protégé by mail, he once said that he hated justice, and in correspondence with Pollock he said that he hated facts. Perhaps the most remarkable thing about him was his willingness to consider and adopt (or adapt) new ideas. After Wu recommended John Dewey's *Experience and Nature* to him in 1927, when he was eighty-six-years old, he wrote Pollock that though the book was "incredibly ill-written" it showed "a feeling of intimacy with the inside of the cosmos that I found unequaled. So methought God would have spoken had He been inarticulate."[11]

In 1908, Louis D. Brandeis, a very successful Boston lawyer who was devoting much of his energy to making a case for social legislation, wrote the first "Brandeis brief" to argue on behalf of the state for the constitutionality of an Oregon law forbidding employers to work women more than ten hours a day. Only two pages of a brief that ran well over a hundred pages were devoted to legal argument; the rest was a survey of scientific and medical literature on the effects of fatigue on women.[12] The defense of the Oregon statute was, oddly enough, an uphill battle, for the Supreme Court three years before, in the high-water mark of its concern for "liberty of contract," had buried a New York State effort to limit the hours worked by bakers. The purpose of the Brandeis brief was to demonstrate that the legislature had good reason to write the law. This was not—and the distinction is crucial—an argument that the Court must decide a case so that justice is served to the litigants or that correct public policy can be created. It was an argument that the legislature is generally empowered to enact laws promoting the public welfare, and that those laws should be protected from judicial interference if the state can produce plausible reasons for enacting them. The Brandeis brief looks backward, and accepting its arguments does not commit the Court to the belief in any philosophy or the promotion of any policy. Courts had been saying for centuries that their measure was what a reasonable man would do. Brandeis was merely trying to uphold the reasonableness of his client.

From Holmes's point of view, though he and Brandeis were allies on the Court, the Brandeis brief was unnecessary and maybe unwise. Holmes had already written three years earlier, dissenting in the *Lochner* case, that "the word 'liberty' is perverted when it is held to prevent the natural outcome of a dominant opinion, unless it can be said that a rational and fair man necessarily would submit that the statute proposed would infringe fundamental principles as they have been understood by the traditions of our people and our law. It does not need research to show that no such sweeping condemnation can be passed upon the statute before us."[13]

When Holmes looked forward to the results of a decision, it was in the most general terms, and it was usually to confirm the judgment of others. Writing to affirm the constitutionality of the Arizona Workmen's Compensation law (it was a concurring opinion, originally commissioned as the opinion of the Court but too strong for his brethren), Holmes noted merely that "there is no more certain way of securing attention to the safety of the men, an unquestionably constitutional object of legislation, than by holding the employer liable for accidents. . . . They probably will happen a good deal less often when the employer knows that he must answer for them if they do."[14] The common law, of course, was mostly the codification of common sense as applied to the times in which the judges wrote it. The infuriated minority opinions in the workmen's compensation cases proclaimed (by Justice James McReynolds) that it would "stifle enterprise, produce discontent, strife, idleness and pauperism" and (by Justice Joseph McKenna, already senile but still furious) that "it seems to me to be the very foundation of right—of the essence of liberty as it is of morals—to be free from liability if one is free from fault. . . . There are principles of constitutional law as there are precepts of moral law that reach the conviction of aphorisms."[15]

3

McKenna was a fool, and McReynolds a vindictive, mean, vicious man who should never have been a judge. (His law clerk in the 1936 term kept notes of his behavior; they were published in 2004, and they are horrifying.[16]) Those who wish to idealize Woodrow Wilson should remember that it was Wilson who put McReynolds on the bench, partly because he agreed with the president on antitrust matters and partly to quell a scandal that had arisen when he was accused of using his position as attorney general to delay the prosecution of a Mann Act offense (transporting women for immoral purposes) against the son-in-law of a politically well-connected Washingtonian. (In those days, judicial nominees were not questioned as they are now by the Senate Judiciary Committee, so the rumors of impropriety did not endanger the confirmation.) But there is a certain grandeur about their statements, appealing as they do to the eternal verities enshrined in existing law (in this case, a previous generation's interpretation of the Fourteenth Amendment to the Constitution). Twenty years later, McReynolds signed on to an opinion by Justice George Sutherland that invalidated the Bituminous Coal Conservation Act of 1935, and they were famously rebuked in a dissent by Justice Benjamin Cardozo, who said, "A great principle of constitutional law is not susceptible of comprehensive statement as an adjective."[17]

The economist Henry Wallich once picked up Oscar Wilde's aphorism that experience is the name we give to our past mistakes and expanded it forward with the addition that *policy* is the name we give to our future mistakes. So long as law is reason, expressed in the inheritance of decided cases, and so long as the purpose of the decision is to resolve an actual dispute, judges can insist that they know best, and the world will nod approvingly. The life of the law has been experience. When a judicial decision changes or makes government policy, it can be argued, and it may indeed be obvious, that judges are much less well equipped for such tasks than legislators, who are elected to represent the variety of users of law and have access to the entire range of opinion (not just the evidence in a case) about what a choice among conflicting policies can achieve. Public policy, an English judge wrote as long ago as 1824, "is a very unruly horse and when once you get astride it you never know where it will carry you."[18]

The myths and clichés of law and its role in the society all rest on the *retrospective* nature of judicial action. Evidence is from the past, law is from the past, the cases are things that happened in the past; the majesty and mystery of law is that its guardians protect tradition and custom. "The third branch," wrote the late Gerald T. Dunne in his history of the Missouri Supreme Court, "sits not to serve the wish of the present but to enforce the will of the past."[19] The judge's obligation is to deal fairly with the litigants, not with the world at large. The "Brandeis brief" with its mass of social data brings before the appeals court great quantities of evidence that was not in fact introduced at the trial. Today, after a generation of "sociological jurisprudence," judicial opinions *predict* the results of decisions, and attack or defend them by arguing about their impact on behavior.

The most significant moment in the Senate hearings on the confirmation of Judge John Roberts to be chief justice came when Senator Edward Kennedy praised an opinion on affirmative action in university admissions by Justice Sandra Day O'Connor, who had written that judges in deciding such cases had to be aware of the impact their decisions would have out in the real world. Did Roberts agree? " 'Well, Senator,' Judge Roberts replied, 'I think I can answer the specific questions you asked, because, as you phrased the question—Do you agree with her that it's important to look at the real-world significance and impact?—and I can certainly say that I do think that that is the appropriate approach, without commenting on the outcome or the judgment in a particular case.' "[20] Though not recognized as such in any of the reports on the hearings, this statement was a coded reassurance to the senators that Roberts would not seek to overturn *Roe v. Wade*, considering the real-world significance and impact of criminalizing an action taken by more than a million American women every year. The statement put him squarely in the mainstream of the modern Court.

Perhaps the most interesting and inevitable—and important—example of the shift from retrospection to prediction, from experience to policy, is in the question of "privity." It was Cardozo who did it, in 1916, as a judge on the New York Court of Appeals in a case involving the new Buick Motor Car Co. A rear wheel on a car belonging to a Mr. MacPherson had spun off its axle, causing grievous damage to the car. The lesser New York courts, following long-established principles in the common law, had required MacPherson to sue the dealer from whom he bought the car because he had no direct relationship with the manufacturer. For the many centuries in Europe and America when the person who made things sold them himself, the old rules of "privity" served both producer and consumer. In twentieth-century America it was obviously nonsense to say that the purchaser of an automobile that blew up could sue only the dealer who had sold him the car, but the reasoning was clear enough. In the law as Cardozo found it, relationship created obligation. The buyer had a relationship with the dealer, not with the manufacturer. A court that permitted the buyer to sue the manufacturer *created* a relationship that had not existed before. But common sense said that if the manufacturer was responsible for the proper functioning of the automobile he would be more careful.

There was a limit to how far Cardozo would go. "Somewhere between worship of the past and exaltation of the present," he wrote, "the path of safety will be found." He would not, for example, allow a stockholder to sue the accountant of a company that had lured the stockholder into purchasing its stock by cooking its books. In the "sociological jurisprudence" Cardozo pioneered, results were central, and the overriding effort was to make similar situations yield similar results. Otherwise, law could not guide behavior. Similarly, in 1961, Roger J. Traynor as chief justice of California withdrew sovereign immunity from the state's publicly owned hospitals, seeing no reason why people injured by medical malpractice in private hospitals could sue but those injured in public hospitals could not.[21] Similarly, in 1977, the Missouri Supreme Court ruled that the state's highway department could be sued for injuries caused by an employee, but then that state's legislature passed a law restoring "sovereign immunity" to state agencies.

(There was of course no way Benjamin Cardozo or Roger Traynor or anyone else could have foreseen a future when law firms would pull a sound truck up to the gates of a factory where once asbestos had been processed and call upon workers leaving for the day to sign up and get their $10,000.)

Like Holmes, Cardozo was a great scholar of the "common law" that grew out of judicial decisions in concrete cases. But "sociological jurisprudence" demanded consonance with contemporary life, not history. The Brandeis brief now became an argument not for the courts to acquiesce in the enforcement of a law passed by the legislature, but for the courts, examining the consequences of the law as it stands, to write new law. Stare decisis, it stands decided, was no longer an unanswerable argument.

In fairness, this was not a brand-new thought. Ruling in the Charles River Bridge case in 1837, Chief Justice Roger B. Taney had simply brushed aside previous opinions that exclusive charters from a state could not simply be revoked by the state. If such views prevailed, "in a country like ours," he wrote, "free, active and enterprising, advancing in numbers and wealth . . . we shall be thrown back to the improvements of the last century, and obliged to stand still until the claims of the old turnpike operations could be satisfied." The states had to be permitted "to avail themselves of the lights of modern science, and to partake of the benefits of those improvements."[22] Justice Story in his 35,000-word dissent wrote that "I stand upon the old law; upon law established more than three centuries ago, in cases contested with as much ability and learning as any of the annals of our jurisprudence."[23]

Chief Justice John Marshall in 1819 had distinguished between "prolix" laws and the concise Constitution, which set goals for the government and gave the Congress the right to take actions "necessary and proper" for the achievement of those goals. ("We must never forget that it is a *constitution* we are expounding."[24]) Chief Justice Charles Evans Hughes in 1934 wrote that "if by the statement that what the Constitution meant at the time of its adoption it means today, it is intended to say that the great clauses of the Constitution must be confined to the interpretation which the Framers, with the conditions and outlook of their time, would have placed upon them, the statement carries its own refutation."[25] But these opinions, too, looked backward, and approved or disapproved the actions of a legislature.

It was not until Earl Warren wrote the opinion of a unanimous court in *Brown v. Board of Education* in 1954 that the Supreme Court took the final step of insisting that the words of the Constitution had to be heard in the context of modern events, and could be construed to command actions by the legislature or the executive, the nation or a state. It was futile to argue that even the Thirty-ninth Congress, elected in the aftermath of the Civil War and strongly weighted to "radical" views, intended to prohibit state-imposed segregation in the United States. The Congress that sent to the states for adoption the Fourteenth Amendment, insuring everyone "due process of law" and "equality before the law," operated itself under rules that segregated the visitors' gallery by race, and ordered the segregation of the District of Columbia schools. In *Plessy v. Ferguson* in 1897, with only one dissent, the Supreme Court cited the law segregating D.C. schools as part of its argument to uphold a Louisiana law that required railroads to offer separate accommodations to "white" and "colored," and equally forbade whites from the colored carriages and blacks from the white carriages. So long as the accommodations were "equal," they could be "separate" without offending the Constitution.

After World War II, moving slowly, slowly to recognize that services segregated by law would never be equal, the Court prohibited the segregation of restaurants and hotels in Washington under the terms of a long-forgotten D.C. law from 1873. At a time when the Senate was not prepared to do *anything* that would interfere with state-required segregation anywhere, the Court, with statements that in these cases "separate" was not really "equal," struck down the insistence of the Southern Railroad that it could limit service to Negroes in its dining cars, ordered the University of Oklahoma to let Negroes sit at any desks and tables available to whites, and denied the Texas University system's claim that a brand-new law school at black Texas State University was "equal" to the long-established Texas University Law School.

The case of Linda Brown and the Kansas law that required her to attend a segregated school far from her home was accepted for hearing by the Supreme Court in June 1952. In October the Court docketed it together with four other cases against school segregation, from South Carolina, Delaware, Virginia, and the District of Columbia. In November, the Court chewed out the Kansas attorney general for failure to file a reply brief, and in December the Court heard three days of argument. Thurgood Marshall argued for Ms. Brown (with an exhibit signed by thirty-two eminent sociologists, anthropologists, and psychologists to demonstrate the evil consequences of racial segregation.[26]) Former Democratic presidential candidate John W. Davis argued on behalf of the state for the maintenance of a "principle so long often announced, so confidently relied upon, so long continued, that it passes the limits of judicial discretion and disturbance."[27] (One notes with some discomfort that this is the argument the "pro-choice" senators made in quizzing Judge Roberts about his attitudes on abortion in his confirmation hearings). The Court was clearly split. As the year ended in June 1953, the justices asked the parties to argue *Brown* again, answering four questions, three backward-looking and one of policy: Should the Fourteenth Amendment be seen as having ended segregation by itself? Did the framers of the amendment contemplate some future Court or Congress doing so? Did the federal government have the power to force states to end segregation? And then, if the court determined that officially segregated schools were unconstitutional, what remedies were available?

Then Chief Justice Frederick Vinson, Truman's crony, died; and the recently elected president Dwight Eisenhower appointed California governor Earl Warren to be the new chief justice. Congress was not in session. Warren came in on an interim appointment, without Senate confirmation, and got to work immediately. Reargument of *Brown* was postponed a couple of months, however, to give him a chance to read the massive briefs.

Which, I guess, he did. Justice Frankfurter had sent a law clerk to the records of the Thirty-ninth Congress to read every word of the debates on the adoption of the Fourteenth

Amendment, and he had reported back that when you asked those records the question of congressional intent in approving the amendment, the answers were "inconclusive." Warren's opinion blandly said without argument or documentation that the historical record was "inconclusive," and in effect added a comment, To hell with it. The Court, Warren wrote, could not "turn the clock back to 1868, when the Fourteenth Amendment was adopted, or even to 1896, when *Plessy v. Ferguson* was written." All this scholarship was a waste of time. Yale law professor Alexander M. Bickel gave the rationale a few years later, on the assumption that the authors of the three post–Civil War amendments were forward-looking people, not an unreasonable assumption. "It is not true," he wrote, "that the Framers intended the Fourteenth Amendment to outlaw segregation or to make applicable to the states all restrictions on government that may be evolved under the Bill of Rights, but they did not foreclose such policies, and may indeed have invited them."[28]

In the orgy of self-congratulation that accompanied the fiftieth anniversary of *Brown v. Board of Education* in 2004, it was all but universally said that the case overruled *Plessy v. Ferguson* and declared an end to "separate but equal." In fact, Chief Justice Warren's ten-page opinion for a unanimous court distinguished education from other aspects of interracial life, and specifically denied the general applicability of the finding that in education separate could not be equal. Indeed, the question, as stated by the Court was "whether *Plessy v. Ferguson* should be held inapplicable to public education." It was not until 1968, long after the passage of the Civil Rights Act, that the Supreme Court denied the relevance of an asserted "equality" in judging public or private policies that promoted segregation.

Comes now Justice Antonin Scalia and says, "Not so fast." He is hostile to the common-law pattern of judging, which he describes as "the mind-set that asks, 'What is the most desirable resolution of this case, and how can any impediments to the achievement of that result be evaded?'"[29] We live in a democracy, Justice Scalia insists, where law is made not in passing by judges deciding cases but by legislators turning bills into acts, and the judge's job is to enforce these laws *as written*. And the words in the laws (and in the federal and state constitutions) must be taken to mean what they meant to the people who wrote them. Chief Justice Hughes may have said it couldn't be done; Justice Scalia says of course it can be done. He calls it "textualism." To look beyond the words of the law to the "intent" of the legislators who wrote the law is to open Pandora's box. Nobody knows what if anything the supporters of a piece of legislation hoped to achieve with it. British judges are not allowed to consider the debates in Parliament that preceded the passage of a law. The "legislative history" in the United States includes the debates on the floor of both houses, but in practice means the "committee report" that passed the bill to the floor for debate and vote. That report is written by staffers, not legislators; most of the time legislators do not read it. Certainly the court seeking to enforce the statute cannot be *bound* by the legislative history. The judges who cite such stuff, Scalia argues, are really common-law judges making law under cover of confusion by amending legislation to make it say what the judges think it "ought" to say.

All of which is true, or mostly true. (Not that Scalia doesn't do it himself: As he said to a Brookings symposium, "You read my opinions. I sin with the rest of them."[30]) No less a figure than Justice Holmes wrote in a letter that "only a day or two ago, when counsel talked of the intention of a legislation, I was indiscreet enough to say I don't care what their intention was, I only want to know what the words mean."[31] The problem is that the words of the law often—perhaps usually—are no more authoritative or meaningful than the legislative history. Legislators don't read the text of the laws they pass any more than they read the committee reports. Many laws on which lawmakers are asked to vote are not in fact readable, consisting as they do of a string of amendments to existing laws, changing three words in subsection 5 of section 2 of article 7 of something already on the books. Speeches on the floor in support or opposition are usually made to empty seats, because debate in the modern legislature is not intended to persuade, just to register. The congressman or state legislator voting aye or nay is doing so because he promised this vote to Teddy or had a phone call from a constituent or a contributor, or is following his leader. The issue before the court may be something that had never occurred to the legislators. John Chipman Gray wrote in the nineteenth century about times "when what the judges have to do is, not to determine what the legislature did mean on a point which was present to its mind, but to guess what it would have intended on a point not present to its mind, if the point had been present."[32]

When laws are indeed novel and start from scratch, they are written in a conference committee by hired legislative draftsman who try to satisfy all the people who are voting for the bill. "Ambiguity" is not the right word; what judges must deal with in many statutes is opacity. And deliberate opacity, too. I once had occasion to quiz the chief of the House of Representatives legislative draftsmen, by common consent the world's best, about a clause I could not understand at all. "Oh," he said, brushing the comment aside, "that was one of those cases—they aren't uncommon—when you could get agreement on language but not on substance." Justice Scalia has it backwards. In modern America, it's the judges who tell the legislators what their laws mean, not the legislators who tell the judges. Judges have to decide cases. Legislators can split votes on procedural questions and duck any real issues for as long as they remain live wires. Fifty years ago, Charles Curtis (lawyer, senior fellow, guru of the Harvard Corporation) noted, "The more Congress says what it means, the less the Court will have to tell Congress what it ought to have meant."[33]

The interpretation of statutes becomes like common law because successor judges assume that the meaning of the act "stands decided" by the first judge to construe it—after all, if the legislature doesn't like what that judge said the statute meant, it can always amend the statute. First decisions on statutes, like precedents in the common law, have what Cardozo called the power of the beaten path. What Justice Scalia proposes is closer than he wants to think to what Henry Hart and Albert Sacks scornfully called "the flagellant theory of statutory interpretation . . . that it is a court's duty to discipline the legislature by taking it literally."[34] This has been known to happen. In December 2004, Judge Jose A. Cabanes, writing for a unanimous three-judge panel of the Second Circuit, remanded for new sentencing procedures the case of Jorge Pabon-Cruz, an eighteen-year-old community college student living with a mentally retarded mother, who helped pay his family's bills by letting his computer be used to distribute child pornography. He was convicted of the maximum charge, and became subject to a law that says, "Any individual who violates . . . this section shall be fined under this title or imprisoned not less than ten years nor more than twenty years, and both." As Judge Cabanes gleefully noted, this makes no sense—and in effect the court remanded the case to trial judge Gerard Lynch (who had felt strongly that ten years was way too much for a first offender who needed money and had nothing to do with procuring the admittedly awful pictures).[35]

Congress *does* occasionally act to overrule a court decision that misinterprets what today's congressmen consider their intent: Between 1967 and 1990 Congress passed legislation to "correct" more than 340 Supreme Court rulings.[36] Usually, however, the legislature has other things on its mind and ignores the court decisions simply because its members don't wish to take the time to revisit legislation. As California chief justice Roger Traynor put it, "There can be idle silence as well as idle talk."[37]

What Justice Scalia is really getting at, of course, is the wild expansion of "rights" that the Court wrote into the Constitution in the back half of the twentieth century. John Marshall himself had noted that a Constitution was to be expounded, and thus expanded, to meet the understandings of the time. In the 1970s, after the deaths of Jackson and

Black and Frankfurter, the intellectual leader of the Court was Justice William J. Brennan Jr., who toward the end of his life proclaimed that "the Constitution embodies the aspirations to social justice, brotherhood, and human dignity that brought this nation. . . . Our Constitution was not intended to preserve a preexisting society but to make a new one."[38] The end result of this mass of decisions, Justice Scalia writes scornfully, is that if "logic fails to produce what in the view of the current Supreme Court is the *desirable* result for the case at hand, then, like good common-law judges, the Court will distinguish its precedents, or narrow them, or if all else fails overrule them, in order that the Constitution might mean what it *ought* to mean."[39] This, too, is not a new problem: Justice Cardozo in the 1920s saw a "wide gap between the use of the individual sentiment of justice as a substitute for law, and its use as one of the tests and touchstones in construing or extending law."[40] There remains the giant difference between seeking justice in the case the judge must decide and seeking to make the law more just looking to the situations of people whose claims are not in fact before the court.

In determining what the Constitution tells him to do, Justice Scalia is a self-proclaimed "originalist," who takes the words of the document to mean now what they meant in the eighteenth century. But we have now lived through a century of logical positivists and semanticists, and if there is one thing certain in the intellectual world it is that words change their meaning. "Citizens" in the Fourteenth and Fifteenth Amendments, which guaranteed the right to vote, did not mean "women" until 1920. In 1873, when Virginia Minor appealed to the U.S. Supreme Court against a decision of the Missouri

Supreme Court denying her the right to vote, the state did not even hire a lawyer to defend itself in Washington; the federal justices did all the work for them. To win women's suffrage, it was necessary to amend the Constitution. Today, for *all* purposes, both "citizens" and "persons" clearly include women, and Justice Scalia, happily married with nine kids, four of them daughters, would not wish it otherwise. There is, moreover, the great simple truth stated by California's chief justice Roger Traynor: "The state acts through its courts as well as through the legislature."[41]

4

By this roundabout route we reach the much-discussed problem of "activist judges" asserting not merely the corrective of judicial review but the power of "judicial sovereignty." Judges are to "find" law, say the opponents of judicial sovereignty, not to write law. This, too, is not a new concern. Carved in stone in the wall of the Missouri Supreme Court building from almost a century ago is a Latin tag "*Jus dicere non dare*"— Speak the law, do not give the law. The argument has not advanced beyond the Latin tag stage—or, rather, has receded from a once significant, even profound discussion to the calling of Latin tags and advertising slogans. For the real issue does not enter the discussion. That issue is the predominance of judicial decisions that are prospective not only in their effects but also in their reasoning, though all the data within them are retrospective.

In 1949, the Supreme Court in *Wolf v. Colorado* ruled that

states were not bound by the federal rule forbidding the use of evidence against defendants if the evidence was acquired through violations of the Fourth Amendment guarantee against search and seizure. (The crime of which Wolf had been convicted, by the way, was abortion).[42] Twelve years later, in *Mapp v. Ohio*, the court ruled that the Fourteenth Amendment did indeed extend judicial rules on the exclusion of evidence to proceedings in state courts.[43] (The crime here was possession of obscene materials, which the police had found during a warrantless and fruitless search for bombs. It is not without relevance to this discussion that the crimes committed by the appellants in these cases would not now be crimes at all.) There now arose the problem that if judges merely "find" the law, all state convictions prior to *Mapp* involving evidence seized without a warrant were garbage to be thrown away. In *Linkletter v. Walker* in 1965, the Supreme Court decided that sleeping dogs should stay asleep, and that convictions prior to *Mapp* should remain kosher.[44] Later, Justice John M. Harlan expressed his dislike for such loose ends and argued that the rule in *Linkletter* had been a legislative, not a judicial, decision, and the Court should have forced the reconsideration of all cases that would have been affected by the exclusion of evidence seized in violation of the Fourth Amendment.

Nearly forty years later, a similar problem arose when the Court in *Blakeley v. Washington* threw out a state procedure that permitted prosecutors to present to judges at sentencing their version of a convicted defendant's historical wrongdoing, so that the sentence for an offense could be based on evidence never presented to a jury. Justice Scalia wrote the opinion, and grounded it in the plain words of the Constitution. Justice Sandra Day O'Connor objected frantically in a separate dissent (looking once again to what she believed would be the real-life impact of the decision) that these new rules on sentencing would invalidate the federal sentencing "guidelines" as well as many state procedures. The Court almost immediately granted certiorari in another sentencing case for the express purpose of easing confusion about the impact of *Blakeley*, just as though it were a congressional committee asked by the constituents of the congressmen to review a new law with effects the constituents didn't like.

(Let us note in passing that the decision in the new case—*United States v. Booker*—did extend the *Blakeley* interpretation of the Sixth Amendment to federal as well as state sentencing rules and guidelines, and did indeed bury as unconstitutional some legislative mandates of specific sentences for specific crimes. But the 124 pages of opinions, featuring debates among the justices about how much of the sentencing law Congress would have wished thrown out with the bathwater of "judicial fact-finding," did not really tell anyone how much flexibility the Court intended to give judges who wished to disagree with federal sentencing rules or guidelines.[45])

One reiterates: Courts speak with authority when they look backward. When they predict the consequences of their decisions, they lose intellectual distinction. Judges do not, after all, know much about how the world's work is done. Not infrequently, they simply assume that others will do the work to carry out their decisions. Robert Tobin tells a story: "Some years ago a court consultant briefed a supreme court on a project to implement a constitutional amendment requiring establishment of a magistrate court system. The project involved a facility plan for the magistrate court, new case procedures, new bookkeeping systems, a magistrate-training plan, records management procedures, and various other aspects of administration. After a summary of what was going on, one justice turned to his colleagues and asked: 'Why are we going through all this? Isn't the constitutional provision self-executing?' . . . This is an extreme example, but anyone long involved in court administration has encountered similar assumptions about the miraculous power of the law to effect orderly change."[46]

By instructing trial judges to regard sentencing rules and guidelines as merely "advisory," the Court took a step backward toward a previous era's recognition that sentencing is the main function of the judiciary in the criminal justice sphere. Thirty-some years ago, Columbia law professor Harry Jones noted, "When the accused enters a plea of guilty to the charges against him, the determination of the sentence to be imposed is the only significant decision made by a court in his case. . . . [T]he trial judge's exercise of his sentencing authority far outweighs everything else he does as a participant in the administration of justice."

Like the future authors of the sentencing guidelines, Jones noted enormous differences in the sentences meted out by different judges. His examples were drawn from studies done in New York City in the 1920s showing that "the percentage of cases in which the accused person was discharged without any penalty at all varied from 74 percent for the most permissive of the magistrates to less than 7 percent for the most punitive and austere." It seemed obvious to Jones that judges imposing sentence had to consider the criminal as well as the crime, and that judges didn't know enough to do this well. "Over the years," he added, "a good many judges and scholars have urged that our system of criminal justice would operate more fairly and effectively if the guilt-determining functions were separated from the sentencing functions and all issues concerning a convicted offender's penalty resolved less hurriedly and by specialists better qualified for the task than most judges are."[47] Such reforms, of course, would require the elimination of sentencing commissions and legislative committees that deal with penalties wholesale, and nothing in the Constitution empowers the Supreme Court to seek, let alone accomplish, such results.

Results-oriented opinions ignore the fact that nobody can predict with anything like certainty how people asked to work together to seek a goal, particularly a governmental goal, will react to their instructions. "Judges," writes political scientist and management expert James Q. Wilson, "see two or more parties arguing about their rights, rights defended by reference to legal principles. The judges learn the facts chiefly from presentations made in a courtroom under rules of evidence. Though they learn a lot off the bench—by reading studies, talking with colleagues, and consulting their own philosophies—the facts on which they base their findings are supposed to be those that have been taken into evidence. After judges decide whose claims are correct, they fashion remedies, judicial orders or rules intended to enforce a right or redress a wrong. . . . Bureaucrats see the world rather differently. They see a loosely coordinated group of people performing a variety of tasks under a complex array of constraints and with uneven degrees of political support. Agency heads often have difficulty learning exactly what these people are doing and frequently have vague and changing standards by which to evaluate those actions they can observe. . . . Court orders are written rules; before issuing them, the judges should ask themselves whether there is any evidence that the agency under review has been effectively governed in the past by written rules."[48] Better—better by far, perhaps—to decide cases that have arisen under the law, and let others work on the problem of what the decision *means.* Wilson quotes the savage comment by Yale law professor Jerry Mashaw that in the administrative law area, where administrative law judges working for the agency find the facts and apply both the law and the policies of the agency, the appellate courts have developed "a range of techniques for intruding without deciding."

In 1965, in *Griswold v. Connecticut,*[49] Justice Arthur Goldberg in a concurring opinion found the universal solvent, the argument that could justify virtually anything the Supreme Court wanted the society to do. In some ways the most remarkable thing about the case itself is that this antique is only forty years old. It was an appeal from the conviction in Connecticut of a doctor who had counseled a married couple about contraceptive procedures, violating a state law that Justice Potter Stewart in a dissent called "uncommonly silly." The justification for the law as argued by the Connecticut attorney general was that the absence of contraceptives discouraged extramarital sex. The Supreme Court declared the law unconstitutional in a rather labored opinion by Justice William O. Douglas, whose argument was that the Fourteenth Amendment had made the states subject to the restrictions imposed by the First Amendment (freedom of speech) and the Fourth Amendment (search and seizure). The doctor had the right to tell his married patients about contraceptives; the couple had the right to use contraceptives in the privacy of their home, and no government could intrude upon them. The law had been passed, of course, at the insistence of the Catholic Church. Douglas did have some fun with the opinion, citing as his strongest precedent *Pierce v. Society of Sisters*, in which the Court had voided an Oregon law that prohibited religious schools.

Goldberg saw an opportunity to go further. Formerly general counsel to the Steel Workers Organizing Committee and the CIO ("Phil Murray was sick a lot, and I had a lot to do with running the CIO," he said[50]), he had recently been appointed to the Court by John F. Kennedy. He was probably not very happy as the ninth of nine (he considered himself always and everywhere the first of one), and he was happy to play left wing. He wrote a concurring opinion, resting his decision on the Ninth Amendment, which says, "The enumeration in the Constitution, of certain rights, shall not be construed to deny or disparage others retained by the People." We posit a "right of privacy," then assume that the Fourteenth Amendment compelled the states to preserve whatever rights the people enjoy under the Ninth Amendment, and the Court has authority over anything that violates "fundamental principles of liberty and justice" or is "contrary to the 'traditions and [collective] conscience of our people.'"

Justice Hugo Black dissented contemptuously: "[T]he scientific miracles of this age have not yet produced a gadget which the Court can use to determine what traditions are rooted in the '[collective] conscience of our people.'" As Sol Wachtler, then chief judge of the New York Court of Appeals, wrote a few years later: "It is difficult to understand how a judge could not be guided by his or her personal notions of right and wrong when considering what rights should be considered fundamental and deserving of full constitutional protection. Thus, to some extent Justice Goldberg did not see the Ninth Amendment as a source of rights but rather as a source of judicial power."[51] The great English legal scholar Glanville Williams wrote in his masterful *Learning the Law* (I have the seventh printing of its eleventh edition) that this was the idea: "The modern movement for the legislative recognition of 'human rights' is in fact a movement for the increased control of legislatures by the judiciary, because the human rights that are claimed are couched in such broad terms, and involve so much balancing of one consideration with another, that they inevitably call for much judicial 'interpretation.'"[52] But Chief Justice Warren and Justice Brennan signed on to Goldberg's concurrence.

It was a high-water mark: Less than a year later, Goldberg was gone, shoved to the United Nations by Lyndon Johnson so the president's buddy and adviser Abe Fortas could have the seat, an action that in the end did no good to Goldberg, Fortas, or Johnson. Goldberg had to defend the Vietnam War in Turtle Bay, then run for governor of New York, and Johnson's failure to sell the Senate on Fortas as chief justice led to Warren Burger and much more. By 1973 even Justice Harry

Blackmun, pulling a right to privacy out of a grab bag of ideas to justify his decision in *Roe v. Wade* to invalidate laws that criminalized abortion, did not rest any weight on the Ninth Amendment.

O'Connor and Roberts had much history on their side when they looked to the impact of their actions. The great men—Holmes, Hand, Brandeis, Hughes, Traynor, Cardozo, Jackson, Frankfurter—all insisted that courts pay attention to the real world that will be affected by their decisions. What Cardozo called "sociological jurisprudence" was generally seen outside the legal profession as nothing more than common sense. "Law and society" went together. This war was definitively won. But there was an opportunity cost, and what was lost on the other side was some measure of authority. Moving sociology into law risked making law nothing but a branch of sociology. The other Latin tag carved on the Missouri Supreme Court building said *Ubi jus, ibi remidium*—There is no right without a remedy. Trying to construct remedies to segregation in the 1950s and 1960s, the Supreme Court slipped into a trap of wishful thinking.

5

"Legal realism" led to judges trying to change the societies in which they lived. "There is no use arguing," wrote law professor Karl Llewellyn, "with any man who does not take the drive for justice as a prime good in law." But the judges plodding the beaten path of precedent could not let themselves be seen as detached from reality. History had protected their fathers and their fathers' fathers, but it could not save them. Judge Richard A. Posner of the Seventh Circuit (Chicago), a pioneering conservative, writes irritably that history "venerates tradition, precedent, pedigree, ritual, custom, ancient practices, ancient texts, armchair terminology, maturity, wisdom, seniority, gerontocracy, and interpretation conceived of as a method of recovering history. It is suspicious of innovation, discontinuities, 'paradigm shifts,' and the energy and brashness of youth. These ingrained attitudes are obstacles to those like me who would like to reorient law in a more scientific, economic, and pragmatic direction."

Indeed, one could say worse, for history was the source of all sorts of time-wasting procedure, some of it simply insane. "Under our system of practice and procedure," the chief justice of the North Carolina Supreme Court said in a talk to that state's bar association in 1914, "a lawyer is trained to look backwards . . . to reverence the opinion of some unknown judge, of unknown capacity and of unknown bias, who happened to be a judge one hundred or two hundred years ago." Judges, he added, are "the most unprogressive of members of their unprogressive profession." He had practical concerns: Somehow, North Carolina had got itself stuck with a system of assignment that rotated the state's twenty judges continuously through its counties. "What inducement is there," he asked bitterly, "to clean up the docket?" Worse yet: Legislation prohibited judges from setting time limits on speeches by the lawyers in the case.[53]

We reach therefore for another social science— economics—as a basis for forward-looking judicial decision. Judge Douglas Ginsburg of the D.C. Circuit Court of Appeals, one of the leaders of the "law and economics" movement, traces its origins back to studies of how taxation affects behavior done by Herbert Simon (the noneconomist who won a Nobel Prize in economics) at the University of Chicago in the 1940s. This work was extended to more general studies of how law and judicial decisions affected economic behavior through altering transaction costs. Most of this theorizing was done at the economics department and the business school, where Milton Friedman was resident guru; the central figures were Ronald Coase and Gary Becker, who also won Nobel prizes. The idea of teaching this material to judges was realized at the University of Rochester in the 1960s, when the school was led by Allen Wallis, a Friedman protégé. The creator was law professor Henry Manne, and his most significant followers were law professors Richard Posner and Frank Easterbrook, who became federal appellate judges. Manne, who was a charmer and a bon vivant as well as a stimulating teacher, moved to Miami and took with him his school of law and economics, which flourished. Many corporations and conservative foundations contributed large sums to the costs of the Law and Economics Center. The main events were seventeen-day seminars offered free to groups of about fifty federal judges (first come, first served) at the nation's best resorts, with gourmet meals, on a schedule that required classes every morning and then left the rest of the day free, though participants were asked to do a considerable amount of reading.

Though the Keynesian economist Paul Samuelson was sometimes on the faculty, there was a bias toward conservative, Friedmanite economists. The most remarkable example was George Benston, another Rochester professor, who had done a study of direct investments by savings and loans in the 1980s and had touted the success of thirty-nine recently chartered thrifts that had acted as intermediaries between government-insured deposits and what turned out to be wildly improper and dishonest enterprises. Within two years of his study, thirty-seven of them had failed, with huge losses to the savings and loan insurance funds. Benston became a permanent part of the Law and Economics faculty, specializing in the difference between values derived by formal accounting methods and market values. Law and Economics was not, like Zweig's ASTAR, an effort to educate judges so that they could deal with scientific evidence and run their trials in a more informed way. It was an effort to influence the decisions they would render by convincing them that inherited common law and unfettered market competition would maximize value for society as a whole. There is a lot of truth to that—and no one should underestimate the stimulus given the American economy by the deregulation that started in the Carter administration and reached flood tide with Reagan—but not all of the truth.

Eventually, after a stopover in Atlanta at Emory University, Law and Economics settled down at George Mason University in northern Virginia, where Manne became dean of the law school. The Law and Economics Center taught economics to judges and law to economists, and as always the participants learned a lot from each other as well as from the courses and at meals, when the faculty scattered to eat with the students. Among today's descendants of Manne's brainchild, teaching economic perspectives on specific controversies (liability for construction defects, for example, rather than antitrust) is a joint venture of two Washington think tanks, the American Enterprise Institute and the Brookings Institution. They assemble eight weeklong conferences a year (each participant judge attends two of them). The cochairs are Henry Butler, who was Manne's assistant for some years and is now a professor at the University of Kansas, and Robert Litan of the Kauffman Foundation, formerly director of economic studies at Brookings and before that an assistant attorney general in the Reagan Justice Department. Litan participates directly in some of the sessions, bringing the judges the benefit of a remarkable capacity to see any issue simultaneously from several quite different perspectives.[54] What must be said for Manne and Butler, and perhaps even George Benston, is that even before Brookings was summoned to balance the lists, the participating judges (who in the 1980s added up to 40 percent of the entire federal district bench), regardless of their own political orientation, found the work enlightening.

Economics, we economists used to say, is the study of the allocation of scarce means to alternative uses. All economic policy making rests on cost-benefit analysis, with cost understood as "opportunity cost"—that is, the benefits surrendered by the allocation of these resources to the use being analyzed. Unfortunately, the values assigned to these benefits tend to be subjective. Judge Posner refers somewhat inelegantly to "the frequent isomorphism of legal doctrines and economic principles."[55] Law and economics as realms of thought are in truth tied together; indeed, they stand shoulder to shoulder with their gaze frozen in the same direction, for both assume that people are rational. Meanwhile, all around them people are acting for noneconomic, irrational reasons. Herbert Simon, pioneer of economic man, settled down eventually as the prophet of administrative man, who wanted not to maximize but to "satisfice."

Those of us trained in economics have learned to put up with the embarrassment when our colleagues find economic causation that assures people will do something desirable or undesirable, though the behavior involved has roots far, far deeper than mere commercial self-interest. Judge Posner especially is fecund with such stuff, most of it cute. In his book *Frontiers of Legal Theory*, he suggests that a doctor who ran a black market in babies for adoption made it less likely that girls in his area would take precautions against becoming pregnant, because they knew that if they did become pregnant there was a market for the baby.[56] And that a law prohibiting resale price maintenance by a manufacturer (upheld by the Supreme Court as long ago as 1911) disadvantages consumers, who lose the benefits that would come their way because retailers who were required to charge the same price would inevitably compete by offering additional services. And that another law prohibiting advertising by casinos in Puerto Rico would in fact increase the use of the casinos, because they would spend the money they couldn't spend on advertising to lower their prices.[57] And that "women who work in a place in which pornography is displayed are compensated for having to put up with it, in the practical economic sense that wages reflect the amenities or disamenities of a job as well as the worker's productivity."[58]

My own favorite in the Posner oeuvre is the statement that "the reduction in deterrence resulting from the abolition of capital punishment . . . might, by increasing the number of murders and hence of murder prosecutions, have added to the number of federal habeas corpus proceedings."[59] Even assuming that the elimination of capital punishment would increase the number of murders, which is an enormous and arguable assumption, one can contend with at least equal plausibility that the absence of irreversible sanction would diminish the incentive for federal judges to entertain habeas corpus motions and thus reduce their number. All Judge Posner's fanciful hypotheses lead in one direction.

In the end, moreover, economics will take over any partnership that joins law and economics. In an article entitled "The Expanding Domain of Economics," the late UCLA economics professor Jack Hirshleifer explained the phenomenon of *"relitigation.* Since precedents are never absolutely binding, attempts will be made repeatedly to overturn an inefficient one. So long as there is a random element in judicial decisions, even apart from any learning factor, the efficient rule will eventually be hit upon. . . . [T]hose standing to benefit from the more efficient decision can afford to make greater investments (for example, to hire better lawyers) and thus are more likely to win the contest."[60] The economists will win their contest, unfortunately, because they have greater access to the power tools: money and mathematics.

Walter F. Murphy, C. Herman Pritchett, and Lee Epstein, in their textbook *Courts, Judges and Politics*, note sourly that much of the legal theory in this material "naively repeats the standard literature of political science in the 1950s. . . . [T]hese judges have made the breathtaking discovery, which any journalist or college freshman who had taken a course in American government would have long known, that most legislation is, in part, the product of intensely negotiated bargains . . ."[61] And there is an odd deficit to decisions tied too closely to economic results. The more the reliance on rational motivation, the less impressive the logic is likely to be. The life of the law may have been experience, but acceptance of the law is tied to the belief that there is something here quite beyond experience—that the lawyers and judges know things the rest of us don't know.

The historian Gordon S. Wood, commenting on Justice Scalia's brief treatise on statutory interpretation, called for "a renewed emphasis on the esoteric and scientifically legal aspects of adjudication. . . . But first I suppose we must reverse some of the reductio ad absurdum tendencies of legal realism and remystify some of what lawyers and judges do. The real source of the political problem that troubles Justice Scalia lies in our demystification of the law, which is an aspect of the general demystification of all authority that has taken place in the twentieth century."[62]

6

In the early seventeenth century, we are told, King James I remarked to Lord Coke, his chancellor, that "if law was founded upon reason, he and others could reason as well as the judges." Coke, the hero of the legal profession to this day, replied that lawsuits were "not to be decided by natural reason, but by the artificial reason and judgment of the law, which law is an art that requires long study and experience before a man can attain to the cognizance of it." The king was not above all: He was subject to God and the Law. Henry Friendly, who went from an intellectual private practice emphasizing work before administrative agencies to a distinguished career on the Second Circuit Court of Appeals, noted the king's "anger at the idea of a government of lawyers, not of men." He also noted the view of the great Scots-American political scientist Charles McIlwain that "if the claim of the lawyers were to be admitted, the supreme authority would be their exclusive possession."[63]

The courts, after all—and despite the ardent arguments of most judges—are not created or purposed to "do justice." They are created and purposed to enforce the law, just or not. As Supreme Court justice Tom Clark noted, "In a democracy the national welfare should be the primary objective of the legislature whose statutes may quickly pattern effective measures to that end. The courts, on the other hand, have the duty of interpreting and enforcing such legislation. Theirs is the machinery through which law finds its teeth."[64] Martin Luther King, attacking from another side, wrote in his "Letter from the Birmingham Jail" that everything Hitler did was "legal."

Judge Learned Hand, for half a century the ornament of the Second Circuit Court of Appeals in New York, liked to tell a story of driving Justice Oliver Wendell Holmes Jr. to the Capitol for the Supreme Court's Conference day, then a Saturday. "It was before he had a motorcar," Hand told a conference on continuing education of the bar in 1958, "and we jogged along in an old coupe. When we got down to the Capitol, I wanted to provoke a response. As he walked off, I said to him, 'Well, sir, goodbye. Do justice!' He turned quite sharply, and he said, 'Come here. Come here.' I answered, 'Oh, I know, I know.' He replied 'That is not my job. My job is to play the game according to the rules.' "[65] In a tribute to Holmes spoken at the Harvard Law School at the unveiling of his portrait, Hand would invent a "Society of Jobbists," of people who correctly defined their jobs and gave their entire energies to the proper performance of those jobs within the boundaries of the work itself. Holmes was the founder and perpetual chairman of the society. The other side of that argument had been given long ago by Martin Luther himself. "Good jurist," he said; "bad Christian."[66]

Early in his judicial career, Holmes famously wrote that "the prophecies of what the courts will do in fact, and nothing more pretentious, are what I mean by the law." This was in 1897, when he was a justice on the Massachusetts Supreme Judicial Court speaking at the dedication of the new school of law in Boston University. In the same speech he insisted that "the rational study of law is still to a large extent the study of history." Law grew out of history—that was the meaning of "precedent," the rule of stare decisis, "it stands decided." But this central proposition of the common law would not last long in the modern world. It was Herbert Spencer, the philosopher of capitalism, who noted that law meant the governance of the living by the dead, and Holmes affirmed the same in a letter to an acolyte. The living would not forever put up with it: "The black-letter man [the man who knows the written law, the collection of precedents] may be the man of the present," Holmes said, "but the man of the future is the man of statistics and the master of economics. It is revolting to have no better reason for a rule of law than that so it was laid down in the time of Henry IV."[67] Jefferson was even stronger: "We might as well require a man to wear still the coat which fitted him when a boy," he wrote in a letter, "as civilized society to remain ever under the regimen of their barbarous ancestors."[68]

As late as the mid-twentieth century, law was one of the great disciplines, whose acolytes addressed each other as "my learned friend." The literature was challenging and distinguished, a higher form of philosophy. The judges drew public prestige and personal satisfaction from their status as masters of the mysteries. Obviously, Anatole France was right to scorn the claims to equal justice in a law that equally forbade rich and poor to sleep under the bridges of Paris, but the combination of equality and justice was not in fact that simple, and we have cases going back centuries to prove it. McGeorge Bundy, then dean of the Harvard faculty of arts and sciences, later Jack Kennedy's national security adviser and then chairman of the Ford Foundation, could tell a conference of judges and law professors that "the fundamental function of the law is to prevent the natural unfairness of human society from becoming intolerable," but he was not a lawyer. They didn't have to listen to him, and they didn't.[69] Judges could beat off or simply ignore (for such things had little to do with their everyday work) the Marxist analysts whose "critical studies" presented law as part of an oppressive superstructure crushing the working class. But now lawyers are businessmen, judges are traffic wardens, and the triviality of the literature, most of it on the level of newspaper editorials, is alarming. Where once the "legal realists"—the authors of the Brandeis brief that demanded attention for the social and commercial context of the lawsuit—had to fight to sever their cause from the mechanical application of old rules; now law itself has become predictive, just like sociology. There is no way one can remystify sociology. It never had a mystery to begin with.

In the end, we need the history, too. "Exercising judgment," Frankfurter wrote in an opinion that forbade the University of New Hampshire to inquire into the political beliefs of economics professor Paul Sweezy, "is the inescapable judicial task . . . and it is a task ultimately committed to this Court. It must not be an exercise of whim or will. It must be an overriding judgment founded on something much deeper and more justifiable than personal preference. As far as it lies within human limitations, it must be an impersonal judgment. It must rest on fundamental presuppositions rooted in history to which widespread acceptance may fairly be attributed."[70] In a sense, we are back to Justice Goldberg and the collective conscience, but here the judge is controlled by history.

7

The loss of autonomy in the law relates in ways that have not been explored to the control modern society has asserted over all the professions. Doctors curse the insurance companies and health maintenance organizations, teachers resent the required tests by which governments (read: politicians) evaluate the relationship between teaching quality and student achievement, accountants are torn between relief that legislation has relieved the pressure on them from corporate clients seeking to misinform the investing public and irritation at the rule-making and supervisory authority now in the hands of people who are not accountants. Where once it was generally accepted that input, not output, was the measure of professional work, that the quality of the work done by a professional could be measured only by another member of the same profession, lay society now insists that it pays for results. Bureaucrats tell doctors what treatments insurance companies or government programs will pay for—and how much they will pay. The corporate CEO for whom the lawyer was once an indispensable counselor now keeps a pet "general counsel" on his payroll, and expects that general counsel to commission work from outside law firms when necessary to meet what the CEO perceives as his company's requirements. Instead of daily dealings as the client's "counselor," the work compensated by a "retainer" signifying loyalty on both sides, the modern lawyer finds himself bidding on the Internet to sell legal services in bulk. In thousands of corporate headquarters, a new King James I sits in his (sometimes her) swivel chair and tells the Lord Cokes of his entourage what's up.

I wrote in the 1960s that by the end of that century battles over the control of professional performance would be central to the political life of the country.[71] And so they were; but the warriors still don't know that's what the war is about. To some degree, as Professor Woods points out, the "demystification" of the courts merely reflects improvement in the educational level of the society as a whole. Before the Great Depression cut down access to executive office in the manufacturing sector and sent the ambitious young to college, even the CEOs of the great corporations had rarely gone beyond high school. Only the professions required formal education. Doctors, lawyers, accountants, engineers, professors, even schoolteachers knew much that their clientele did not know. They were gurus. Their patients, clients, pupils, feared to contradict, to show their ignorance. No more.

One creates mysteries through the education and training of mystics. In the years ahead, we will have to learn to train judges, not only in the work of judging but also in the disciplines required to understand the background of the cases they hear. The practice of law today is as specialized as the practice of medicine, but anyone with a law degree and acquaintances in the political world can don a robe and preside over cases in which those specialties are central. If anything, we have been going in the wrong direction, "unifying" a judiciary that increasingly cannot perform well without expertise. If the American Bar Association had had its way, judges deciding cases about nuclear energy for the Nuclear Regulatory Commission would simply have been pulled at random from a single body of administrative law judges. Most of the failures of our judicial system have multiple causes, and it is conceivable that today's social workers would handle child protection problems even worse than today's juvenile court judges, but that means only that we must train social workers, too.

Only history can offer an excuse for the patterns of failure we see in family cases, juvenile cases, patents, contract cases (most of which have now disappeared to Alternate Dispute Resolution, where the arbitrators have some expertise), personal-injury cases (where the average cost of the process is about 50 percent of the award), even cases of statutory interpretation. History, previously the impregnable defense, no longer helps: That is what Professor Woods means by demystification. Having irrevocably lost its own mystery, the justice system will have to borrow the mysteries of others. What lies ahead is the age of the specialist judge.

15 OPINIONS

There should be specialized judges. As cases of a certain class become numerous and require that a specialist consider them, judges should be delegated from the staff of the whole court for that purpose and the cases should be assigned to such judges . . . by some functionary.

—**Preliminary Report on the Efficiency of the Administration of Justice,**
Charles W. Eliot, Louis D. Brandeis, Moorfield Storey,
Adolph J. Rodenbeck, Roscoe Pound[1]

Unless some basic problems are considered and solved, our judicial branch will become increasingly faceless and anonymous. The President will nominate, the Senate will consent, but the bureaucracy will decide.

—Judge Alvin Rubin[2]

BACK IN THE MIDDLE OF THE TWENTIETH century there was an institution in New York called the Second Panel Sheriff's Jury. Its solemn duty was to try cases alleging the insanity of public officials. In return for holding themselves available to perform that service, the hundred or so political leaders, insurance brokers, and big-time investment bankers who were members of this panel were exempt from all other calls to jury duty. Annual dues to be a member of the panel were four hundred preinflation dollars, but members got a little value back at an annual dinner, usually in the rooftop ballroom of the Biltmore Hotel, where one could see the leaders of the Democratic and Republican parties sitting side by side on the dais, with judges of both political persuasions scattered around the room. Everyone, panel members and their guests, received a rather expensive party favor, something like a gold-plated pocket watch or Cross pen and pencil set. But the real reward, of course, was the guarantee that the members of the panel would never receive jury summonses.

"Jury duty" was a great and recurring pain in the rear for New Yorkers, because it involved two weeks of sitting around on hard polished benches in a cavernous, assembly room, with nothing to do. Every so often lawyers elsewhere in the courthouse would proclaim themselves ready for a trial, the telephone would ring on the desk in the middle of the room, and the clerk behind the desk would spin a bingo wheel and take out slips of paper with names on them. Forty jurors would be shepherded by an armed police officer to a dirty room down the corridor where twelve would be put in jurors' chairs at the front and the other twenty-eight would sit in a gallery and listen while the lawyers chose a jury through the rites of the voir dire, translated by lawyers as "to speak the truth."

In federal court and in many states, judges conduct the voir dire, asking questions submitted to them by the lawyers. In New York, judges were excused from participation in the voir dire, and the questions counsel asked potential jurors would be premised on all sorts of unproven and maybe untrue "facts" that improved their clients' chances. As I put it in 1965, "Nobody can write calmly about the New York system who has ever been compelled to waste literally days of his time while the yahoos of the New York bar (with the consent of the judges, who have ratted out and do not preside at the voir dire) run through stereotyped and often illegitimate series of questions, separately for each juror in the box, all for the purpose of frustrating the only excuse there is for a jury trial, that the facts are to be found by an unselected mixed bag of the community."[3] Often the task of selecting a jury, let alone trying the case, could not be be completed the same day.

After each round of the voir dire, the lawyers would dismiss some of the twelve on the original panel (for whatever reason or no reason; nobody was supervising), and the policeman would once again spin a wheel and pick other names from the group in the voir dire gallery. And the whole process would start all over again, the lawyers paid well for their time, the jurors paid scarcely anything. Rejected jurors often had to stay in the room until a jury satisfactory to the lawyers had been chosen. Those not chosen for this jury at the end of this process would be returned to the assembly room to become cannon fodder for the next trial—as would jurors who had actually served and turned in a verdict in another trial. Meanwhile, the lawyers on both sides would look over their notes on the jury they had chosen, and often as not settle the case. (This is literally true: for not much short of half the cases on the calendar, the lawyers made their deal *after* choosing a jury.)

Summonses to jury duty were for two weeks. For those receiving and obeying a jury duty summons it was almost impossible to get away losing less than a week of your life, though if enough jurors summoned for next week's cohort actually showed up, it might be possible on the following Monday to duck the second week with the consent of the clerk. And almost everybody who was called then found himself or herself on a list to be called again every two years. Not surprisingly, the percentage of recipients who obeyed the summons to jury duty declined with the passage of time, and pressures from the public continually increased the categories who could legally beg off. That included proprietors of small businesses who would have to close shop, mothers of small children, doctors, schoolteachers during the school year, policemen and firemen, and, of course, lawyers and clerks associated with the courts.

When Judith Kaye became chief judge of the New York Court of Appeals in 1993, her first mission was to make jury duty dignified and fair. Virtually all exemptions were eliminated—lawyers and even judges included. Instead of a universal summons for all to come in on Monday morning, jurors called for this week were given a phone number to call each day until they were needed. The obligation was for a single case, and everybody impaneled for a jury, whether or not they actually served, was immediately excused from further jury duty for four years. Each morning, a judge came to each redecorated jury room in New York State and thanked people for coming.

In 2004, accepting the recommendations of a task force appointed by Judge Kaye, the court administration announced further improvements: insistence that lawyers meet to settle cases *before* the jury panel is chosen, requiring that "a judicial officer" be present during the voir dire to police the behavior of the lawyers, and imposing penalties on lawyers who come repeatedly late to their engagements associated with jury trials. Exemption from future jury service was extended to six years for people who merely reported to jury rooms, eight years for people who actually served in trials. The experience of serving as a juror in New York has been totally transformed.

The jury service revolution was only the beginning of the changes Chief Judge Kaye planned for the New York courts. Some things she could do by herself. Appointments to lucrative referee posts, special guardianships, and the like are controlled by the judges sitting on the cases, and one reason to become a judge is the opportunity to reward friends, former partners, and colleagues. These appointments are made pursuant to Rule 36 of the Chief Judge's Rules. Judge Kaye amended those rules to forbid judges to grant to their former law partners and clients fee-paying posts yielding more than $5,000 a year—and forbade the award of such benefices to any firm or individual who had received more than $50,000 in such fees the previous year.

Random assignment of cases to judges had meant in New York that sophisticated cases and counsel could come before judges who knew little about the customs of the industry involved or the applicable law. Not surprisingly, the result was that legal business leaked away from the state courts. If the lawyers involved could find an argument why the case should go before federal judges, it went there; if they couldn't, they were increasingly likely to opt for arbitration. Only weeks after she became chief judge, Kaye authorized the creation of a "commercial part" in Manhattan, to which New York County business cases could be sent, regardless of where the random-number table wanted to send the case, and she appointed two much-respected judges to handle the work. The big Wall Street law firms liked the idea, and Judge Kaye proceeded to form a "task force" of judges and lawyers to write rules. Nobody wanted to get on the wrong side of the new chief judge, and people with resentments kept their feelings to themselves.

The commercial part opened with four judges in New York and one in Rochester. After a few years, the Manhattan commercial part expanded to seven judges who did nothing else, and corporate lawyers in other counties began asking for similar favors. Soon Buffalo, Rochester, Albany, Syracuse, and other New York and Long Island counties had commercial parts of their own, with judges selected for such duty by Judge Kaye, and the program had won prizes nationally from both the American Bar Association and the Chamber of Commerce. "The Commercial Division," says the Web site, "was intended as a vehicle for resolution of complicated commercial disputes. Successful resolution of these disputes requires particular expertise on the part of the court across the broad and complex expanse of commercial law." Meanwhile, Judge Kaye and her chief administrator—Albert Rosenblatt before his elevation to the Court of Appeals, then Jonathan Lippman, who had been chief clerk in New York County—organized a "Litigation Coordinating Panel" to consolidate at least the pretrial phase of similar cases filed in different counties. Rosenblatt also created an "Advisory Committee on Judicial Ethics," a panel of judges that meets seven times a year to consider written requests for guidance from judges. Between its founding in 1987 and 2003, the panel delivered 2,500 written opinions. (Can a judge pass the plate in church?)

In theory, New York has had a "unified court system" since 1975, with a state budget line of more than a billion dollars, but in fact there are nine different kinds of trial courts, and different courts for different counties. New York County has forty-seven family courts (the judges appointed by the mayor), and a single judge may handle every day more than a hundred requests for orders of protection. Twenty-five of these judges also handle cases of neglected and abused children. Judge Kaye has managed to stretch her authority to start community courts (so far, only a few of them) with an "integrated judge" who has the powers of a family court judge, a criminal court judge, and a divorce judge. There is a gun court in Brooklyn to which all gun offenses are sent, and a single court to process parole violations citywide and make sure they are punished. Though in principle cases are assigned at random, Judge Kaye likes to arrange the world so that judges with experience, affinity, and education in a specialty hear cases in that specialty. Three judges in New York County, for example, handle the county's medical malpractice litigation.

In the same system, some fifty housing court judges handle more than 300,000 filings a year. What with the summons, the response, and the motions, a housing case may take six months to get on the calendar. New York still has rent control, and a large book of rules that protect tenants. (Nothing of course protects the property. The manager of a large trade-union-based housing co-op once explained that "After a generation of rent control, people know that rent goes to the landlord, services come from God, and deterioration— deterioration is something you get used to.") Nonpayment of rent, however, triggers a summary proceeding that puts the matter before a judge after only twelve days. Almost 200,000 such accelerated cases are heard every year. Judge Kaye's predecessor said he thought the New York housing court was the worst court in the country. Judge Fern Fisher-Brandwein, the deputy chief administrative judge who handles the civil courts, says that the same lawyers work on all the cases, and both litigants and lawyers hate each other. "It's worse than divorce." New York is now pioneering a court where housing and family matters are considered by the same judge.

The lungs of the system in New York is the civil court, with 120 judges, seventy of whom on most days are on loan to the criminal courts, the family courts, or the supreme courts. Everything is complicated. The required interpreters run a gamut from Creole to Cantonese, through all the European and several of the Asian languages. Matrimonials are different in different parts of the state, the courts ordering discovery (pretrial interviews and rummagings through papers) upstate but not in the city. And, says deputy administrative judge Jacqueline Silberman, matrimonials demand "a high skills level. Equitable distribution law is quite complex. We have made property out of lots of things not usually regarded as property." Among Judge Silberman's innovations was an insistence that once a judge was assigned a contested matrimonial, that judge remained in charge. In 1987, she appointed an outside expert to value property, and a lawyer who had expected to get a valuation from a jury protested. "You can't do that." "Yes, I can," said Judge Silberman. "Inherent powers of the court." And the appellate division sustained her, after which

Albert Rosenblatt as chief administrative judge put it in the rule book, and then the legislature codified it.

Judge Kaye found a very messy system. In some parts of the system, this waste was entrenched. Elected "surrogates," for example, probated the state's wills, separately in each county. Some courts could lend judges to others; most could not (housing court judges, for example, are not "constitutional" judges and can sit only in housing court; elected justices of the peace can sit only in their own courts). Most judges were elected. Some were appointed by the governor, some by the judges of the appellate division, others by the mayors of the cities. The clerks, who do not report to the judicial administrators, continue to play an immense role. Courts become involved in cases only when an RJI—Request for Judicial Intervention—is filed with the clerk's office, which may not be in the courthouse. In New York City, county clerks are appointed by the appellate division; outside the city, they are elected.

Still, progress was possible. During the boom years of the 1990s, the New York courts got money to greatly expand the information technology sections, and in the process to ramp up the number and powers of administrative judges. Supervised by those administrators, a new computerized case management system greatly increased the productivity of the New York trial courts (though it remains in use in only a minority of the judicial districts, because so many judges and clerks are still uncomfortable with computers). Motions and scheduling are available through electronic media. A model electronic courtroom is on display in the New York County courthouse, with eight flat screens in the jury box; pictures and documents scanned into the system at the lawyer's podium are available to the jury during deliberations on demand. The electronic courtroom is to be spread through the system as funds become available.

In 2005, Judge Kaye was still crusading with the legislature for a simplified court structure that would make possible better use of the 14,000 employees of the New York State courts. And she may get it, though many judges are not on her side. Roy Schotland says he likes to come up to New York every once in a while to watch Judge Kaye walk on water.

2

Judge Kaye's most cherished initiative, however, is in the string of "problem-solving courts" her leadership has scattered through the state's urban communities. We have looked at the Brooklyn Treatment Court, which is atypical because it is in a downtown courthouse. Others—there are now five dozen of them in New York, two hundred in the country—are mostly in community centers of various kinds. The coordinating and research mechanism is a Center for Court Innovation established under her guidance in 1996 and celebrated in an impressively sensible book titled *Good Courts: The Case for Problem-Solving Justice*,[4] written by its former and present directors John Feinblatt and Greg Berman. It may be significant that the concept of problem-solving courts has won a unanimous vote of approval from the Conference of Chief Justices.

What characterizes the problem-solving court is an intense

concentration on the practical consequences of a trial and punishment in the future behavior (and by extrapolation the future lives) of the accused. Conservatives worry about a touchy-feely emphasis on rehabilitation, which for a substantial fraction of the defendants is simply not possible (especially in the domestic violence area). Liberals worry about the loss of rights when adversarial challengers cannot be mounted against a benignly defined "problem" that has to be solved. This is an argument where everybody is right, and it doesn't matter. Stern adherence to "law" means sentences to "time served" for prostitutes and wife-beaters and first-time drug-possession offenders, who then walk out of court free. The punishments meted out to shoplifters, vandals, and beggars don't yield any measurable deterrence. The same people are back in court on the same charges a few months or even weeks later. On the other side, full-bore advocacy in lower criminal courts doesn't happen because it's time-consuming—and when it does happen, defense counsel loses motions something more than 95 percent of the time. From both the conservative and liberal points of view, the current system cannot be saved. The most important argument for the problem-solving court is that its opponents cannot intelligently support retention of the existing rules and regulations.

When the problem-solving court works right, offenders take responsibility for their own behavior. As in Alcoholics Anonymous, they confess before their fellow sinners and promise to do better. Moreover, the judge in accepting that confession takes a certain amount of responsibility herself. Typically in the problem-solving courts, the offender returns weekly or monthly while his program is under the jurisdiction of the court, subjects himself to a drug test, explains absences from the program, if any, and receives praise for living up to promises. The conventional court puts a convicted offender on probation, with an obligation to report to the probation officer. But the probation officer is not a judge, his caseload is ludicrously too high, and many people cheat on him without consequences.

In the problem-solving court, the offender's obligation is to the judge, the same judge that imposed whatever the punishment may be, and failure to turn up normally triggers the imposition of the jail sentence previously suspended. Quite apart from fear of consequences, there is a value for an offender in his relationship with a judge. And he knows that if he does not appear in court when his name is on the docket, the judge automatically orders his arrest. There is a sense in which the judge, having accepted this miscreant into the drug treatment or anger-management program, or reduced a penalty to community service, has put her own judgment on the line in a way that the sentencing laws increasingly forbid in conventional courts. "This notion," Berman and Feinblatt write, "that judicial authority carries weight, that judges can make a difference, goes to the heart of the problem-solving enterprise."[5]

Central also to the enterprise is the idea that courts need not always create winners and losers. "Adult education," Learned Hand said in 1958, discussing post–law school legal education for lawyers, "means we have got rid of inveterate advocacy." In the Brooklyn Treatment Court, as we have seen, the same prosecutor and defense lawyer work together month after month. The interests of society and the interests of the defendant are not at all in conflict when the subject is drug addiction, domestic violence, prostitution. Once one has abandoned the childish idea that truth is best discovered by unlimited advocacy on two sides of any issue, the "trial" court to which Americans are accustomed can be seen as the horse-and-buggy device it really is. And the black-or-white winner-take-all decision making of the appellate court carries a lot less authority than it did a generation ago.

No doubt much of what goes on in these courts is highly manipulative. Dockets are organized to present successes first, so the judge can exude confidence in a courtroom full of defendants (and, not infrequently, family). Petty criminals in one of the therapeutic programs are encouraged to read to the room their self-descriptions written for job interviews. The participants whose urine sample tested dirty may be made to sit in the courtroom in the jurors' box, where everyone who enters the room sees them and their shame. The computer screen on the judge's desk shows details about the individual before the court, allowing the judge to ask, for example, how the baby is doing when the interlocutor is a mother whose child has been restored to her from foster care as part of her reward for testing clean on three straight scheduled visits to the courtroom.

In general, the judge in the problem-solving court is expected to know much more than the judge in a normal court about the crimes alleged to have occurred, the social background from which the defendant springs, and the patterns of behavior associated with overcoming the conditions that brought this miscreant before the court. The intake process is much more informative at every step. The objection does remain that this extra information does not assure that the judge

knows what this individual or this society should do. Yale's
Alexander Bickel wrote scornfully of judges who "view themselves as holding roving commissions as problem solvers."[6]
Denver's Morris Hoffman puts the case violently: "I cannot
imagine a more dangerous branch than an unrestrained judiciary full of amateur psychiatrists poised to 'do good' rather
than to apply the law. . . . Judges have become, in the flash of
an eye, intrusive, coercive and unqualified state psychiatrists
and behavioral policemen, charged with curing all manner of
social and quasi-social diseases, from truancy to domestic violence to drug use."[7] Lots of people remind us that juvenile
courts started off a hundred and ten years ago with objectives
and procedures not that different from the new problem-
solving courts, and deteriorated into the loading dock for the
people warehouse that they are today.

3

In the end, these objections miss the point, more easily because it is a point the proponents of problem-solving courts
make only reluctantly and badly, fearing backlash from colleagues and political leadership. Yes, most of the judges we have
today, by a big margin, cannot handle the challenge of the
problem-solving court. But the tasks they do undertake in today's court system—the tasks they are asked to undertake by
today's court system—are not worth doing well. A court system
that does not solve problems offers significantly less than what
a twenty-first-century society will require.

Learned Hand once said that a good lawyer had what he

called "a bathtub mind." He filled it with one case, became a master of the subject matter in that case, then pulled the plug and refilled the tub with the next case. As the United States has set up its judicial system, this talent does not well serve a judge. American judges are not supposed to know anything about a case other than what the lawyers have presented to them, in good time and within the rules of evidence. The idea of a judicial inquiry designed to get at the truth is foreign to American jurisprudence, but the modern judge is forever encountering situations where one counsel or the other wishes to introduce "expert" testimony, and the judge has no way to decide whether this witness really is an expert and this piece of evidence really does prove something.

The concern that judges are not trained to be scientists or psychiatrists or social workers hides the worry that they are not trained to be judges, either. Indeed, the easiest and perhaps most important reform of the American judiciary in the years ahead is the establishment of a career path that will lead to professional judges meeting professional criteria. This starts with education. On the European continent, law students divide early on into future advocates and future magistrates. Per capita, the core states of the European Union have more judges and fewer lawyers than the United States, and serious consideration should be given in America to the argument that in the modern world the European systems of justice are more fair and more effective than our own. In minor criminal cases, this has been true for years, and those who doubt that statement need merely find a library that has Sybille Bedford's old book *The Faces of Justice*, from which comes the first epigraph of chapter 1 in this book. Recent improvements in labor law, securities law, antitrust, and financial regulation have given the European Union codes and means for enforcing those codes that may give the citizens of those countries greater benefits from their legal order than we now receive from ours. The codes are often too detailed and the enforcement can be ham-handed, but its principles are right.

In any event, American lawyers are now trained in three-year programs, of which the last year is widely regarded as a waste. We can at least begin programs in our great university law schools that offer an option of preparation for judicial office in the third year, with a general public bias and eventually a requirement that candidates for judgeships be graduates of such programs. Such advance preparation is better for sure than one- or two-week (or maybe overnight) postelection summer camps or making arrangements for a newly elected judge to get help from an appointed "mentor" whose status on the court is the same as her own, which is about the best the state courts offer these days. The federal courts, with the growth of a corps of about five hundred federal magistrates, may have lucked into a system that offers a true apprenticeship. The federal magistrates already handle an increasing share of the routine work of the federal courts. Federal magistrates are chosen by the judges of their circuit, serve eight-year terms, and something like a dozen of them have already been nominated by the president to be district judges.

Philosophically the burdens are greater—even apart from the life raft of the myths sunk in chapter 2—because so many of our judges, lawyers, and political leaders are not just content but proud of the (charitably) second-rate judicial system we have today. In the long view, the true importance of the problem-solving court may turn out to be its more or less inadvertent demonstration that our justice system has been moving in the wrong directions. What the country—any country—needs is courts on the lower level that are acutely conscious of the practical impact of their decisions—in short, of something that might be called justice—and courts on the higher appellate level that start their deliberations with trust in history and the accumulated wisdom of precedent. The trial courts, because they know more of the situation before them, should have greater freedom. The appellate courts, because they must live in the partial vacuum of the printed record, should be more tightly constrained. Instead, we have trial courts supposedly tightly bound by law from the past, held to that law by the advocacy of the lawyers in the courtroom, staffed by judges who come into their jobs with practical experience as lawyers but without noticeable training and sometimes without much aptitude for the work. And we have appellate courts staffed mostly by law professors and former government counsel who are not, to quote lawyer-journalist Stuart Taylor Jr., "familiar with the everyday workings of the political and judicial systems, and with the beliefs and concerns of everyday Americans,"[8] but have great authority to change the rules.

As Judge Kaye has expanded the experiment of problem-solving courts, it has become apparent that not every judge can handle the work. Nobody is arguing that assignments to problem-solving courts, like assignments to "general jurisdiction" courts, should be managed by random-number tables. Indeed, if we can lick the corruption worries that brought random assignment to us two and three generations ago, we should be able to recognize in a formal and practical way that

the judges who succeed at specialized work tend to have special training—pharmacology and the psychology of addiction
for judges in the drug courts, accountancy in the tax courts,
social psychology in the family courts, medical procedures in
parts devoted to malpractice litigation, finance in the courts
that process securities law cases, hydrology for water allocations. We must learn to make use, in the law as well as in the
lab, of the immense gains in information we have achieved in
the last generation. There is an upside to law professor Harry
Kalven's elegantly stated fear that through the agency of the
computer mankind may lose its benign capacity to forget. If
we render unto Caesar only what Caesar is most competent to
do, it is only the antiques, the laws of wills and estates, real
property conveyance and crime, that should go by random selection to the randomly trained judge who became a judge because he knew a politician.

The rise of political advertising in judicial elections—and
the ugly, growing prominence in our political discourse of beliefs about the personal views of federal judicial candidates—
should lead to a reconsideration of our cherished tradition
that our judges, unlike European judges, are not civil servants.
American court systems with ten and twelve employees for
every judge are no less bureaucratic than European magistra-
cies. Protecting the independence of civil servants is easier
than protecting the independence of elected judges. The
courts of the European Union have demonstrated that judges
who are civil servants can indeed interpret a charter and give
orders to the political authorities above them on the organization charts. And the orders will be obeyed, especially when
the court seeks to enforce treaties for human rights and civil

rights, the areas that correctly trouble the most thoughtful defenders of our present judicial procedures.

Admittedly, this is not a time for easy optimism. Calling for greater involvement by universities in training judges clashes in 2006 with the decision by the University of Virginia to suspend the only master's program in the country for sitting judges. American political leadership these days clearly does not wish to reinforce the independence and authority of the judicial branch. The judges themselves are insufficiently unhappy to think hard about what has gone wrong.

Historically, the law and the role of law in governance have been subjects that commanded the best minds in the nation. We don't have that quality of discourse now, perhaps because the best minds have been sidetracked into intellectually trivial stuff by the enormous rewards in the market for both corporate and tort lawyers. But the most important subjects tend over time to draw the attentions of the best people, and the defects in our judicial system have become damaging enough to qualify.

NOTES

CHAPTER 1: THE MONASTIC BENCH

1. Sybille Bedford, *The Faces of Justice* (New York: Simon & Schuster, 1961), p. 101.
2. Message to Congress, reprinted in Benjamin N. Cardozo, *The Nature of the Judicial Process* (New Haven: Yale University Press, 1921), p. 171. Note that the president and the Congress were both lame ducks, and that their lameduckery under the rules of that time had four more months to run.
3. Bureau of Justice Statistics, Department of Justice, *State Court Organization 1998*, National Center for State Courts, p. 7.
4. Jerome Frank, *Courts on Trial* (Princeton, N.J.: Princeton University Press, 1950), p. 171.
5. Patricia M. Wald, "Some Thoughts on Beginnings and Ends: Court of Appeals Review of Administrative Law Judges' Findings and Opinions," *Washington University Law Quarterly* 67, no. 3 (1989): pp. 661, 665.
6. Felix Frankfurter, *Of Law and Men* (New York: Harcourt, Brace, 1956), p. 109.
7. Frank M. Coffin, *The Ways of a Judge* (Boston: Houghton Mifflin, 1980), pp. 9–10.

8. Frankfurter, op. cit., p. 32.

9. James F. Simon, *What Kind of Nation* (New York: Simon & Schuster, 2002), p. 276.

10. Frances Kahn Zemans, "The Accountable Judge: Guardian of Judicial Independence," 72 S. *Cal. L. Rev.* 625, 636.

11. Joyce Purnick, "Judges Data? The Objections Are Overruled," *New York Times*, Feb. 10, 2005, p. B1.

12. *Chambers Handbook for Judges' Law Clerks and Secretaries* (Washington, D.C.: Federal Judicial Center, 1995), pp. 17, 175.

13. Martin Mayer, *Today and Tomorrow in America* (New York: Harper and Row, 1976), pp. 155–56.

14. Zemans, op. cit., pp. 637–38. The Pound quote appears on p. 636.

15. In Walter F. Murphy, C. Herman Pritchett, Lee Epstein, eds., *Courts, Judges, and Politics*, 5th ed. (New York: McGraw-Hill, 2002), p. 224.

16. William M. Bowen, Jr., "The Judge As a Professional," *Court Review*, Summer 1993, p. 5.

17. John A. Martin and Brenda J. Wagenknecht-Ivey, "Courts 2020: Critical Trends Shaping the Courts in the Next Decade," *Court Manager* 15, no. 1 (2000): pp. 6, 10.

18. Frank H. Easterbrook, "What Does Legislative History Tell Us," 66 *IIT Chicago-Kent Law Review* 441, in David M. O'Brien, *Judges on Judging*, p. 234.

19. Sandra Day O'Connor, *The Majesty of the Law* (New York: Random House, 2003), p. 254.

20. Sheldon Goldman and Thomas P. Jahrige, *The Federal Courts as a Political System*, 3rd ed. (New York: Harper & Row, 1983), p. 220.

21. Francis L. Wellman, *Gentlemen of the Jury: Reminiscences of Thirty Years at the Bar* (New York: Macmillan, 1944), p. 126.

22. Martin Mayer, *Making News* (New York: Doubleday, 1987), p. 8.
23. *Branzburg v. Hayes*, 408 U.S. 665.
24. Readers should know that Judith Miller, the reporter in question, has been a friend of the author for more than twenty-five years, and of his wife for more than thirty years.
25. Adam Liptak, "Judges Skeptical of First Amendment Protection for Reporters in C.I.A. Leak Inquiry," *New York Times*, Dec. 9, 2004.
26. *Times Co. v. U.S.*, 403 U.S. 713, 717.
27. *Hadley P. Hanson v. Globe Newspaper Co.*, 159 Mass. 293.
28. Chief Justice William H. Rehnquist, Address to the American Bar Association, Oct. 21, 1993, pp. 16–17.
29. Neil Lewis, "Raise for Judicial Employees, Hidden in Bill, Angers Judges," *New York Times*, Nov. 22, 2002, p. A19.
30. Frank M. Coffin, *On Appeal* (New York: Norton, 1994), p. 310.

CHAPTER 2: CONFRONTING THE MYTHS

1. Morris Raphael Cohen, *American Thought: A Critical Sketch* (New York: Collier Books, 1962), p. 150.
2. Charles E. Wyzanski Jr., *Whereas* (Boston: Atlantic–Little, Brown, 1965), p. 84.
3. Abbot Gasquet *Lord Acton and His Circle* (London: Abbot, Gasquet & Co., 1906), p. 166; cited in *New York Times v. Gonzalez* (2005), typescript opinion by Judge Robert Sweet.
4. Gerald Gunther, *Learned Hand: The Man and the Judge* (New York: Knopf, 1994), p. 665.
5. Ibid., p. 596.

6. Benjamin N. Cardozo, *The Nature of the Judicial Process* (New Haven and London: Yale University Press, 1921), p. 33.

7. Steve Bogira, *Courtroom 302* (New York: Knopf, 2005), p. 88.

8. Richard A. Posner, *Law, Pragmatism and Democracy* (Cambridge, Mass., and London: Harvard University Press, 2003), pp. 120–21.

9. *In re J. P. Linahan, Inc.*, 1943, 138 F2d 650, 653.

10. Antonin Scalia, *A Matter of Interpretation* (Princeton, N.J.: Princeton University Press, 1997), p. 24.

11. Greg Berman, Aubrey Fox, and Robert V. Wolf, *A Problem-Solving Revolution: Making Change Happen in State Courts* (New York: Center for Court Innovation, 2004), p. 181.

12. Michael Wines, "Justice in Russia Is No Longer Swift or Sure," *New York Times*, Feb. 23, 2003, p. 3.

13. Brian C. Ostrom and Neal B. Kauder, eds., *Examining the Work of State Courts, 1998: A National Perspective from the Court Statistics Project* (Williamsburg, Va.: National Center for State Courts, 1999), p. 72.

14. Bogira, op. cit., p. 336.

15. *The Challenge of Crime in a Free Society: A Report by the President's Commission on Law Enforcement and the Administration of Justice* (Washington, D.C.: GPO, 1967), p. 106.

16. All these figures are from Ostrom and Kauder, *Examining the Work of State Courts, 1998.*

17. Alexis de Tocqueville, *Democracy in America* (New York: Vintage Books, 1954), pp. 205–6.

18. Roscoe Pound, *The Spirit of the Common Law* (Boston: Beacon Press, 1963), p. 128.

19. T. D. Weldon, *The Vocabulary of Politics* (London: Penguin Books, 1953), pp. 65, 68, 69.

20. Charles Wyzanski, *Whereas: A Judge's Premises* (Boston: Atlantic Monthly Press, 1965), p. 107.

21. Posner, op. cit., p. 281.
22. Jerry Mashaw, *Due Process in the Administrative State* (New Haven: Yale University Press, 1985), p. 2.
23. Oliver Wendell Holmes, *The Common Law* (New York: Dover, 1991), p.
24. Leo Levin and Russell R. Wheeler, eds., *The Pound Conference* (St. Paul, Minn.: West Publishing, 1979), p. 112.

CHAPTER 3: THE ORIGINS OF THE SPECIES: HISTORICAL PRECEDENTS

1. U.S. Constitution, Art. III, Sec. 2.
2. Russell R. Wheeler, *Origins of the Elements of Federal Court Governance* (Washington, D.C.: Federal Judicial Center, 1992), p. 7.
3. Robert W. Tobin, *Creating the Judicial Branch: The Unfinished Reform* (Williamsburg, Va: National Center for State Courts, 1999), p. 45.
4. Henry Friendly, "The Historic Basis of Diversity Jurisdiction," *Harvard Law Review* 41: 483, 497.
5. Earl Warren, "Celebrating the Hundredth Birthday of Chief Justice Taft," *Yale Law Journal* (March 1958): p. 361.
6. Alexis de Tocqueville, *Democracy in America* (New York: Vintage Books, 1954), pp. 288, 289.
7. Ibid., p. 290.
8. See Oliver Wendell Holmes, *The Common Law* (New York: Dover, 1991), p. 274.
9. *Cohens v. Virginia*, 6 Wheaton 64, 204.
10. National Conference on the Causes of Popular Dissatisfaction with the Administration of Justice—"the Pound Conference"— West Publishing, 1976, p. 5.
11. W. A. Bogart, *Consequences: The Impact of Law and Its Complexity* (Toronto: University of Toronto Press, 1992), p. 10.

12. Thomas F. Burke, *Lawyers, Lawsuits and Legal Rights* (Berkeley: University of California Press, 2002), p. 2.

13. Tocqueville, op. cit., p. 297.

14. David M. O'Brien, ed., *Judges on Judging* (Chatham, N.J.: Chatham House, 1997), p. 75.

15. Bernard Botein, *Trial Judge* (New York: Cornerstone Library, 1952; repr. 1963), p. 53.

16. Tobin, op. cit., p. 59.

17. See Felix Stumpf, *Inherent Powers of the Courts* (Reno, Nev.: National Judicial College, 1994); note especially *In Re Janitor of Supreme Court*, 35 Wis 410 (1874), cited p. 48.

18. *Wachtler v. Cuomo*, No. 6034, 91/NY Sup. Ct., Sept. 25, 1991; *Cuomo v. Wachtler*, No. 91-CV-3874 (E.D. N.Y. Oct. 1, 1991).

19. Dr. Roger B. Hartley, "State Budgets and Judicial Independence," *Court Management* 15, no. 4 (2003): pp. 16, 17.

20. "National Briefing," *New York Times*, Oct. 12, 2005, p. A17.

21. Bruce Jackson, *Law and Disorder* (Urbana and Chicago: University of Illinois Press, 1984), pp. 6–7.

22. See Gerald T. Dunne, *The Missouri Supreme Court* (Columbia, Mo.: University of Missouri Press, 1993), pp. 168–71.

23. Tobin, op. cit., p. 55.

24. Walter F. Murphy, C. Herman Pritchett, and Lee Epstein, eds., *Courts, Judges, and Politics*, 5th ed. (New York: McGraw-Hill, 2002), p. 192.

25. Joseph Borkin, *The Corrupt Judge* (New York: Clarkson N. Potter, 1962), p. 23.

26. William Glaberson, "Former Justice Said to Have Deal on Bribery Plea and Jail Term," *New York Times*, Aug. 3, 2002, p. B1.

27. Frederick Pollock and Frederic Maitland, *A History of the English Common Law* (London, 1898; 2nd ed. 1968), p. 48.

28. Richard E. Messick, "The Origins and Development of Courts," *Judicature* 85, no. 4 (January–February 2002): p. 75.

29. Kenneth W. Starr, *First Among Equals: The Supreme Court in American Life* (New York: Warner Books, 2002), p. 115.

30. Botein, op. cit., p. 52.

31. Friendly, op. cit., pp. 497–98.

32. Tocqueville, op. cit., p. 289.

33. Steve Bogira, *Courtroom 302* (New York: Knopf, 2005), p. 88.

34. Tobin, op. cit., p. 59.

35. Ibid., p. 57.

36. Ibid., p. 52.

37. Ibid., p. viii.

38. Harold W. Laski, *The Danger of Being a Gentleman* (New York: Viking Press, 1940), p. 88.

39. Starr, op. cit., p. xiv.

40. O'Brien, op. cit., p. 27.

41. Learned Hand, *The Bill of Rights* (Cambridge, Mass.: Harvard University Press, 1958). It is interesting to note that Gerald Gunther's admirable and very long biography of Hand, *The Man and the Judge*, does not quote this devastating phrase in its long discussion of the Harvard lectures.

42. *Annals of Congress* 437 (Washington, D.C.: Gales and Seaton, 1834).

43. In Frank M. Coffin, *The Ways of a Judge* (Boston: Houghton Mifflin, 1980), pp. 28–30.

44. See John T. Noonan, *Narrowing the National Power* (Berkeley: University of California Press, 2002), pp. 58 et seq. The argument here follows Noonan, except that the *South Carolina State Ports Authority* case was subsequent to Noonan's book.

45. Ibid., p. 156.

CHAPTER 4: IN PRACTICE: THERAPY COURT IN BROOKLYN

1. All quotes are from *Brooklyn Treatment Court: Five Year Report, June 1996–December 2001.*
2. *Drug Courts* (Washington, D.C.: General Accounting Office, April 2002). GAO 02-434, pp. 4, 76.
3. "National Briefing," *New York Times*, Apr. 17, 2003, p. 20.
4. "A Victory for California," *New York Times*, Apr. 10, 2006, p. A22.
5. Donald P. Lay, "Rehab Justice," *New York Times*, Nov. 18, 2004, p. A29.
6. Steve Bogira, *Courtroom 302* (New York: Knopf, 2005), p. 118.
7. Judith S. Kaye, "Making the Case for Hands-on Courts," *Newsweek*, Oct. 11, 1999.
8. Carl Baar and Freda F. Solomon, "The Role of Courts," *The Court Manager* 15, no. 3 (2000): pp. 19, 26.
9. Benjamin N. Cardozo, *The Nature of the Judicial Process* (New Haven and London: Yale University Press, 1921), p. 31.

CHAPTER 5: DECISIONS, DECISIONS, DECISIONS

1. From *Beale's Treatise on Conflict of Laws*, section 118, cited in Charles P. Curtis, *Law as Large as Life* (New York: Simon & Schuster, 1959), p. 87.
2. Sheldon Glueck, 1963, p. 252.
3. Quoted in a speech by Circuit Judge Patricia Wald to the Federal Bar Association Reception for Administrative Law Judges, Oct. 14, 1998, p. 3.
4. In Curtis, op. cit., p. 15.

5. Learned Hand, *The Spirit of Liberty*, ed. Irving Dilliard (New York: Vintage, 1952), p. 33.

6. "Evidence Advocacy: The Judge's Perspective," *Litigation* 28, no. 1. (Fall 2001): p. 3.

7. Henry J. Friendly, *Benchmarks* (Chicago: University of Chicago Press, 1967), p. 2. The inner quote is from Oliver Wendell Holmes Jr., *The Path of the Law* (Whitefish, Mont.: Kissinger Publishing, 2004), p. 167.

8. *Judicial Writing Manual* (Washington, D.C.: Federal Judicial Center, 1991), p. 7.

9. Ibid., p. 17.

10. Gunther, *Learned Hand*, p. 142.

11. Ibid., p. 147.

12. Harry T. Edwards, "The Effects of Collegiality on Judicial Decision Making," *U. of Pa. L. Rev.* 151, pp. 1639, 1648–50.

13. Roger Traynor, *The Traynor Reader* ed., pp. 27–28.

14. Charles Evans Hughes, *The Supreme Court of the United States: Its Foundations, Methods and Achievements* (Frederick, Md.: Beard Books, 2000).

15. Frank M. Coffin, *On Appeal: Courts, Lawyering and Judging* (New York: Norton, 1994), p. 286.

16. Roger A. Hanson, *Appellate Court Performance: Standards and Measures* (Williamsburg, Va.: National Center for State Courts, 1999), p. 3.

17. Lynn Mather, "Policy Making in State Trial Courts," in John B. Gates and Charles A. Johnson, eds., *The American Courts* (Washington, D.C.: Congressional Quarterly Press, 1991), p. 120.

18. Thomas F. Burke, *Lawyers, Lawsuits and Legal Rights* (Berkeley: University of California Press, 2002), pp. 7, 175.

19. Benjamin N. Cardozo, "Law and Literature," 14 *Yale Law Review* 699, pp. 715–16.

20. In Walter F. Murphy, C. Herman Pritchett, and Lee Epstein, eds., *Courts, Judges, and Politics*, 5th ed. (New York: McGraw-Hill, 2002), pp. 112–13.

21. "The Judges Do Their Job," *New York Times*, June 24, 2003, p. A31.

22. Warren E. Burger, "A Sick Profession?" *Tulsa Law Journal* 5, no. 1, pp. 2–3.

23. Sandra Day O'Connor, *The Majesty of the Law* (New York: Random House, 2003), pp. 217–18.

24. Marvin E. Frankel, "The Adversary Judge: The Experience of the Trial Judge," 54 *Texas Law Review* 465 (1976). In Murphy et al., op. cit., pp. 381–82.

25. Mary Ann Glendon, *A Nation Under Lawyers* (New York: Farrar, Straus & Giroux, 1994), pp. 147–48.

26. Roger Traynor, op. cit., p. 79.

27. Melvin J. Urossky and David W. Levy, *Half-Brother, Half-Son: The Letters of Louis D. Brandeis to Felix Frankfurter* (Norman, Okla.: University of Oklahoma Press, 1991), p. 431.

CHAPTER 6: IN PRACTICE: THE TAX COURT

1. Louise Story, "Secrecy Is Lifted in Some Tax Court Trials," *New York Times*, July 12, 2005, p. C1.

CHAPTER 7: 30,000 JUDGES, 100 MILLION CASES: THE SCOPE OF THE ENTERPRISE

1. Cited in Alvin B. Rubin, "The Bureaucratization of the Federal Courts," *Notre Dame Law Review* 55: 648, 654.

2. Ruggero J. Aldisert, review of *Super Chief: Earl Warren and His Supreme Court*, by Bernard Schwartz, *Ca. L. Rev.* 275

(1984), vol. 72, p. 275. Cited in *Chambers Handbook for Judges' Law Clerks and Secretaries* (Washington, D.C.: Federal Judicial Center, 1994), pp. 14–15.

3. Frank M. Coffin, *On Appeal* (New York: Norton, 1994), p. 310.
4. *Journal of American Judicature Society* 6 (December 1922): p. 37.
5. Bureau of Justice Statistics, Department of Justice, *State Court Organization 1998* (Washington, D.C. U.S. Dept. of Justice, p. 7.
6. *Summa Theologica*, Second Part; no, 67, Article 1.
7. *Federal Court Governance* (Washington, D.C.: Federal Judicial Center, 1994), p. 78.
8. All this salary information is from *Survey of Judicial Salaries*, published by the National Center for State Courts in Williamsburg, Va.
9. Robert W. Tobin, *Creating the Judicial Branch: The Unfinished Reform* (Williamsburg, Va.: National Center for State Courts, 1999), p. 288.
10. Ibid., p. 69.
11. *Federal Court Governance*, op. cit., p. 34.
12. Doris Marie Provine, *Judging Credentials: Nonlawyer Judges and the Politics of Professionalism* (Chicago: University of Chicago Press, 1983), p. 148.
13. Ibid., p. 84.
14. Statistics are from *Examining the Work of State Courts, 1998* (Williamsburg, Va.: National Center for State Courts Court Statistics Project, 1999), and from Court Statistics Project, *State Court Caseload Statistics, 2004* (National Center for State Courts, 2005).
15. David C. Steelman, with John A. Goerdt and James E. McMillan, *Caseflow Management* (Williamsburg, Va.: National Center for State Courts, 2000), p. 19.

16. *Federalist Papers*, No. 82 (New York: New American Library, 1961), p. 494.
17. John Chipman Gray, *The Nature and Sources of the Law* (Boston: Beacon Press), p. 253.
18. 115 U.S. 1 (1885).
19. 19 U.S. 264.
20. Roger Traynor, *The Traynor Reader* (Hastings, Nebraska: Hastings College of Law, 1987), p. 54.
21. Victor Eugene Flango, "Creating Family-Friendly Courts," *Family Law Quarterly* 34, no. 1 (Spring 2000): pp. 115, 121.
22. All these numbers are from *Survey of Judicial Salaries*, published by the National Center for State Courts, Williamsburg, Va., Winter 2002.
23. These figures are from Roy Schotland's Report, June 2005, to the California Judicial Council.

CHAPTER 8: IN PRACTICE: THE COLORADO WATER COURTS

1. *Yunker v. Nichols*, 1 Colorado 551, 555. This reference, and most references to law and judicial opinion in this chapter, are drawn from Gregory J. Hobbs Jr., "Colorado Water Law: An Historical Overview," *University of Denver Water Law Review* 1, no. 1 (Fall 1997).

CHAPTER 9: ELECTING AND SELECTING JUDGES

1. Francis L. Wellman, *Gentlemen of the Jury* (New York: Macmillan, 1924), p. 187.

2. Joyce Purnick, "A Judiciary in Disrepair (and Denial)," *New York Times*, Dec. 1, 2005, p. B1.

3. Ron Howell, "Justice Came at a Price," *Newsday*, July 17, 2003, p. A3.

4. Clifford J. Levy, "Picking Judges: Party Machines, Rubber Stamps," *New York Times*, July 28, 2003, p. A1.

5. "New York's Farcical Judicial Elections," *New York Times*, Nov. 2, 2002.

6. Leslie Eaton, "State Commission Seeking Ouster of Surrogate Judge in Brooklyn," *New York Times*, Feb. 15, 2005, p. B1.

7. Doris Marie Provine, *Judging Credentials: Nonlawyer Judges and the Politics of Professionalism* (Chicago: University of Chicago Press, 1983).

8. Ibid., p. 99.

9. William H. Rehnquist, *The Supreme Court* (New York: Knopf, 2001), p. 99.

10. Charles P. Curtis and Ferris Greenslet, eds., *The Practical Cogitator* (Boston: Houghton Mifflin, 1945), pp. 413–14.

11. Ibid., p. 14.

12. Rehnquist, op. cit., p. 99.

13. Robert H. Jackson, *That Man: An Insider's Portrait of Franklin D. Roosevelt* (New York and Oxford: Oxford University Press, 2003), pp. 54–55.

14. Ibid., n. 58, p. 232.

15. Harry W. Jones, ed., *The Courts, the Public, and the Law Explosion* (Englewood Cliffs, N.J.: American Assembly, Prentice Hall, 1965), p. 160.

16. David Alistair Yaloff, *The Pursuit of Justices* (Chicago: University of Chicago Press, 1999), p. 11.

17. James F. Simon, *What Kind of Nation* (New York: Simon & Schuster, 2002), p. 148.

18. Friendly, *Benchmarks*, p. 497.
19. Luke Bierman, "Beyond Merit Selection," *Fordham Law Journal* 26, no. 3, pp. 581, 584.
20. Carl Baar, *Separate but Subservient: Court Budgeting in the American States* (Lexington, Mass.: D. C. Heath, 1975).
21. Robert W. Kastenmeir and Michael J. Remingon, "A Judicious Legislator's Lexicon to the Federal Judiciary," in *Judges and Legislators: Toward Institutional Comity*, ed. Robert W. Katzmann (Washington, D.C.: Brookings Institution 1988), p. 72.
22. Gerald T. Dunne, *The Missouri Supreme Court* (Columbia, Mo.: University of Missouri Press, 1993), p. 126.
23. L. Aspin and W. K. Hall, "Thirty Years of Judicial Retention Elections," *Social Science Journal* 37 (2000): p. 1.
24. Mark Kozlowski, *Regulating Interest Group Activity in Judicial Elections* (New York: Brennan Center for Justice, NYU School of Law, 2002), p. 2.
25. Alexander Tabarrok and Eric Helland, "Court Politics: The Political Economy of Tort Awards," 92 *Journal of Law and Economics* 157.
26. Kozlowski, op. cit., p. 4.
27. *USA Today*, Nov. 2, 2000.
28. Roy Schotland, *Financing Judicial Elections*, unpublished.
29. Tobin, *Creating the Judicial Branch*, p. 37.
30. These numbers are from unpublished papers by Roy Schotland, as is the three-word quote. Schotland has been point man on these issues for the National Conference of State Supreme Court Justices and is the source of a great deal of the material in this chapter, and others.
31. Martin Mayer, *Madison Avenue, USA* (New York: Harper Bros., 1958), pp. 295–97.

32. David G. Savage, "Running Stance," *ABA Journal* (August 2002): p. 32.
33. *N. Ky. L. Rev.* 37, pp. 400–01.
34. *Republican Party of Minn. v. White*, texts in supremecourtus .gov, 2001 term slip opinions, majority opinion, p. 18.
35. Ibid., p. 4.
36. Justice Ginsburg's dissent, ibid., p. 11.
37. Justice O'Connor's concurrence, ibid., p. 4.
38. Justice Kennedy's concurrence, ibid.

CHAPTER 10: IN PRACTICE: AT THE POVERTY LEVEL IN PHOENIX

1. www.admc-org/Lenten.
2. www.superiorcourt.maricopa.gov/ssc/info/gen.

CHAPTER 11: TEACHING JUDGES TO JUDGE

1. Glenn R. Winters and Robert E. Allard, "Judicial Selection and Tenure in the United States," in Harry W. Jones, ed., op. cit., pp. 172–73.
2. Robert S. Thompson, "Comment," *USC Law Review* 72, pp. 559, 563.
3. Thomas E. Willging, "Past and Potential Uses of Empirical Research in Civil Rulemaking," *Notre Dame Law Review* 77, no. 4 (April 2002): p. 1124, n. 15.
4. *Imposing a Moratorium on the Number of Federal Judges* (Washington, D.C.; Federal Judicial Center, 1993), pp. 38, 41.
5. *Federal Court Governance: Why Congress Should—and Why Congress Should Not—Create a Full-time Executive Judge, Abol-*

ish the Judicial Conference, and Remove Circuit Judges from District Court Governance (Washington, D.C.: Federal Judicial Center, 2000), p. 63.

6. *The National Judicial College 2002 Course Catalog*, Reno, Nevada, 2002, p. 23.

7. William E. Melone, "Ethics Issues in Judicial Education," *NASJEN News/Quarterly* 20, no.1 (Winter 2005): p. 19.

8. Robert G. M. Keating, "The New York State Judicial Institute: Transforming the Educational World of the Judiciary," *New York State Bar Association Journal* 17, no. 4 (May 2005): pp. 11, 12.

9. *Environmental Health Perspectives* 111, no. 4 (April 2003).

10. William G. Schulz, "Judging Science," *Chemical and Engineering News*, Feb. 27, 2006, p. 36.

11. 43 F2nd 1311, 1316.

12. Ibid., p. 39.

13. Schulz, op. cit., p. 39.

CHAPTER 12: IN PRACTICE: ADMINISTRATIVE LAW

1. Frank M. Coffin, *On Appeal* (New York: Norton, 1994), p. 304.

2. Paul R. Verkuil, Daniel J. Gifford, Charles H. Koch Jr., Richard J. Pierce Jr., and Jeffrey S. Lubbers, *Administrative Conference of the United States, Recommendations and Reports*, vol. 2 (Washington, D.C., 1992), pp. 782, 787–88.

3. Antonin Scalia, "The Administrative Law Judge Fiasco—A Reprise," *University of Chicago Law Review* 48, pp. 57, 79.

4. Ibid., p. 57.

5. Karl Llewellyn, *The Common Law Tradition: Deciding Appeals* p. 263.

6. Speech by Chief Judge Patricia M. Wald to the Federal Bar

Association Reception for Administrative Law Judges, Oct. 14, 1998.

7. Verkuil et al., op. cit., p. 781.
8. Ronnie A. Yoder, "The Role of the Administrative Law Judge," *Journal of the National Association of Administrative Law Judges* 22, no. 2 (Fall 2002): pp. 321, 323.
9. *Butz v. Economou*, 438 U.S. 478, 513.
10. Verkuil et al., op. cit., p. 1037.
11. See Frank S. Black, Jeffrey S. Lubbers, and Paul R. Verkuil, "Developing a Full and Fair Evidentiary Record in a Nonadversary Setting: Two Proposals for Improving Social Security Disability Adjudications," *Cardozo Law Review* 25, no. 1 (November 2003).
12. Jerry L. Mashaw et al., *Social Security Hearings and Appeals* (Lexington, Mass.: Lexington Books, 1978), pp. xi, xiv, 99.

CHAPTER 13: THE POLITICS OF SUPREMACY

1. Quoted in Charles E. Wyzanski Jr., *Whereas* (Boston: Atlantic–Little, Brown, 1965), p. 61.
2. Linda Greenhouse, *Becoming Justice Blackmun* (New York: Times Books, 2005), pp. 164 et seq.
3. Justice John Paul Stevens, "Deciding What to Decide: The Docket and the Rule of Four," *New York University Law Review* 58 (1983): p. 1; cited in David O'Brien, ed., *Judges on Judging* (Chatham, N.J.; Chatham House Publishers, 1997), p. 93.
4. Learned Hand, *The Bill of Rights* (Cambridge, Mass.: Harvard University Press, 1958).
5. Quoted in Max Lerner, *The Mind and Faith of Justice Holmes* (Boston: Little, Brown, 1945), p. 390.

6. Wyzanski, op. cit., p. 162.
7. Gerald T. Dunne, *Hugo Black and the Judicial Revolution* (New York: Simon & Schuster, 1977), p. 316.
8. Gerald T. Dunne, *Justice Joseph Story and the Rise of the Supreme Court* (New York: Simon & Schuster, 1970), p. 382.
9. Ibid., p. 351.
10. Frankfurter, *Law and Politics* (New York: Capricorn Books, 1962), p. 6.
11. Felix Frankfurter, *Of Law and Men* (New York: Harcourt Brace, 1956), p. 141.
12. Ibid., p. 117.
13. Felix Frankfurter, *Law and Politics*, p. 15.
14. William H. Rehnquist, *The Supreme Court* (New York: Knopf, 2001), p. 115.
15. David Alistair Yalof, *Pursuit of Justices: Presidential Politics and the Selection of Supreme Court Nominees* (Chicago and London: University of Chicago Press, 1999), p. 89.
16. Gerald N. Rosenberg, *The Hollow Hope: Can Courts Bring About Social Change?* (Chicago and London: University of Chicago Press, 1991), p. 5.
17. Sheldon Goldman and Thomas Jahnige, *The Federal Courts as a Political System*, 3rd ed. (New York: Harper & Row, 1985), p. 191.
18. Sheldon Goldman, *Picking Federal Judges: Lower Court Selection from Roosevelt Through Reagan*, (New Haven and London: Yale University Press, 1997), p. 130.
19. Ibid., p. 78.
20. Ibid., p. 3.
21. Donald D. Jackson, *Judges*, p. 266.
22. Goldman, *Picking Federal Judges*, p. 206.
23. Yalof, op. cit, p. 133.
24. Greenhouse, op. cit., p. 186. Greenhouse quotes Southern

Methodist University's Joseph F. Kobylka, that Blackmun was with Burger in divided cases 87.5 percent of the time in the first five years, 45.5 percent in the second five years, and only 32.4 percent in the last five years.

25. *The Oxford Companion to the Supreme Court of the United States* (New York and London: Oxford University Press, 1992), p. 804.

26. Quoted in Greenhouse, op. cit., p. 242.

27. Brandeis, op. cit., p. 97.

28. Goldman and Jahnige, op. cit., p. 155.

29. John T. Noonan Jr., *Narrowing the Nation's Power: The Supreme Court Sides with the States* (Berkeley: University of California Press, 2002), p. 144.

30. *Federal Maritime Commission v. South Carolina State Ports Authority*, May 29, 2002.

31. Bernard Bailyn, *To Begin the World Anew: The Genius and Ambiguities of the American Founders* (New York: Knopf, 2003), p. 128.

32. Bailyn, op. cit.

33. Wyzanski, op. cit., p. 52.

CHAPTER 14: THE LOSS OF AUTHORITY

1. Morris Raphael Cohen, *American Thought: A Critical Sketch* (New York: Collier Books, 1962), p. 204.

2. *Barnette*, 349 U.S. 624, 639.

3. Jerry L. Mashaw, *Social Security Hearings and Appeals* (Lexington, Mass.: Lexington Books, 1978), p. 161.

4. "The Law," a speech by Justice Oliver Wendell Holmes Jr. to the Suffolk Bar Association Dinner, Feb. 5, 1885, in Max Lerner, *The Mind and Faith of Justice Holmes* (Boston: Little, Brown, 1945), p. 29. Also in steel letters on marble on the wall

of Boalt Hall, the Law School of the University of California, Berkeley.

5. Roscoe Pound, *The Spirit of the Common Law* (Boston: Beacon Press, 1963), p. 83.

6. William James, *Pragmatism* (Cambridge, Mass.: Harvard University Press, 1975), p. 116.

7. John Chipman Gray, *The Nature and Sources of the Law* (Boston: Beacon Press), p. 99.

8. *Fortnightly Corp. v. United Artists Television, Inc.*, 392 U.S. 398.

9. Lerner, op. cit., p. 432.

10. Ibid., p. 444.

11. Mark DeWolfe Howe, ed., *Holmes-Pollock Letters* vol. 1 (Cambridge, Mass.: Harvard University Press, 1941), p. 273.

12. 208 U.S. 412.

13. 198 U.S. 45.

14. *Hammer v. Dagenhart*, 247 U.S. 251.

15. Lerner, op. cit., pp. 162–63.

16. Dennis J. Hutchinson and David J. Garrow, *The Forgotten Memoir of John Knox* (Chicago: University of Chicago Press, 2004).

17. *Carter v. Carter Coal Co.*, 298 U.S. 238, 327.

18. *Richardson v. Mellish*, 2 Bing 229, 252.

19. Gerald T. Dunne, *The Missouri Supreme Court* (Columbia< Mo.: University of Missouri Press, 1993), p. x.

20. Sheryl Gay Stolbert, "Nominee Is Standing on Precedent, and Setting His Own, with Hearings Responses," *New York Times*, Sept. 15, 2005, p. A26.

21. *Mushkopf v. Corning Hospital District*, 359 Pad 457, 459.

22. *Charles River Bridge v. Warren Bridge*, 11 *Peters* 542.

23. Ibid., 598.

24. *McCulloch v. Maryland*, 4 Wheaton (17 U.S.) 316, 407.

25. *Home Building and Loan Assn. v. Blaisdell,* 290 U.S. 398, pp. 442–43.

26. 347 U.S. 483, 492.

27. Cited in Gerald T. Dunne, *Hugo Black and the Judicial Revolution* (New York: Simon & Schuster, 1977), p. 309.

28. Alexander M. Bickel, *The Least Dangerous Branch* (Indianapolis: Bobbs-Merrill, 1962), p. 103.

29. Antonin Scalia, *A Matter of Interpretation: Federal Courts and the Law* (Princeton, N.J.: Princeton University Press, 1997), p. 13.

30. In Robert A. Katzmann, ed., *Judges and Legislators* (Washington, D.C.: Brookings Institution, 1988), p. 175.

31. In Walter F. Murphy, C. Herman Pritchett, and Lee Epstein, eds., *Courts, Judges, and Politics* (New York: McGraw-Hill, 2002), p. 491.

32. John Chipman Gray, op. cit., sec. 370, p. 165; cited in Cardozo, *The Nature of the Judicial Process* (New Haven, Conn.: Yale University Press, 1997), p. 15.

33. Charles P. Curtis, *Lions Under the Throne* (Boston: Little Brown, 1947), p. 105.

34. Hart and Sacks, op. cit., p. 1201.

35. Benjamin Weiner, "Court, Taking Time to Proofread, Says Law's Wording Nullifies Sentence," *New York Times*, Dec. 7, 2004, p. A23 The draft opinion, *U.S. v. Pabon-Cruz*, pp. 19–23, is solemnly funny.

36. William N. Eskridge Jr., "Overriding Supreme Court Statutory Interpretation Decisions," *Yale Law Journal* 101, p. 331.

37. Roger Traynor, "No Magic Words Could Do It Justice," *California Law Review* 49: pp. 615, 620.

38. In David O'Brien, ed., *Judges on Judging: Views from the Bench* (Chatham, N.J.: Chatham House, 1997), p. 201.

39. Scalia, op. cit., p. 39.

40. Cardozo, op. cit., p. 140.

41. Traynor, op. cit., p. 44.

42. 338 U.S. 25.

43. 367 U.S. 43.

44. 381 U.S. 618.

45. The syllabus of the case reveals that Stevens, J., delivered the opinion of the Court in part, in which Scalia, Souter, Thomas, and Ginsburg, JJ., joined. Breyer, J., delivered the opinion of the Court in part, in which Rehnquist, C.J., and O'Connor, Kennedy, and Ginsburg, JJ., joined. Stevens, J., filed an opinion dissenting in part, in which Souter, J., joined, and in which Scalia, J., joined except for Part III and footnote 17. Thomas, J., filed opinions dissenting in part. Breyer, J., filed an opinion dissenting in part, in which Rehnquist, C.J., and O'Connor and Kennedy, JJ., joined.

46. Robert W. Tobin, *Creating the Judicial Branch* (Williamsburg, Va.: National Center for State Courts, 1999), p. 110.

47. Jones quoted in Andre M. Scott and Earle Wallace, eds., *Politics USA*, (New York: Macmillan, 1974), pp. 398–99.

48. James Q. Wilson, *Bureaucracy* (New York: Basic Books, 1989), p. 291.

49. 381 U.S. 479.

50. Martin Mayer, *All You Know Is Facts* (New York: Harper & Row, 1969), p. 237; from a reprint in a book of an article I wrote about Goldberg in 1966 for *The New York Times Magazine*.

51. Sol Wachtler, "Judging the Ninth Amendment," 59 *Fordham Law Review* 597 (March 1991).

52. Glanville Williams, *Learning the Law*, 11th ed. (London: Stevens & Sons, 1982), p. 11.

53. Walker Clark, "Address on Reform" before the North Carolina Bar Association, 1914, pp. 2, 3.

54. I was a Guest Scholar at Brookings for a decade, watching Litan at work. In spring 2006 I gave talks to the judges in this program.

55. Richard A. Posner, *Frontiers of Legal Theory* (Cambridge, Mass., and London: Harvard University Press, 2001), p. 37.

56. Richard A. Posner, op. cit., p. 47.

57. Ibid., p. 76.

58. Ibid., p. 79.

59. Richard A. Posner, *The Federal Court* (Cambridge, Mass., and London: Harvard University Press, 1988), p. 328.

60. Jack Hirshleifer, *The Dark Side of the Force* (Cambridge: Cambridge University Press, 2001), p. 333.

61. Murphy et al., op. cit., pp. 482–83.

62. Scalia, *A Matter of Interpretation*, p. 63.

63. Henry J. Friendly, "The Place of the Expert in a Democratic Society," in Harry W. Jones, ed., *The Courts, the Public and the Law Explosion* (New York: American Assembly, Columbia University, 1965), p. 83.

64. Tom Clark, "Random Thoughts on the Court's Interpretation of Individual Rights," 1 *Houston Law Review* 75, 75 (1963).

65. This version from Charles P. Curtis, *Law as Large as Life* (New York: Simon & Schuster, 1959), p. 157.

66. In Sheldon Glueck, *Roscoe Pound and Criminal Justice* (New York: Oceana Publications, 1965), p. 60.

67. Max Lerner, ed., *The Mind and Faith of Justice Holmes* (Boston: Little, Brown, 1945), pp. 75, 83.

68. Thomas Jefferson to Samuel Kercheval, July 12, 1816.

69. Arthur Sutherland, Jr., ed., *Government Under Law* (Cambridge, Mass.: Harvard University Press, 1958), p. 366.

70. *Sweezy v. New Hampshire*, 354 U.S. 234.

71. See Martin Mayer, *The Teachers Strike* (New York: Harper & Row, 1969), p. 118: "On a higher level of generalization, our problems in education are merely a special case of the root problem of politics in a modern society: the control of professional performance."

CHAPTER 15: OPINIONS

1. National Economic League, *Preliminary Report on the Efficiency of the Administration of Justices* (Boston, 1913), p. 16.
2. Alvin Rubin, op. cit., p. 658.
3. Martin Mayer, *The Lawyers* (Harper & Row, 1967), p. 481.
4. Greg Berman and John Feinblatt, *Good Courts* (New York and London: New Press, 2005).
5. Ibid., p. 220.
6. Alexander M. Bickel, *The Supreme Court and the Idea of Progress* (New York: Harper & Row, 1970), p. 134.
7. In Curtis, *Law As Large As Life*, p. 159.
8. Berman and Feinblatt, op. cit., p. 111.
9. Stuart Taylor Jr., "Remote Control," *Atlantic Monthly* (September 2005): p. 37.

ACKNOWLEDGMENTS

Over the five years that this book was in work, I interviewed more than three hundred people who worked in various capacities around the court systems. My debt to those who are quoted is on the page; but most judges and administrators and clerks did not wish to be identified as the source of a quote, and I have protected their anonymity.

There are a few people, however, to whom no promises of confidentiality were made, who were helpful well beyond the utility of interviews. Professor Roy Schotland of the Georgetown Law School, who performs various services for the Conference of Supreme Court Justices, was a source of bibliographies and introductions; I hope our friendship will survive the publication of the book. Robert W. Tobin's book, *Creating the Judicial Branch: The Unfinished Reform*, written for and published by the National Center for State Courts, was an indispensable asset in the early phases of deciding what this book should cover and supplies much enriching detail to these pages.

Jeffrey Lubbers of American University introduced me to the complexities of the administrative law judges. Felix Stumpf of the National Judicial College in Reno, pioneer of continuing legal education, was a font of information and scholarly guidance. William Vickrey, chief administrator of the California courts, educated me about procedures there and in Idaho. John Werner, chief clerk of New York County, guided me through the complexities of those courts and introduced me to other clerks. (Irving Kahn, an old friend from the world of finance—and I do mean old: He will turn 100 the year this book is published and is still going to the office every day—introduced me to John Werner.) Chief administrator Marcus Reinkensmeyer and his public relations assistant J. W. Brown made my visit to Phoenix and the Maricopa County courts by far the most efficient period in the work on the book.

Russell Wheeler, then deputy director of the Federal Judicial Center, answered more questions than anyone else and supplied months of reading matter. He later did me the great kindness of reading the manuscript and catching literally scores of errors, though some doubtless remain that even his attentive concern did not catch. Robert Litan of the Kaufman Foundation, my colleague at the Brookings Institution in Washington from 1993 to 2001, invited me to participate in several educational seminars for judges in 2006, which he and Henry Butler of the American Enterprise Institute were running in Washington; and I learned there, too.

Among the great pleasures of writing this book was the chance to work again at the law library in the Library of Congress and the library of the Association of the Bar of the City of New York (I used my card of invitation from 1963—issued the morning of the day John F. Kennedy was assassinated—which rather bewildered today's librarians, but they coped).

Like everyone else who tries to write these days about real people and places, I owe a debt to Google, and in this subject to its servitors at Findlaw.

The dialogues on this subject will intensify in the years to come. I hope that with all its faults *The Judges* will make a contribution to those dialogues.

Martin Mayer
Shelter Island, N.Y.
July 2006

INDEX

INDEX

INDEX